AMERICA: RETURN TO INDEPENDENCE

Green Energy as the Key

Nicholas Notarberardino

BOOKS
ACADEMY
LEARNING LIFE FROM EVERY PAGE

BOOKS ACADEMY
LEARNING LIFE FROM EVERY PAGE

Books Academy LLC
112 SW H K Dodgen Loop,
Temple, Texas 76504
Hotline: (254) 800-1189

Ordering Information:
Quantity sales. Special discounts are available on quantity purchases by corporations, associations, and others. For details, contact the publisher at the address above.

Printed in the United States of America.

ISBN-13: Softcover   978-1-964929-62-0
         eBook   978-1-964929-61-3

Library of Congress Control Number: 2024921882

Table of Contents

PART 1

CHAPTER 1

INTRODUCTION

My fellow Americans, we have reached a point in this country where we must look at the problems that face us and address them in a positive and actionable manner. The problems have been piling up for decades. We continue to push them aside, hoping that someone will deal with them later. Later is now. We have reached critical mass. We are within moments of collapse. Moments in historical terms can be years or months, and -as we've seen in the past - can come in a day. The problems are complex, but the answers are simple. In order for us to come up with the answers, we must ask "What is the United States of America." How was it conceived? What are its basic principles? What has made it work for so long? What are the issues that are tearing it down? And how do we solve these problems? In this book, we're going to address all of these issues, but we're going to do it from a single platform. We're going to look at sovereignty, which is the basis for our success because sovereignty enables and protects freedom. We're going to look at what enables sovereignty.

One of the things that we must start with is economics. A nation and the people who live in that nation cannot be free if there is no sovereignty. They cannot have sovereignty in the midst of economic collapse. The concept is simple. When you depend on others for your existence, those who are in control get to make the rules. The thing that has made this country so great is that we have enabled the people of this country to make the rules by which they are governed. That brings sovereignty down to the level of the individual. The individual decides how much power it will give to the government. The individuals decide who will run the government. In the end, it is always the people who are the body that runs the country. This has been tried and tested, and it works. It was put together by founding fathers who claimed - and they were right - that there was divine intervention in building this plan. Why is this so? You see, as explained in the Constitution of the United States, the people have been given inalienable rights - life, liberty, and the pursuit of happiness. This means they get to decide what course of action they will take through the course of their lives. This enables them to choose between right and wrong. What is the righteous path of society? The most important factor in preserving this is the right of the people to be in control of their own lives. Therefore, individual sovereignty is the key that unlocks the door to actionable freedoms - those which we call liberty.

My concern is that these liberties are being compromised. We will endeavor to understand all of the functions of this country and why those liberties must be protected at all costs. The purpose of this book is to explain the relationship between economic status and the liberties that we wish to protect. We will discuss a number of scenarios that will bring home the points that are most important to keeping our liberty - sovereignty and the economic status that enables it.

The first thing I would like to do is ask you to read the Constitution of the United States of America. It is born of divine intervention in order to proliferate freedom. It is that freedom that allows us to worship, live, and act as free people.

The economic and military strength that we have makes us the hub of righteousness in the world. We are the most generous. We are the most compassionate. We are the most caring. We are the leaders who fight for the rights and freedoms of people around the world. Without us, tyranny will most certainly dominate. What happens if the United States were to fail? I'm about to give you two scenarios. These scenarios are not just predictions.

They are the result of logic and the observation of historical events.

We have seen history play out over and over in places where dictators and tyrants control the people. They cannot control their thoughts, but they can control their actions. After a while, the people become indoctrinated into a philosophy that is what the tyrants wish them to believe. They succumb to fear. It is fear that is the main tool used to control the masses - fear of retribution for using your God-given right to speak out in opposition to any particular controlling body - fear that enables that body to have control. The fear comes with physical violence. Anyone not in compliance will be punished physically. We look through history, and it happens over and over again.

Pharaohs, emperors, dictators, and monarchs used this as a means to control the people. They not only control their actions, but they control their belief system. The ability to maintain our liberty is what makes the United States so special. As we look around, we see that our liberties are slipping away - not only individual liberty but the sovereignty of our state and the sovereignty of our nation. We are the victims of what is known as creeping socialism. This is the belief that the government not only has the right but the obligation to control society. This is to control what the people believe and how they act.

We're going to discuss what I call rational sovereignty in Part I of this book. Also, in Part I we will look at how the nation was formed, why sovereignty is so important, mistakes that we have made in trying to protect sovereignty, and what is the future of our sovereignty. In Part II of this book, I will offer to you a plan. This plan is based on the concept that sovereignty cannot be maintained without economic strength. It is the economic strength of this country, and the freedom of thought and action, that has allowed us to invent and innovate and pay for all of the things that make us great. At the top of this list is our military might. In order to be a sovereign country, you must be able to protect that country from any invaders. Invaders don't always come with weapons. Sometimes they seek to control and dominate by breaking the economy of a nation, thereby disabling the ability to build and sustain a strong military force.

There is one item that in our time is the key to the economic strength that we need. This is energy. Without a means of supplying and distributing energy, this country will fall economically. The military will be dismantled, and we will become victims. We have now the three legs of sovereignty: Energy, Economics, and Military. In Part II of this book, I will propose a plan, a plan that will bring America to the greatest era in its existence to date. The Golden Age of America is upon us because of what Americans do. We respond to adversity. We are in a time of adversity. We are going to rebuild this country from top to bottom, and we're going to do it without the help of the federal government. We are going to restore sovereignty to the people, and the people will rebuild America. This is nothing like the hope-and-change scenario and fundamental transition that was promised by our President. This will work. It will work because it will involve all of America from the ground up. The plan, though complex, is simple in its concept. When you read Part II of this book, you must keep an open mind and remember how America was built. It was built by entrepreneurs, businessmen, by corporations. It was built on capitalism. Without capitalism, the economic strength will be gone. I'm about to explain that to you.

First, I want to tell you about Part III of the book. Part III is called Miscellaneous Options and Opportunities. You see, whenever a plan is put into place, it must have the ability to expand and diversify. Each time we reach another level, we open doors to solve other problems. The problems that we're going to look at in this part are problems of immigration, education, healthcare, as well as our partnership with other countries that have similar economic woes, and how we can help them. When another country is sovereign, and that means economic strength, there is trade. They buy our products; we buy theirs. That makes the world economy strong. We're also going to look at possible scenarios to enable us to protect our nation, not by building forces that can stop another country as they engage in war against us, but by putting up a barrier built on military strength that reaches far beyond our borders and keeps the pressure off of our borders by putting military might in places around the world that can deter other nations from seeking to engage America in a war scenario. This will all be in Part III of the book.

In Part IV of the book, we will look at means by which we can increase our energy production with new ideas and innovation. Remember, energy is one of the three legs of sovereignty. It is through the proliferation of clean, affordable, environmentally safe energy that we create all of the jobs that provide the economic strength that enables our military to stay strong and provide for the masses, including the safety nets that we call entitlements, which we all believe in as a loving, generous, caring nation. That can come to pass without bankruptcy in this country. It's all based on economics. Energy - being a universal need - can be the means to create 15 million jobs and provide the answers to how we get people out of the ghettos, immigrants on the books paying taxes, living wages for all of those that have any skill. This enables us to build educational systems that will move our children and grandchildren to a new and higher level of satisfaction in their lives. This is what we as responsible adults must do. It is imperative. The time is now.

Now I'm about to give you several scenarios that, as I said, are not uneducated predictions but have a fairly high degree of likelihood. This is what happens when the United States economy fails. I'm also going to explain to you exactly how the economy is going to fail. Let's start with 2008. A bubble bursts. The bubble is created when people over-speculate on stocks. When people over-speculate on stocks, it means that they drive the price of the stock disproportionately higher than what the value of the company is. Let me explain this: The way it is supposed to work is that a publicly traded company has a product they sell and assets they own. Each quarter, when the revenues are tallied, the profits are divided amongst the stockholders. These are called earnings. When you see a company giving out big checks in earnings to their stockholders each quarter, this entices the stockholders, and others who don't have the stock, to buy that stock. It is that check that they get every quarter that makes the stock valuable to them. There is another value to the stock: If the earnings are high, the stock becomes desirable. People want to buy that stock. Therefore, the market price of the stock naturally increases and finds a balance. How much are you going to pay to own the stock compared to how much earnings you are going to get? That's the way it's supposed to work.

Here's the problem: When people buy the stock not based on its earnings but based on speculation that the price of the stock will go up, it creates a bubble. There are actually companies out there that don't even have a product, but they sell stock. The big players invest billions of dollars into owning this stock. That drives the price of the stock up. When the stock reaches a certain level, they sell the stock. Millionaires and billionaires can be made overnight with smart investments in stock, by speculating that their investment in the stock will cause other people to invest. The price will go up, and then they will sell and make a ton of money, even though the stock has limited or no value, as far as earnings go. Smart long-term investors want to see a stock that goes up incrementally based on the amount of earnings that it pays. They want to get that check every quarter. Because of speculation and what we call over speculation, stocks begin to rise disproportionately to what their true value is. You can buy a stock at $50 and in the next three months, it goes up to $75.

Theoretically, you've made $25, even though at the end of the quarter, your earnings are little or nothing. That doesn't matter to a speculator. When we look at 2008, we see exactly that. It was based on housing. The speculators on housing were buying stock in that market, which is technically considered to be a financial market - those run by banks and investors - expecting that the stock price would continue to increase even though the value was nothing or near to nothing. An event occurs that causes the investors to panic. The investors start selling the stock in massive quantities because there are no assets or very few assets, or certainly not enough assets, to warrant the price of that stock. When they panic, the bubble collapses. Who wants to buy a stock that is dropping like a rock and has little or no earnings value? That's what happened in 2008. The housing market bubble collapsed. It caused what we now call the Great Recession. We compare it to a time that we call the Great Depression - the stock market collapse of 1929. What is the difference? Why was that a great depression and this only a great recession? You see, in 1929 the bubble was not just one market. It was not just financials. It was an across- the-board bubble. All stock values were inflated beyond a rational capability for them to ever pay off the investors if the bubble collapsed. The stock market at that time was just a fraction of what it is now. It was not globally entrenched. It wasn't as massive and it wasn't dealing with GDP of $16 trillion a year. Still, when it collapsed, we saw the damage – an unbelievable amount of suffering and loss. Our government decided to adopt Keynesian economics. That is when the government takes control of the financial section and artificially props it up simply by printing money. They print money and give it to the banks so the banks can pay off their debts, and this brings the financial sector back to solvency. That works great for the financial sector.

Because our collapse in 2008 was primarily in the financial sector, it helped. It kept the country and the world from falling into a full-blown depression. Here's the problem: When the nation produces money artificially with a printing press, not based on assets or the earnings that can come from a company that utilizes these assets, it begins a new bubble. Unlike 2008, where the bubble was strategically a financial bubble, the government is building an across-the- board bubble. Its inflection of money into the economy is building higher prices of stocks, and that is because there are no other options for investors to make money. Normally investors will turn their money towards building a business. Small businesses will be coming up in large quantities every day. Because there is no market and no economy, no way to realize earnings from starting a business, the investors now just invest in the stock market. The more they invest, the higher the prices of the stock are.

You can see how, by doing what we call quantitative easing-which is in the hundreds of billions of dollars and has been going on for four years - we are not boosting the economy. Manufacturing is growing at a snail's pace. The growth of the earnings is less than the growth of inflation. Therefore, all investments that are going into businesses are losing money. There are a handful of stocks that are holding the country up. God forbid if they burst! The fact that our country is now teetering on an economy that is artificially propped up by the government is a matter of great concern. What happens if it bursts this time? This time it won't be just a bubble from one sector. It will be an across-the-board collapse, the way it was in 1929, only this time it is 1000 times worse because the economy has grown so much and the inflation has grown so much. All the countries of the world now are involved with each other. If the United States falls, the world falls. There is no way around it.

There is no country that will survive. No country at this point is sovereign. In order to be sovereign, you must have the ability to stand on your own economically. There is no country that can do that. We are in terrible shape, yet according to the other countries of the world, we are actually way better off than they are. If we fall, how will they stand alone? They cannot. They are not sovereign. They do not have sovereign economic status. They are not able to stand on their own. They rely on us and us importing from them. When we break, we will not be able to do that anymore.

What happens next? I'm going to try to do this quickly and painlessly. The bubble bursts. The stock market crash is 1000 times worse than anything we've ever seen. There are no jobs. American currency becomes worthless. The only way to prop up America is by printing money, and the money has nothing to back it up. We say, "We can back it up with gold." First of all, we have no gold. Secondly, when this catastrophe hits, the only thing the people will care about is food and energy. Without energy, we cannot grow and distribute the food. Energy now becomes #1, alongside food. You cannot eat gold. You cannot burn gold for fuel. Anybody that thinks we'll go back to a gold standard is out of their mind. When this happens, people are starving. What do people do when they're starving? They revolt. They gather en masse and attack government institutions, demanding the government do something about it. What can the government do? This will happen around the world.

There will be militias that will go out to anyone who has any of these resources and take them by force. Whole countries will engage in this activity.

Countries that have not will turn to countries that have and demand help. The countries that have will not even be able to supply their own people; they will resist. Do I need to draw you a picture of what started World War III?

Conventional weaponry will be used in the beginning, but there will be no means to manufacture and sustain the amount of ammunition to fight a war. Someone will point a nuclear weapon, first as a threat, a bluff. When the country resists, the nuke will fly - expecting that this show of strength will get them to break. Because of alliances, countries that are under siege will turn to their allies, who will then fire their nuclear weapons. It's going to be ugly.

Another scenario: In order to control the masses when the riots begin and the militias start to form, the only alternative will be for the government to impose martial law. When martial law is imposed, the Constitution goes out the window. It is now up to the military force of the government to control the people, to get control of whatever assets and resources are available, and to ration them as they see fit. What do we call this scenario? We call it socialism. In basic socialist philosophy, the military is not needed. The government supplies for the people based on their needs. They take from the people what they have in resources and abilities to distribute the wealth. In a scenario where there isn't enough to go around, the government must choose who gets the resources and who doesn't. This is done by looking at the capabilities of an individual and deciding what level of productivity and worth they have to provide for the masses. This is communism 101. Communism is a philosophy. Socialism is the implementation of that philosophy. This is what we'll come to. You'll get educated but only to a certain degree, and for certain individuals.

You will get indoctrinated into the communist philosophy. You will lose your belief that God is the ultimate Supreme Being and you will exist for the welfare of the state. This will take three generations. By the time the third generation is old and dying, the generation that is young will have been indoctrinated and then there will be no one left with the old-school mentality of freedom, capitalism, and freedom to choose actionable freedom. Liberty and the pursuit of happiness will no longer exist. That is the best-case scenario. After all, the worst-case scenario is World War III with nukes.

Is that what we want? Do we want to live in a socialist society controlled by the military, where we get rationed according to our usefulness? The United States, being the country with the most resources and the most ability to produce, will not be able to use that to feed its citizens, but must put it into a huge kettle that will be divided up between the nations that are determined to be worthy. Who will determine this? The most worthless idiotic group on this planet, the most inept, moronic imbeciles on this planet - those whom we call the United Nations - will now be in charge of the world. They will decide.

America, please read this book the whole way through. Please stand with me. Implement the plan that I'm going to offer you. Protect the sovereignty of the people, the state, and the nation. Keep us as the hub of righteousness in the world, as you will soon learn the Economics of Sovereignty.

CHAPTER 2

DEFINITIONS

1 : **Rights of the People.** These Rights are outlined in the Constitution and the Bill of Rights. They are, as stated, the inalienable rights that are given to us by God. Everyone has these rights. They are life, liberty, and the pursuit of happiness. The important thing about rights that must be understood is that just because you are born with these rights, it does not necessarily mean you are able to use these rights in your daily life. What we find is, though you may have rights, if you are oppressed and these rights are suppressed by any other individual, the government, dictators, monarchs, or even by another country that affects you in a negative way because of the leverage that they have over you for any reason, then 'rights' are simply abstract. You can't use them for anything. They are of no concern to you. Rights are the precursor to freedom.

2: **Freedom**. Freedom is an extension of your rights. Freedom is the ability to act upon these rights. If you are unable to act upon the rights, then you are not free, and the word 'freedom' is, again, just an abstract word. If a man is put in prison, then his ability to act upon his rights has been seriously compromised;

therefore, his freedom has been compromised. He is free to do only what is allowed by those who put him in jail. Therefore, we should never mix freedom with human rights. The rights always exist; the ability to use those rights may be taken away. This usually is a result of law. In some cases, the jailer may put you there for any reason that he may have. In cases of dictatorships or monarchies, etc., these reasons may not be because of the rule of law; they may simply be at the will or the whim of the person who is in charge. We see this across the world, where people riot, screaming for their freedom. This is because they know that those rights that they were born with - that they instinctively feel they should be able to act upon - have been compromised. Those that strive for freedom will often rise up against the suppressor and are generally met with physical violence. We see this, as Americans, in our own history. The roots of our country came from a desire to be able to act upon our human rights in a free manner. We, therefore, revolted – the Revolution against Britain. There was much physical violence and much bloodshed. Had we lost, we would have never been free. Because we won, we are now able to act upon our rights, and we therefore have freedom.

3: **Sovereignty**. What we see is that freedom must be protected. Now, what protects the freedom? What protects freedom is sovereignty. The definition of sovereignty is being independent from all others. Pretty simple, pretty clear, yet it goes very, very deep. First, to be independent requires some very important items. In our world today, there are three things necessary to be sovereign. First, you must have a strong military. If you are not able to turn your oppressor away from your borders, then the invader will conquer and suppress. Freedom will disappear. Although you still have the rights given to you by God, you will not be able to act on them. Again, it becomes simply an abstract term. The second thing that you need is a strong economy.

Throughout history, it is the one that has the wealth that commands the power to rule. In ancient times, land was wealth.

The land supported all human needs. Therefore, if you had the land, you had the wealth. Of course, as always, there would be those who would choose to come to your land, remove you from power, and assume that power, therein increasing their land and their wealth. Again, you see the importance of the military. Now we ask, "How do you get a strong military?" You must have a good economy. You must have the means to pay for a strong military. Therefore, in the economy, the distribution of wealth and the ability to gain wealth are paramount in being sovereign. If you cannot pay the bills, you cannot be sovereign. The third thing that you must have to be sovereign is a source of energy. In ancient times, that was not a big issue because energy was in the form of fire. The land produced the trees, the trees were made of wood, and wood would burn. Even when the first steam engines were produced, they ran on steam produced by fire that came from the burning of wood. Those times were much simpler, and you could almost discount energy as being important to sovereignty because it was so abundant. In the days of our fathers and today, we've seen energy rise to a level equal to, and possibly even greater than, the economy. The military needs a strong source of revenue to fund it; the economy produces that. Yet, how does a nation function without an abundant source of energy? Electricity depends on it. Fuel depends on it. Vehicles run on that fuel. The military is lost without a source of fuel and a source of energy. Without the economy and without the military, you cannot be sovereign. Now we have a dilemma. In the United States, we call ourselves a sovereign nation, implying that we have the economic means to support ourselves, the military to protect our borders, and the energy sources to run the country. Problem: Our economy has tanked so badly at this point, that we are well over $17 trillion in debt. How can we be sovereign, and independent from all others, when we are so strongly tied to those to whom we owe the money? In essence, we work for them. They influence our daily actions in enormous ways because without them we have no funds and no ability to run our country. Therefore, it is obvious to me that because of this debt and because of the slow economy - and our inability to not only pay the debt off but even stop borrowing - the first leg of sovereignty has been broken. Let's look further. Because energy is so important, much of the economy depends on energy. It influences nearly everything in every way. When the price of energy goes up, it hits every person in the country. Our dependence on sources of energy that come from other countries again gives those countries leverage over us. They can now dictate terms, ask for favors, get away with unscrupulous acts, and not be punished for these deeds because we cannot afford to lose that source of energy. Also, since the energy costs go up and down under their control, it directly affects the economy. When we depend on another country for that source of energy, that influence is always negative. Therefore, we have just broken the second leg of sovereignty. The only leg left now is the military, and how long do you expect it to withstand the downslide of a poor economy? What if the energy sources are cut off? How will they function? We still have a strong military, the best in the world; how long is this going to last? Our third leg of sovereignty is teetering; it is dependent on the first two. We still have control over that, but for how long?

We, I claim, are not a sovereign nation. We are not independent of all others. This is what we have fought for, and our fathers fought for, and their fathers, and son, back to the first Pilgrim that ever-set foot on this land. The original people who ran away from their oppressors could find a place where they could be sovereign, where they could be independent. It's simple: That's why we had the Declaration of Independence. That's why we have Independence Day. Where is that independence now? We have lost our sovereignty. We are puppets for much of the rest of the world, yet we refuse to accept and realize that we need to stand up and turn this around. Sovereignty, if you recall, protects freedom. How will we remain free when sovereignty is lost? If you have sovereignty, you will know freedom. Give me sovereignty, or give me death.

CHAPTER 3

STATE SOVEREIGNTY

In the previous chapter, we discussed the importance of sovereignty as a nation. We explained the three legs that support this sovereignty, that enable this sovereignty, that create this sovereignty. What about the States? In the Constitution, the states are given more power than the Federal Government: Why is this? What made them do it this way? It's actually simple.

The people in any state deal directly with the government of that state. The government of that state is in touch with the needs of the people of that state. This has to be because every state is different. Some states need some things; other states need others. The people of each state are different. People in one state may feel that a law should be enacted because of problems that they have in their particular state. When you go to another state, you find they don't have the same problems, and therefore laws may differ or may not even exist. Why address a problem you don't have? Because of this close relationship between the individuals and the state government, the founding fathers decided that the states needed to have more power when governing the people. They, therefore, need to be independent from the Federal Government. Therefore, they need state sovereignty. Because of the Constitution, the state is protected. Their sovereignty is protected. Therefore, they don't necessarily need an army. They don't necessarily need their own sources of energy. However, economic conditions in any state are absolutely the number one item of importance. Because the state has responsibilities to its people, it needs to provide for them. It needs to provide things such as Unemployment Compensation, entitlements for the poor and homeless, and types of medical insurance. It needs to address the problems found in that state. The people of that state are of utmost concern. This is a very difficult scenario. It's difficult because states cannot print money, like the Federal Government. They have to continuously balance a budget while providing for their people. What happens when they fail? Let's just look around the country.

States are failing all over the place. They then try to borrow money. As their failure gets more pronounced, those that would lend do not want to lend any more. The people fall on hard times. Unemployment runs amok. The entitlement programs are flooded by those who cannot provide for themselves. The tax revenues that keep the state afloat dwindle. The bills are going up as the revenues are going down. It's double trouble! The alternative is that states must then turn to the Federal Government and ask for help. How can the Federal Government help?

All 50 states have individuals who are paying taxes. Those tax revenues go to the Federal Government. For the particular states that get in financial trouble or cannot meet their bills, the Federal Government takes out of its pocket, which in essence is the people of the country's pockets, and gives it to that particular state. Now you have 49 states propping up one bad one. Of course, as Americans, we don't let our neighbors fall on those types of hard times. What happens when other states begin to fail when the bad economy moves from state to state like an infection? Every state becomes financially sick. The revenues that go into the Federal Government are greatly diminished, while more and more states are asking for handouts. Soon the Federal Government runs out of our money. Major problems now occur.

First, they try printing more money; that only inflates the dollar and makes our conditions worse. Now, instead of having $5 and a loaf of bread is $2, you only have $2 and the loaf of bread is $5. That's what we get when we just print money and spend it without getting anything in return. No profits, no dividends; just emptying the pockets of the people. That would be okay if the people had lots of money in those pockets, but let's look: We've got a national crisis. The people have no money. We're in depression and we're in recession. What do we do?

Simple: The Federal Government then goes out and borrows the money to give to the states to pay their bills, and to take care of the people that are suffering terribly. Of course, in that case, they can't really give the people a lot because there are so many, so everybody gets a meager subsistence allotment. We get just enough to survive. What happens along this path? Just as the Federal Government is now indebted to the suppliers of their energy as well as the suppliers of their money, the states are now indebted to the Federal Government. Since we are the people who live within the borders of those states, it falls on us, but we don't have any money. What is the state going to do? They basically sell off their sovereignty. They let the Federal Government come in, make the regulations, make the rules, and set up basically anything they want. If the states refuse to comply, their funding can be cut off. This gets very complicated.

The representatives of that state are in Washington. They're supposed to be there to represent that state, yet the Federal Government, especially the executive branch, is trying to dictate to the states what they will accept and what they won't. Battles go on in Congress. Months and months go by.

Representatives from states that would benefit from the government being there want more. Representatives who don't believe the Federal Government should be there in the first-place fight back. These wars rage inside the halls of Congress. In the end, they try to compromise. They try to make a plan that will benefit every state, all states the same. This is not even possible! The states are too varied; they are too many in number. You cannot find a one-size-fits- all plan for anything in our country.

When we look at the Constitution the Federal Government is not even permitted to dictate to all 50 states. That state is supposed to be sovereign. It is supposed to have its own independence. It is supposed to deal with its own problems in its own ways. Once the trend of taking away state sovereignty began, the Federal Government realized that there could be no limit to the amount of power that it could amass.

CHAPTER 4

INDIVIDUAL SOVEREIGNTY

In this chapter, we will study the atrocities that were caused when the Federal Government tried to impose its will, successfully, on state sovereignty, and how this damaged individual sovereignty. It ended up in a bloody war.

Initially, the moral high ground was taken by many in the North, though the South had a number of people who were in agreement with the morality of the issue of slavery. On the whole, it became a battle between North and South for the state rights of sovereignty. It ended up with the Emancipation Proclamation, which defined the rights of the individual to be free. We have discussed the difference between rights and actual freedom, and how sovereignty protects these, as well as what the basis is for accepting these values. Let's look at the Civil War, and all this blood and treasure that was spent - 650,000 lives. What was the actual plan, how did it progress, and of what value was it?

Let's start with some of the basic issues. The people wanted to set slaves free. That was morally correct. There were issues on what the limits of freedom were and what limitations should be on their individual statuses as American citizens. Previously, they had not been recognized as citizens.

Supposedly, this freedom would allow that. Yet the bias of the people, and I mean A LOT of people in the North and the South, was quite evident in the way the African Americans were treated. They were given freedom by the stroke of a pen on a piece of paper. The real freedom comes when the human rights given to us by God are brought to fruition through the actions of the individual. Therefore, real freedom is an actionable commodity. It is an extension of the human rights. Therefore, if one cannot enact their rights through freedom, again freedom is just another word.

What we have is a condition where this point becomes very important. By the demeanor of the white man towards the black man, the black man was not able to utilize his rights in a free manner. Everywhere they went, they were belittled, condemned, physically abused, pushed away, laughed at, hated. They were hated enough to spawn, in later years, the Ku Klux Klan, which was merely an exaggeration of the hatred for the black man that existed all along. In fact, at one point, we even decided that the black man was only three-fifths of a person. Does that mean he had three-fifths of a soul? Does God see him as only three-fifths of what his creation was all about? Did God see the black man as a mistake? Does God see the black man as being secondary in the overall plan that He has for his children? Is the black man the crippled child of God?

Does he not deserve equal amounts of love and consideration from God? Does not God require us to follow and address His will, to glorify Him by having compassion towards all of his children, to want to help all of our brothers and sisters equally, with equal love and equal compassion and equal care? These issues were so dominant, and have been for so long, that it has caused us to try to find a path through the confusion. This path is where we can clear our souls and our guilt by doing something, rather than nothing, yet not having to embrace or uplift our black brothers and sisters. What we do is create a Welfare system. We will talk a little more about that later in the chapter.

In the original plan - as it was spoken of by the proponents of the Emancipation Proclamation - the black man, though never envisioned as an equal and never treated as an equal, should at least be given some opportunity to lift themselves. This was all a good idea; however, the plan was flawed. It was spoken and printed that the black man should receive a mule and 40 acres. Let's remember: Women did not get their sovereignty until the 1900s. It was well into the 1900s - in the first half of the century - but many years later. Black women, therefore, were left out of the picture. Of course, children were the possessions of their parents and were given no rights. You have to look at this from the perspective of the black people. First of all, there better be a male adult in the family if there were to be any way that the inalienable rights could be extended into freedom - actual, realized, tangible freedom.

Let's say that occurs. Most male slaves of adult age took a wife and immediately began to propagate the race. They had babies. This was great for the slave owners, who became very interested in which slaves mated and which were deemed not useful in the mating process. Of course, when a slave child was born, he became the property of that owner. That owner wanted that slave to be big and strong and healthy, so he could do much work. He could have other children who were big, strong, and healthy. When freedom was given, you would expect that the black man would immediately break away from his owner, if not for any other reason than to be able to pick their own spouse, whom they would mate.

Problem: The black man had never been allowed to become fluent in English or whatever language was preferred by their owner, pretty much any of the languages that were prevalent at that time. They were not allowed to be educated. A slave could face mortal punishment if the owner caught him with a book, trying to learn, or having been slightly educated and learning to possibly read and write. If they were caught engaging in those activities, it was very bad for them. The point I'm making is, how does a slave in the deep South, or really anywhere but mostly where they were isolated, find out that he is a free man? You see, even though all the blood was shed - the Federal Government intruded on the state's sovereignty- it really wasn't going to change things, not for a long time. Now that they were freed, they could learn to read and write. They could go out and be educated. Since they were no longer owned by anyone, anyone who tried to stop them would be in violation of the law. Big deal!

The fact of the matter is that for a long, long time they didn't even know.

Slowly but surely, the word started getting around. You would think that black people would rise up, stand against their oppressors, take their newfound freedom, and go on their way. Wrong! This would be the position of a black slave: He finds out the freedom that was fought for has actually come about.

He knows the bias and the bigotry of the white man towards him, even in the states that fought for their freedom. He looks at his position and says, "Where am I going to go? How will I get there? What will I do when I get there? I can't read or write. I don't even know how to count money. I can't even communicate effectively, in many cases. I have no money. I have no tools. I don't have an ox, a mule, or the 40 acres that I'm supposed to get. Where are these acres and where is my mule? Is anyone down here handing out mules and certificates of ownership to the property? I don't think so! Big talk, Mr.

Lincoln." Big talk. So, the slave owners pretty much won after all, on that issue. But they lost state sovereignty, and therein lies the crime. Even though the Federal Government mandated it, the southern states just ignored it. The slaves had no way of capitalizing on it. Therefore, to them, freedom was just a piece of paper.

We look back and say, "But we did the right thing." After a while, we start feeling a little bit guilty. Slowly but surely, the black man begins to integrate into everyday society. Now what do we do? There are those of us Bible-toting, gospel-spouting phonies who want to show that they glorify God and emulate Jesus. They really don't want the black man around, though. They start rumors of how the black man rapes the white woman. Women and children are pulled from the street when the black man walks into town. They take positions of subservience to those with enough money, those who would have servants in their houses, and servants tending to their properties. These privileged people make a deal that they will not physically abuse - ha, ha - and that they will treat their servants properly. Some of the more righteous ones do; others slip right back into their abusive ways because they still don't see the black man as their equal.

Oh, yes, they're at church on Sundays. They're praying and dropping their two cents in the basket, then going home and patting themselves on the back, expecting to be whisked up to heaven when they die because of their righteousness. The people - let's use the term loosely - "working" for them are still slaves. They still have nowhere to go, no means to get there, no money to start a life. No white man will accept them. They can't get work. The only work that will be given to them will be under the condition that they basically remain as slaves. This was termed servitude. There were some who would say, "If you serve me for a period of time, we will release you and help you to make your own way."

When the time would come, many would renege and extend the length of servitude. It was a legal slavery system. We were 'doing right by the poor, helpless, heathen animals that lived among us.' It makes me sick!

Now the black man and his family have served their time in servitude if they had taken that approach, and expected to go out and make a life. Again, he is met with resistance, the righteous resistance of the same people who go to church on Sundays and pat themselves on the back. They still don't want him around. They actually fear him. Why? They know that anyone who has been treated that way would - when given the chance, or certainly would be expected to - come back and fight to try to even the score. A little revenge would be appropriate. They were afraid to give them the vote. They thought that they would take over Congress because there were so many of them.

They would take over the government. This was what was put out there by the fearmongers, the ones who really hated the black people. They regarded them as undesirable, and unequal. They felt they should remain as property. Nothing can be further from the truth. History shows that.

The black man struggles, struggles, and struggles. The suffering may be not as bad as when in slavery, but in some cases may be worse. The suffering is just unbearable. What are they going to do? They still have no money. They have no education. A very few have been lucky enough to meet someone with a true heart, and true compassion who helps to educate them. Of course, those who have been educated go and try to educate others. Brilliant minds are found amongst the black people. There is much for them to be proud of. In fact, few races have ever survived such an onslaught of bigotry and hatred.

That alone is something of which to be proud.

As time goes on, it is a long, slow, hard-fought battle. Finally, as we move into the 20th Century, the Industrial Revolution is the era of progressivism and the era of massive gains by the Federal Government in the way of control of the country. Finally, Civil Rights again become issues. This time, the black man has begun to mass into groups and stand up. Leaders from within those groups stand up and make themselves known. They begin to demand that they have more opportunity, and more means to advance their cause. There is a problem still: Though some have come around, many of the white people have yet to find compassion in their hearts. No matter what the law would demand of the people. The government may force whites to comply with ordinances, state and Federal laws, regulations, and mandates. They could not pluck the bigotry from the hearts of the white man. That can only be done within the soul of the individual. Slowly, this guilt becomes pronounced, and decent white people take up the cause alongside their black brothers and sisters. They try to bring to the forefront what has been there all along but has been repressed. The racist whites whisper about the 'nigger' but don't want to stand up and shout it out loud. What happens is they form groups.

One in particular is the Ku Klux Klan, those that whisper about the 'nigger' and decide to take action. Being the cowards that they were and are and always will be, they had to cover their faces. Of course, they wore white because they were so righteous. They stood alongside decent people in the churches. They worked alongside them in the mills and the factories. At night, they were killed. They set houses, and sometimes even people, on fire. They thought that everybody really would admire them for that. Some did: The latent racists, the ones that remained whisperers. Others, seeing the atrocities, finally had to face their guilt and say, "What can we do? Of course, we still don't want them to stand alongside us. We don't want them in our churches.

We don't want them in our communities. But we have to help the poor heathens, in order to answer to our guilt and to appease our consciences. What should we do?" Idea: Let's take the worst, most miserable, rat-infested, unheated part of town, with no plumbing, and put them there, where we don't have to worry about them. We don't have to work with them. We don't have to face them every day. We can put them there and forget about it. How will they live? We will create a welfare state. We will give them the absolute basic needs to survive. We will spend as little as possible. We will not ever go up to that part of town to check on how they are or the way they're living. But now we have appeased our consciences and served our guilt. The welfare state is born.

Slavery has been renewed, but slavery is different this time. The slavery is an invisible chain that attaches the black man to the state and to the Federal Government. The chain is an economic chain. They are dependent on the government for their mere existence, for their everyday survival. This is still slavery! Of freedom and of human rights - what have they? Do you remember the definition of sovereignty? Sovereignty means independence. They are not independent, in any way. Everything they have in life depends on the government. They have no sovereignty. We gave them freedom on a piece of paper, written in blood, but we never gave them sovereignty. We never made them independent, so that they could learn and grow and prosper, so that they could become viable members of society and be accepted into society, with their rights and freedoms protected by their sovereignty.

Their sovereignty would only be allowed because of some improvement in their economic status. They would have prospered. They would have amassed wealth. They could afford sovereignty. They could afford to walk away, to break the chains that bound them to government. Instead, what did we do?

Little by little, year after year, we tried to give them a little bit more, maybe some healthcare. We promised them education but did not deliver. We put them in schools - big deal! What if they do get educated, and they are bright? When they come out of school, where is there to go? Here we are again. We are back in the 1860s. "Where is there to go? What will I do when I get there? Will I be accepted or shunned?"

A young child is born in the ghetto. For several years, he has been tended to mostly by his mother. At a certain age, he steps out of the house onto the streets and looks around. What does he see? Violence. Drugs. What doesn't he see? A future. A way out. A means by which he can claim his sovereignty, his independence. A means to break the chain, walk out with his head held high- a free man, a sovereign man with a goal, with necessary education and skills, with the jobs out there waiting so that he can live an independent life. Does this exist? There are those who would make points of some who have gotten lucky, some who have ancestors who pushed their way into positions where they gained some wealth. There are some that have actually become Congressman and Senators, one even a President. So, we stand back and say, "They're doing just fine, all because we gave them their freedom." Yea for us! Pat us on our backs. Let's count how many are still slaves, compared to the number that have become sovereign citizens. The atrocities continue.

There is a way. Let's go back to the beginning. You see if we had addressed this problem in a logical way, it would be over by now. The acceptance by the white man of the black man would have been accelerated. We would have much more quickly realized that they are of value. They are people, they are God's children, and they are valuable, not just to God but to our Nation. How should we have done this? The landowners of the southern states, those that were economically dependent on slave labor, could have found a way around this. If they had, the issue of slavery would have been addressed by state and local governments. Therefore, there would have been no need for the Federal Government to intervene. Therefore, the sovereignty of the states would not have been challenged. Therefore, there would have been no Civil War, and this country would be a much different place. What should we have done?

Let's look at the economics. A plantation owner needs workers. He needs them as cheaply as possible. The markets for their products are great, but the supplies are in abundance. Competition between slave owners creates a demand for inexpensive labor. That's what started the whole thing. They would just go to Africa, where the animals live, and rip the people away from what, for them, was a sovereign tribe or nation, and make slaves out of them; that solves the problem. The thing is the people that went to get the slaves had expenses. They needed big boats. They needed people to man the boats. They needed weapons. They needed to make it the whole way to Africa, round up these people, and bring them the whole way back. Why would they do that?

There must be profit in it. There was! There was a huge profit in it. Where did the profit come from? It came from the people that they sold the slaves to.

How about that?

Suddenly, slaves are not free; I mean, in having no money invested in them.

You don't just go out and pluck them from a tree. You have to pay for them. They start looking at them as commodities. They want the biggest, the strongest one that is not a child but not a full-grown man. They want to get their mileage out of this person because he is very expensive. Of course, you have to breed him in order to propagate your herd. Yes, I said 'herd', like cattle in a herd. Therefore, you have to buy some women as well. Women, when they have babies, run the risk of losing their babies. You don't want that; as a slave owner, you want new generations. You're even choosing which slaves to mate with which women. You want great big strong women. You buy them; they cost more. If they have a couple of children who appear to be healthy and strong, with the potential to grow, you might throw a couple of bucks in for that as well. Now your investment amount has considerably grown. Let's not stop there. You have to buy chains. You have to buy shackles. You have to hire people to beat and whip them into submission, to make sure that they are producing a maximum amount every day. You have to put clothes on them.

You have to feed them. If a valuable slave would take ill, you didn't just throw him away. You needed to get him healthy again. He was no use to you otherwise. If he became deathly ill, then you just kicked him out into nowhere or threw him in a hole - whatever you wanted to do with him.

Those who were belligerent, who would not let you subject them to this torture, were taken to Market. Hopefully, they looked big and strong. They couldn't really speak English. They couldn't stand up for themselves. Then you would find some sucker out there that would pay you equal or near to equal what you paid for him. You could get your money back, hopefully. If that came to pass, he may just be ripped away from his spouse and his children, and that would be it. Family gone. It was bad enough that they tore him away from the families when they kidnapped them from Africa, but now that they've finally settled with a new spouse and new family, they at any moment can be ripped away and sold. My God! Could you imagine if you were in your house and you had several children and your husband was the only provider, and the only way that he provided was by being useful to the man that owns you, and the man that owns you decides your husband wasn't useful to him anymore and ripped him away from you and your children? You never saw him again. How on God's earth could we live with ourselves?

Now we think we are better because we don't do that anymore. How about this? This is what should have happened. Suppose before the war ever started, individual states and big landowners got together with important people from the North and the

33

politicians. The politicians say about an impending war: "Look, you see what's coming. This is going to be a major blowout. No one needs this, and no one wants it. We understand the position that you're taking for state sovereignty. We don't want to do this, but we will. Let's figure out a plan. We know how much that slave costs you. We know how much it costs you to keep him and his family, to breed, to house, to clothe, to feed. No wonder you cannot afford to give him any money. They're already expensive enough. Suppose we set up a system where we give them their freedom. The state really does not even need to mandate that. As an owner, as a sovereign individual, you have the right to give any of your possessions their freedom. Of course, where will they go? How will they survive? You see, you have them over a barrel. Whether we fight this out, whether we sign this piece of paper or not, you have them at a disadvantage, a serious disadvantage."

How about this? Suppose we come together and ask our states to mandate certain conditions. First, you have the right to keep your slave if you want. If you choose to set them free, though, this is what will happen. You will be required to give the slaves fair payment for their work. You will pay them hourly or daily, but there will be a maximum of what you can ask them to do. If you need more hours from them, you can negotiate. You can say, "If you continue to work for me today, I will pay you more." This wage needs to be determined by what is considered, and that would mean some study and analysis on what it would take to live. We'll take a look around and see what the average worker/farmhand/subservient person would make if being paid a fair wage. We'll use that as a basis. What you're going to do is give these people and their families a small patch of dirt suitable for farming, maybe just a few acres - two, three, four. You have thousands and thousands of acres. Put them down in a corner, give them that dirt, supply them with basic hand tools for farming, and supply them with wood to put up some shacks to live in. For that, you will take a small amount of money from their pay each week. The strong males would be under your employment. They would be required to show up at work when the sun comes up and work the required amount of hours before they go home. The required amount of hours should leave time in the daylight. They can go home and tend to their own gardens. They would be allowed to set traps and to try to feed themselves from the land. You wouldn't give them guns. As the employer and owner of the land that they are leasing from you, you can demand that. If they don't comply, they have the right to leave. You can fire them. You can't kill them, you can't beat them, but you can fire them. As the children grow, they can tend to the land. You, of course, as the employer, would supply them with their first seeds to start. The wife tends to the house, and the cooking; any spare time she has, she is out in the field working with the children. The families inevitably would join together, and for those who can't keep up with their crops, the community would help. What they do for a living is farming; this fits perfectly into this scenario because they would be required to farm some land for themselves. At this point, you no longer clothe them or feed them; they must take care of themselves. They get a small amount of money, which they bring home with them, which they can use to buy a little bit of livestock, some chickens, and maybe even a cow for milking. They may wish to take their money and purchase an upgrade in tools. The men get up every morning; they are loyal to their employers. This is how they survive, just like the rest of us. They would be free to go if they wanted. They could be fired. They would pay a small amount, a previously established amount, of rent for the land and the shack.

Our Northern Politician may point out that the community would become smarter. They could go out and buy a book or two. They could find someone, or even send someone out, for basic education: reading, writing, arithmetic. This person could come back into the community and teach the rest new ways of farming. They get smarter. Their crops are doing better. They divide the chores up amongst the community. "Who can grow this? Who can grow that?" Not everybody grows everything. Some grow corn, some grow wheat, and some grow vegetables. Some supply eggs and chickens. When one entity weakens, the others come to their rescue to pick up and help. This is the way America started, the reason why America and Americans prospered. You see the growth of America. You see the prosperity. Giving the black man that opportunity would have been what was righteous. That is what God would hope that we would do. The black man, in a short amount of time, would become sovereign and independent while, just like the rest of us, would give up a little bit of his independence and tie himself to his employer, just as the employer ties himself to his employee. What works for one also works for the other. The relationship between employer to employee should and could, and sometimes will, be a sacred bond. No employer under the sun wants more than to have a hardworking, loyal employee. The landowners would have found this in the black man. They would have found it times ten. The black man would have respected the white people, and the white people would have learned to have respect for the black man.

Let's fast-forward: 100, 120, 130, 150 years go by. Are there ghettos? Yes.

Are there people who can't or won't help themselves? Yes. Do we have the obligation, because of the desire for social justice, to help those people? Yes. How many would there be? Not too many. Most would be working, sovereign American citizens. Many would have banded into communities that, while open, would still be mostly or all-black. Why? Perhaps they would prefer it that way. If they didn't, perhaps they would want to move into your community - Because you may have a better school there, and they want the best for their child. Over all these years I submit that we would have learned to respect and honor the wishes of our equal partners in life. The minorities, whether the black, the brown, or - those who used to be the worst abused- women, would be embraced by our communities. We would not have feared them. We would never have said blacks are three-fifths of a person. The economic changes that were forced on them - yes,

I say 'forced' on them- because of the condition that was created for them, would not exist. There would be levels of dependence. Anyone who cannot help themselves will be dependent on the kindness of someone else.

As these black communities would have prospered, business would have grown and entrepreneurship would have been at a high level. Success would have been at a high level, breaking out into worldwide markets and national markets. They are not stupid. They can work every bit as hard as any of us.

They are not motivated. They are not driven. They do not see a future. They do not create goals that they think they can ever achieve. We propagate that. We keep them tied to our economic chains, and the Federal Government loves it.

They grow, and they grow, and they grow; every time they do, they give us another entitlement, a bigger and stronger chain. It is a new chain. Sometimes they make it out of chrome and make it nice and shiny. We can't wait to try it on, but it is a chain. You give up freedom because you lose sovereignty, and sovereignty protects our freedom.

What would the world look like? The money that entitlements cost us is unbelievable. The waste of human life is atrocious. All along, the landowners could have balanced their books if the state had demanded that all employers use this method, not just with the blacks but even the poor, wretched white people who were also shunned. Maybe the price of cotton or other commodities would have risen a little bit, but let's look at it this way: Rather than create a welfare state, we could take a little bit of money - which we do all the time - and give some subsidies to those employers. Help them to make sure that they can remain competitive. I submit that in the long run, it would have been cheaper for the employers, the landowners, etc. to put the black man on the clock, to pay him, to arrange for him to be able to live as a sovereign, free man. They would have saved money and about 650,000 lives.

America would look so much different. Maybe if we had stopped that grab for sovereignty by the Federal Government when they initially stood against the South and broke the sovereignty of the state, just maybe we wouldn't be dealing with the bloated, huge, inefficient, demanding government that we know today. Maybe we would have stopped this progressive cycle 150 years ago. Let's try to stop it now. We can't go back (maybe in little bites) but we sure as hell don't have to continue with this madness. With my plan comes millions of jobs. Let's take a look at what we can do now.

First of all, the jobs, as you will see later, are going to grow in number at a phenomenal rate, an exponential rate, to the point where we cannot keep up, to the point where the labor force is barely able to supply the need of the employers. There will be more jobs than there are working forces. In ten years, 20 million American citizens will give up their jobs to move into retirement. This has everyone scared. How are we going to be able to pay them their Social Security and keep Medicare alive? Their problem is this:

Because of our stunted growth, we simply haven't been able to keep up. Now, with the growth still stunted, and all of the people who have paid in their entire lives coming out of the workforce wanting what they were promised, we can't do it. Why? What happened to all that money that was paid in? It was stolen! There was so much because everyone was paying in and no one was taking out. There was so much that the greedy politicians could not stand it.

They had to have their hands on that money. They got it, and they blew it! They never paid it back. Now we, the baby boomers, are screwed. Now what do they want us to do? They want us to work longer. Add three more years to our already tortured 40 years of existence in the workplace, for many of us.

Add three more years to it - that'll save us some money. Do you know what else is happening? At the rate of 2 million people a year going into retirement, that would be 2 million jobs a year that do not open up for our kids who are coming out of high school and college. What do we tell them? What is three more years, when we're looking at 20 or 30 years that this problem is going to last? Oh, big deal. It won't work. It's stupid. If anything, we should be retiring earlier so that the young people can get a job. They are going to have to carry the burden to keep us safe and alive, with healthcare, with money, with other programs that help the dis- abled and crippled and elderly that can't get around. That burden will fall on our youth, and they damn well better have a job. They better get married to a woman or married to a man that has a job.

They better be trained, and they better be educated. There better be a lot of them because they're going to have to take on this burden. You must outrun the problem. You must outgrow the problem.

How do we get this thing up and running? We forget about the three-year extension. We just let people retire at 65. We don't want to raise taxes. Let's look at my plan. I will bring this plan in detail in the second part of this book. Let's just take some numbers: I'd say my plan creates 10 million jobs in five years, from the time that it actually goes into operation. It'll take a year to get it set up, but from the time we sign the first contract over to start rebuilding this country, jobs will be created. In five years, I submit the number will be in, on, or around 10 million new jobs. Many of them will actually be old jobs that will come back to life. Ten million people will go to work. That is 10 million people who will now be paying into Social Security. Their employers will now be paying taxes on them. For every job we create, we increase the revenue and remove the demand. That's a double positive now. Every job. I'm telling you I'm going to put 10 million people to work in the first five years. Do you think that might help our situation with Social Security and Medicare, as well as Medicaid? How many of these people who are unemployed end up on welfare? What about the welfare payments? What about the food stamps? What about Medicaid? Again, double negatives. They used to pay taxes to supply these things. Now they're on the line taking out instead of putting in. That's a double negative. Everyone we take off of that welfare line and put back to work, we turn a double negative into a double positive. He now is paying taxes. He is contributing, while at the same time, he is being eliminated from the people that are removing money from the system.

We have to outgrow. We have to outrun them. We have to create jobs. That's how we're going to stabilize these entitlements. That's how we will have the safety net that we so desperately need and deserve. We won't use it unless we have to, but it will be there. We must outrun the problem. Let's add up the total: 10 million in five years. I'm saying 15 million in ten years, because some of the people working on projects will be done in the first five years, and they will move on to the second stage of projects. Some will remain behind; therefore, the job market will expand at a rate of 50% per five years, in the second five years. That's what I claim. I would love someone to do serious statistical analysis, as my abilities are limited. Let's add that 15 million jobs in ten years to the 20 million jobs that will be open because of the retirement of our senior citizens. Tell me now: Where are we going to get 35 million people trained, and skilled? Let's go back to African Americans, who have been waiting patiently (some not so patiently) for hundreds of years, to get their shot at the American dream.

How about this? I will walk you through my plan. This is my plan for education: First of all, I don't believe Americans are undereducated like the statistics tell us. Yes, the other countries love to rub our noses in it – while everything great always comes from America. If we're so stupid, why is that so? Here's the reason the numbers stink: We have some of the brightest, most educated people on the planet, and we have a lot of them. At the same time, all of these people that I've been telling you about, that are chained to the inner- cities, take the tests and it's abysmal. It's embarrassing. The national average plummets. It's not because we don't spend enough money. We keep adding to the amount of money, but it does nothing. The teacher's unions demand more, and they eat up the money. They get away with it because they are the Union. People like Barack Obama, rather than help straighten this mess out, stab us in the back and let Unions Walk all over the taxpayer so that he can get votes. It makes me sick.

Suppose we do this: We go into the inner city. I don't care if it's a black ghetto or a barrio ghetto. I don't care if Italians live there; I don't care if it's Russians or anybody, Muslim or Jew. We go into these areas of poverty, into the areas where the people are chained to the government. We look at the kids from first grade on up. We see who is the brightest. Of course, some IQ tests can be helpful. Let's see where our strengths are. Now we've identified our strongest force. Let's make a proposition. Suppose you do this: You graduate from grade school and move into middle school, do well and move into high school, do well there. We want to see a motivated, intelligent, well-balanced individual who has some compassion and cares about the plight of the community that he or she lives in. I'll tell you what we'll do: We will pay for you to go to a fine college. Pretty much up to a dollar amount that we have preset, you can pick the one you want, but we're going to pick the curriculum. You are going to learn to be a teacher. Choose your level: Grade school, middle school, or high school. You're going to learn to be a teacher, and you are going to come out of there with at least a C average. Anything below that and you may be subject to us pulling your funding. I said 'funding.' We will pay for that education, all elements of it. All fees, housing, food, and an allowance for clothing and miscellaneous. We will pay for it. There will be a contractual agreement between us. Here is your end of the bargain: When you come out of college, you will go back to your community or a similar community where the ghetto exists, where the people are in the greatest need of a good education.

You will spend the next five years there, at any particular level that you've been trained at. You will develop new teaching methods. You will learn how to motivate. You will learn how to deal with the problems. You will learn how to bring our children along, to instill goals in them, to instill the values in them.

Make them love their community and love their country. I say 'make them'; you can't make them, but you sure can influence them in a positive way. You will do this for five years. You will be paid well. We will subsidize the average payment, which I hope will be made reasonable, and the benefits made reasonable, in the future. We will throw in a few bucks based on performance when we see your kids coming out with some good scores. I want to see your kids moving on to the next grade. At the end of five years, you will take these teaching methods and go back to college, this time as a professor, with a professor's wages. Good money. The job is guaranteed as long as you perform in the first five years.

In the meantime, we will have chosen others. They will have come up through the system and will have shown that they have an above-average ability. They will have shown that they have desire and determination and that they care about their community. Hopefully, they will have been involved in some community actions, and some community service, to make us want them. We will put them through the same program that we put you through, only this time you will be their professor. You, as the one who has studied the problem for the last five years, and who has shown an ability to motivate and get results, will now take your teaching methods and teach the new teachers. It will be a special program. In order to qualify, you have to have come from poor surroundings. You have to have an understanding of the problem. You have to have come from those communities that you wish to go back to and serve. For five years, you will train a new group. They will follow the same process. It will be five years in their community, or any community that is similar and that needs their help. I am not racist, but I would like to see blacks helping blacks;

there is much easier bonding when you're dealing with one of your own who understands you and has gone through what you are going through. There are cultural differences between different races. I think it would just be more efficient. Hopefully, we will put you right back into the very community from which you came. If we do this repeatedly, every year putting new people into the program who come out with this special knowledge, having gone through the special training, it won't be long. Maybe 10, 15 years, but certainly by the time this generation has grown, we will have an army of qualified, specially trained operatives. Our Navy Seals of the teaching community. We will have an army. We will invade every corner of every ghetto in this country. We will bring the education, we will bring the motivation, and we will bring the opportunity. We're going to start in high school training them in a number of different trades and skills. We're going to give them the opportunity to spend some time in each area to see what they like. We will make a promise to them: If you qualify because of your economic status, and you graduate from high school - just get through it, just graduate - and have taken the prerequisite training in your junior and senior years, we will put you into a training program. We will give you a grant to go to a tech school. You will learn the construction trade or some electronics. It won't be expensive. You've already had a hands-on experience with them. Now you will work with this every day, for whatever time the trade school or tech school believes is necessary for you to come out a viable candidate for a job.

Now you remember my plan to open up 35 million jobs. Without the jobs, the whole thing is for nothing. All we will do is bring out millions and millions of educated, trained people with no job to go to. Our promise and our goals will be compromised. We will be facing failure. With my plan, we create those jobs. Now, we seriously put a dent in the huge bills that we call entitlements. We recoup that money. We give the minority people - let's hear that word one more time - sovereignty because they now are no longer dependent on the government. They have broken the chain. They are now taxpaying, viable, valuable citizens - sovereign citizens of the United States of America. We will have finally done what we should have done long, long ago. Now we can sleep with a clear conscience. We can wash away the guilt. We can look to God and say, "I'm your child. I tried to emulate Jesus. I tried to glorify you. Will you accept me back into your home?"

One last point in this chapter: I want to mention the Indians - or as they are more commonly known these days - Native Americans. These are the ones that we slaughtered, and destroyed. We called them thieving Indians and spit on them. Why? Because we wanted their land. We talked them into coexistence, then we stabbed them in the backs. We gave them parcels of land, where nobody lived. Then when our population expanded and settlers came out and started inhabiting their land, they fought back. Instead of going and removing the settlers as per the agreement, and instead of telling the settlers we promised the indigenous peoples they would be a sovereign nation - there's that word again, sovereign, independent from the rest of us - and you have to leave, we brought on the first Americans the most incredible slaughter in our nation's history, besides the Civil War. Maybe - I don't know the count - more lives were lost in the years we spent destroying the sovereignty of the Native Americans. We went along with Colonel Jackson down the Mighty Mississippi and fought the British in the town of New Orleans. The British, after the Revolutionary War, weren't happy to just sit it out from here on in.

They wanted their land back. They wanted their power back. They were bound and determined to get it. They made another run at us. After we defeated the British for the second time, 'our hero', Colonel Jackson, became President. The red man who fought with him side-by-side, who inhabited sections of Florida and other places in the South, was forgotten. Their loyalty, their bravery were forgotten. The expansion of the colonies dictated that the land they lived on would be more useful in the hands of the white man. We literally threw them out. Have you ever heard of the Trail of Tears? We removed the red man from his land, but did we put them in wagons, on trains? Did we give them horses? No. Most walked, carrying only what their frail bodies could bear. They walked for miles, hundreds and hundreds of miles on the Trail of Tears, which for many was the trail of death. That's what they got from the white man, for fighting for us. For the second time, others helped us remain a sovereign nature, helped us protect the sovereignty of the states and the sovereignty of the individual, and the rights and freedoms that came with that. What did we do? How about that President Jackson? What a guy! Don't you love him? We should put his name and his face on some of our money! Oh, yeah, we did. We displaced a number of tribes all over. We just kept pushing them and pushing them further, into areas that had no value to anyone. When it was found that there was gold on their land, we slaughtered them and kicked them out again, breaking our treaties, breaking the promise that they could remain sovereign. We sent General Custer, that ignorant, arrogant, sociopathic piece of garbage, to take hundreds of men to their deaths. He thought that no matter how many Indians there were, he was invincible. I hope they sliced him to bits before he died. He is not in heaven. He is not one of our national heroes. He is a boil on the integrity of the United States and is an embarrassment to our past.

My God, I'm afraid that we may be committing the same atrocities in other parts of the world again. I think we're trying harder not to. At least this time, the fight was brought to us - the way it was in the Second World War - which justifies things but not all things. To slaughter men, women, and children because there was gold in the hills where they lived is just unbelievable.

What do we do about it? Finally, we gave them the most barren, garbage land in the country that, to this day, no one wants. We gave them their sovereignty, and for the most part, have honored that sovereignty. They are independent. Unfortunately, no matter how hard they try, they do not have the means to be able to prosper as a sovereign nation on the land that they inhabit. I submit to you this: The plan for the education of our inner cities applies every bit as much to the Native American as it does to any other American. We owe them. Let's use the same plan for education and empower them to lift themselves to a higher level of prosperity. As well you will see when you read the second part of this book, that the jobs and the need now for some of the resources that are on the land that they inhabit can create a new day for the American Indian. We can help them develop clean sources of energy that fit perfectly into our plan that fit perfectly into our need to become energy-independent. We can help, because we're going to put $200 billion a year into this plan. They certainly should be a part of it. They certainly should reap some of the rewards and benefits that I will lay out in the plan for all of the people of this country. Finally, we may be able to settle with those people for the torture and indignity that such proud people had to suffer. I love the red man. I love his spirit. I love his traditions and his religion. I love his love for nature and the earth. We can be so well served to study and try to emulate the integrity and pride that is so rich in their heritage. God bless them. Stay safe. If I have my way, if I can just get back this book into people's hands and get people to listen, we'll be coming to help soon.

CHAPTER 5

RATIONAL SOVEREIGNTY

From the earliest times, man has cohabitated. There were the Oppressed and the Oppressor. Naturally, the Oppressed would dream of a place... a new place, a land far away, where the Oppressor did not exist, a place where he could go and be unencumbered by the rule of law handed down from the powerful. This is no more obvious than the European migration to the Americas. Once this land was discovered and was found to be under no control of any established government or hierarchy, it was thought that it could be a land of freedom. The idea that those who were oppressed in Europe, England, etc. could come here and live a sovereign life became very enticing to many. They boarded their ships with nothing but hope in their hearts, and they came to this land to start anew. It is said that they came for freedom. This is true. It is said that they came for religious freedom. This is true also. The common thread that bound each and every one of the Pilgrims together was sovereignty. It was independence. When independence has been achieved, freedom is a naturally occurring result. We know that freedom is an extension of our God-given rights and that it cannot exist without sovereignty. Sovereignty protects freedom; therefore, in its essence, sovereignty is what the Pilgrims, their children, and their children (up to today) are actually seeking.

When the first Pilgrims arrived, something became evident. It became evident that in order to cohabitate the people would need a rule of law. Although this seems in direct opposition to what they originally came for, it became apparent that it must exist in order for society to exist in peace. They began to wonder, "How do we do this in a sane, rational way?" It started out very simple. If you would presume to take another's freedom by stepping on their God-given right, then you would be deemed undesirable. The community would reject you, and you would be forced to live without the conveniences and safety that the community provided. As things progressed, the communities got larger. There became more and more need to outline in detail and expand on the laws that were pretty much accepted without any governing body or any enforcing body. They realized that there must be a system that provided for continuing sovereignty for maximum independence while protecting the people from those who would seek total sovereignty.

You see, total sovereignty is not rational. In total sovereignty, you have made yourself independent from family commitment, community commitment, laws, government, and even God. This type of sovereignty is not only irrational but detrimental to anyone who seeks it and detrimental to any community that accepts it. It is nothing short of anarchy, a total willingness and ability to revolt at any time, to take law into one's own hands, to plunder the goods that belong to another, to encroach on their property, and to even take away one's spouse and family.

In the early days, this is what drove the people to find this rational sovereignty. You cannot come onto my property. I am the king of my castle. I say what goes in my castle. If you try to compromise the integrity of my authority while on my property or in my castle, I have the right to turn you away by any means necessary. Early on, everyone carried a musket. Firearms were common. They were so common and so important that they became the second amendment to the Constitution. The Right to Bear Arms did not come from a society wishing to attack its neighbor but instead from a society that needed to protect itself from a neighbor that would attack it. The concept of rational sovereignty grew with the ever-growing population and the needs of society.

All government from the beginning of time and all people that have either chosen a leader or let themselves be led came from the needs of the people. It all began with protection. As we see through history, those who would acquire this position generally would abuse this authority and power, would compromise the needs of the individual, and, in many cases, would even hold themselves as high as God. They had total sovereignty. No matter what they said or what wish they had, it was up to the people to fulfill the needs of the single most powerful entity. People were stillborn with God-given rights we always have had, but we didn't have freedom because we didn't have sovereignty. We didn't have the independence from that ruling authority.

Therefore, we were slaves. Slaves are simply men, women, and children with souls that were given inalienable rights by God but cannot extend those rights to know freedom because they have no means of sovereignty. They are not economically or militarily strong enough to withstand the power of the dictator.

When we come back to America, we find that the people that came here knew this. They absolutely knew it; it's why they came here - for a new beginning, a chance to get their sovereignty, to turn it into freedom, to be able to use their given rights, to pursue happiness. As it turned out, the conundrum was that in order to pursue happiness, there had to be guidelines. There had to be rules. They also found out that individually one man and a musket cannot stand against a gang of thugs. Therefore, they realized immediately that they were dependent upon each other. They had to band together in a force that was greater than the force that pushed against them. At the same time, they found that the very authorities that they ran away from had followed them here and began to impose their will upon the people. The people weren't yet organized enough to turn away those would-be monarchs. It was at this time that militias were born. For the purposes of government, land areas had been cut into sections. They now had borders. It turned out that the existence of a border - any border - is one of the most important ideas ever conceived. The border gave rights to people in one area; these may not be given in another area. Different "governors", let's call them, would make rules as they saw fit. Generally, these rules, those based on primary edicts of the homeland, would be distorted to meet their own personal ideals. They used it to amass wealth, power, and position. Suddenly the people realized that this new system, this new land, this newfound freedom was not really happening for them because they did not have their sovereignty. They were dependent.

The militias, on the other hand, were able to stop lawbreakers in small communities, but the overwhelming authority to invoke and enforce the law came from the very authority from which they had run.

At this point, their concept of rational sovereignty is a sovereignty that is compromised only when the will of the people dictates that it be compromised. Let's take an example: Murder, the ultimate sin. It can not only impede upon one's rights but also take away their freedom. Obviously, if a person has no means of defense, their sovereignty is really nonexistent.

Therefore, the intruder can impact his will. The people said, "This is not only against rational behavior; it is breaking the rule of God." Therefore, one of the first rules - and now we will make it legal, which makes it the first law that we will impose - is that of murder. You cannot kill your neighbor - for any reason. This is rational sovereignty. To the would-be murderer, he has given up his right and his freedom to express himself in a manner that causes someone else's death. Irrational! Certainly, a little bit of one's sovereignty has been compromised. As rational, caring, compassionate people, we get together and decide if we're willing to give up this little piece of sovereignty. Are we willing to say that part of our rights and freedoms don't include murder? On down the line that includes beating someone half to death, assault, kidnapping, rape. All are mortal sins. Let's start there. Let's outlaw these things and begin a trend of what I call rational sovereignty.

Of course, what good is a law if you have no means of enforcement? It is useless. It need not even exist. Therefore, we must join together and figure out a way to enforce these laws. Certainly, we realize that each and every time throughout history when someone comes into a large amount of unimpeded power, it will be abused. There is no doubt about it; it happens every time.

There are those who would fight to carry out justice, but they will be few and far between. Even the ones that come into the system with those intentions may soon find themselves being indoctrinated into corruption.

Now we have a lawmaking system and we have an enforcement system, but we have yet to put in place a means of control. As time goes by, we see the powers from across the sea come to our land and compromise our sovereignty, our belief system, and our ability to govern ourselves. This was all part of the great plan, and we know now that Britain was the biggest perpetrator of the plan to eliminate our sovereignty. The situation worsened. Taxes were imposed on people while the people had no means of representation. The governors, leaders, and generals - those that had the power to make law, to enforce law, to compromise our freedom and sovereignty at any moment that they deemed necessary - eroded away the reasons behind why we had originally come here.

We turn the page to a time years later. The discontent of the people has become an outrageous movement to take back their sovereignty. Now we see something happening. The movement turns into a frenzy. It borders on rebellion. It borders on anarchy. It borders on complete annihilation of the system that was imposed upon them. We have the Boston Tea Party, one of the most significant days in our history, a day when people stood up and said, "This is it! We've had enough!" We see documents being drawn up: The Declaration of Independence, Independence Day, our celebration when we came together and decided once and for all that we would not stand for this totalitarian force that is amongst us. The Declaration of Independence: what is the definition of sovereignty? It is 'independent from all others'. Now we come together as a people and say, "Our group, on our land within our homes, denies your right to treat us as slaves." We declared our independence, and that day we struck a blow for sovereignty.

The question is, were we sovereign? Did we have the economic might? Did we have the means of production, which all comes down to sources of energy, manpower, fuel, and something that can drive machinery? Did we have the military might to stand against the strongest country on the earth? We weren't sure because it was so important, because it was life or death to us.

Give me liberty or I will die trying to get it! We did.

Now we come back. Okay, we have struck a blow for independence. We have achieved our sovereignty. We are now 'one nation under God with liberty and justice for all. Sweet words; how are we going to pull it off? The important words in that statement are "with liberty and justice for all." We realized our founding fathers knew that in history a government that rules from the top down inevitably enslaves the people. The very thing that we ran away from, we will, in our ignorance, bring right back into our lives. They said, "This cannot happen!" That's the answer: A government ruled by the people, for the people. We, the people, will decide what is rational and what is irrational.

Therein lies the importance, the monumental importance of national sovereignty. We cannot let others - those who think they're strong because they have a better weapon, those who think they're stronger because they have higher intellect or education, or because they've come from wealthy families - take away the rights and freedoms of the individual. Therefore, we must preserve individual sovereignty. We must come together and make the laws fit the crime, and make our judicial system work. This is why our founding fathers drew up the Constitution of the United States of America. It outlined what the people would need in order to remain in control.

Throughout history, in the future, however long it may be, it was designed for people to decide between rational and irrational.

Certainly, when you have 300 million people, there are differences of opinion. That is why we must all be involved. We must all look at the laws. We must all look at the enforcement techniques and the people doing the enforcement. We must look at the judicial system and those that are sitting on the bench. We need to protect the constitutional rules that have been laid out for us. That means that everyone must stay involved and make sure that our leaders aren't leading us astray. Why is this of concern? We know that when they get the power, they fall away from the initial intention, which was to preserve the Constitution. They all take an oath to preserve the Constitution. Cops take an oath, judges take an oath, and politicians take an oath. We must preserve the Constitution and the rights of the people. Yet when I look around, I am appalled! They actually believe that they know best and that we are stupid. Why do they think we're stupid? Because we keep letting them get away with it, over and over. We have a problem, so we throw it at them. We don't have the desire to get our hands dirty, to get out there in our communities and join together. Within the churches and ministries, the people should take up issues of morality within their own confines, and then join together to make a loud voice - through elections, through the media, or simply by standing on the steps of Congress holding a sign. They need to say, "You cannot do this. It is irrational. It serves you and a few of your special chosen people. It does not serve the masses." We see this over and over again. The politicians cannot make a law without attempting to extend the reach and scope of their power. They can't make a rational law anymore. Every law starts with rational ideas and the people's support behind it. Suddenly it's pushed beyond the scope of rationality.

Let's take the power that is given to the EPA. They have now been given the power to regulate everything in this country. Everything! If you eat it, if you drink it, if you breathe it, if it is near your community, if it is anywhere to be found within the borders of the United States - they can regulate it. What in God's name is going on? Who gave them that kind of power? How could they possibly get away with that much power? We, the people, stand by and let it happen. This is wrong. This is not rational. Now our sovereignty is not rational anymore. We've given up the rational sovereignty because we just don't want to be bothered anymore. Let the politicians do it. Once every blue moon we come out and vote on one or two of them. They have massive propaganda machines that influence our votes. They flat-out lie to us over and over. They flat-out lie to us! They stand there and make promises that they would never be able to keep, nor do they intend to keep. Anything! They let our borders be compromised by criminals. They take innocent people and put them in jail.

They have a law for everything. No matter what they do, they can come onto your property or come into your house. They can just say "I saw him do it" and therefore you're guilty. Do you believe that a police officer has a right to say, "I saw him driving funny so I arrested him, and it just so happened that I caught somebody that had been drinking that day?" The police have no right to assume that you have made a criminal act, and they have no right to stand up in a court of law. Because they say it is so, then it is so.

We look at laws designed to keep drunks off the road - certainly a great moral high ground, certainly a great place to stand. People who cannot control their cars should not be behind the wheel - period! However, 18,000 people in my state alone were taken into custody and drained of hundreds of millions of dollars. The insurance companies - the ones that take all of their losses and put it on our premium costs because they can't afford to encumber the losses - are the ones that are paying for it. The government makes anyone who uses any kind of alcohol or drug or even over-the-counter pharmaceuticals, incur thousands of dollars in liability, whether the drug is legal or used properly under a doctor's care. The state has the right to claim impairment simply because the officer said that he saw you doing something, even if he is lying.

Hundreds of millions of dollars! Insurance fraud is what it comes down to. It is insurance fraud! Those in the position started up little businesses and said to send these poor, addle-brained, alcoholic, drug addicts to us; we'll cure them at the cost of $85 per hour per person in groups of 10, 15, 20 at a time with a counselor. Would you like to have $850 an hour to tell people that they have stinkin' thinkin'? A bunch of community college graduates who think they all need Dr. Phil. You and your friends are paying $850 an hour for that person.

You tell me that this isn't a fraud? These people save no one. They don't care to save anyone. They are raping the insurance companies. If you don't have insurance, the county will pay. Who gives the county the money to pay this? It's us! We're the ones that give the county the money to pay. Then the insurance companies tack on all this cost to our premiums and now we can't afford healthcare anymore. Employers are dropping like flies. Everybody is bailing out. What do we do? We watch our

President and Congress come up with some lame-brained idea that is supposed to help us. Where is this rationality? Where is the rational sovereignty? There is none. We've let it go. It has gone too far. We have to stop it, and we have to stop it now. We have to get involved. We have to quit laying around, being lazy, cry-babying, worrying about whether we're going to have a job tomorrow or what we're going to do, and screaming at the government to save us. This is all craziness. We must regain our sovereignty.

Go to the second part of my book: You will see the plan. You will see how it starts with the people. It goes through the progress and ends up in the hands of the state. It cuts out the federal government. It keeps their hands out of the plan. It gives us, the people, the opportunity to make this happen for ourselves, and we get to reap the rewards. This plan is built and based on individual sovereignty and how it relates to state sovereignty, and how that relates to national sovereignty. Of course, the end result will be national sovereignty, but we do not skip over individual and state sovereignty to get there. In fact, it's the opposite. We cannot get national sovereignty without having the individual get involved, without having the state involved. The greatest tool we have as individual citizens is the state government. We, in the state of Pennsylvania, can go directly to our governors, senators, and state representatives, and we can scream bloody murder. We can get things done. If you don't take care of the problem in Pennsylvania, the sovereignty of the state will soon be gone. If we protect the sovereignty of the state, then any state has the right for its voice to be heard by the Federal Government. There are fifty states each with their own needs. The Feds have the idea that one plan suits everyone. They think every state will benefit in the same way, that the cost to every state will be the same, and that the results will all be the same. This isn't true. It is not possible. It is not rational. It takes away the sovereignty of the individual who lives in Pennsylvania just because someone out in Arizona needed something done. Instead of letting Arizona take care of the problem of immigration law, the federal government came in and presumed to come up with an idea that would solve the problem in every state in the country. This is ludicrous! They found out it was ludicrous; they couldn't do it. So, what did they do? They just let it go. They made immigration laws, but they never enforced them. Now you have states suffering terribly while others are doing just fine. That is not rational!

We must look at our sovereignty through the objective eyes of rationality. It must be based on truth. It must be backed up with facts. It must be desired by the people. Too many times we see a small group of distraught people. Maybe they're 2% (quite often far less), but they come together and make a lot of noise. They claim that they'll be standing at the pole, telling people about the rotten politicians who wouldn't listen to them and their plight. They force the politicians to do something, to do exactly what the politicians would want to do in the first place. They make a new law, a law that doesn't serve the 2% of the people while preserving the freedoms of the other 98%. No! They make a law that encompasses every person in the country, no matter where they live what state they're in, or what their individual circumstances are. They make it so outrageous that rational people cannot comprehend what good could possibly come from this law, other than helping to satisfy the voice of the 2%. We look at these and ask what happened to state sovereignty. Who gave the federal government the power to impose legislation across the board on every man, woman, and child in the country, while leaving the states unable to deal with the problems within the state on their own? What of us, the other 98% that sit here cheering the basic intent, the reason that the law was conceived in the first place? We cheer it and support it without taking a closer look at the law. What we find out is buried in the details, sometimes in 2500-page bills; there are all kinds of ways in which the enforcers can exceed the authority given by the Constitution and impede upon the rights, freedoms, and sovereignty of the individual. How do we let them do that? They make it so complicated that no one person could possibly ever figure out the maze that is laid out there by our legal system. What do we do? We must remain diligent!

We must continually challenge! The most important thing is to learn the Bill of Rights and the Constitution and challenge these laws on that ground alone.

That is the rule. That is the system that our forefathers came up with, that we hailed as the greatest that has ever been designed, that has brought us so much prosperity and so much freedom, that has lasted hundreds of years and put us head and shoulders above every other country on the planet. Now what we see is that great system collapsing before our eyes. Individual sovereignty is being laid to waste. Borders are being challenged. The governments within those borders and the people within those borders are being rounded up and herded like cattle into a 'one size fits all' society, into an entitlement society, a nanny state. We will all be chained to the federal government by those invisible economic chains because we need their help with healthcare. We need the Food Stamps because there are no jobs anymore. This is what we're headed for because we have let them take away the rationality of rational sovereignty. Pull back the reins and let us solve the problems ourselves. Let's formulate a plan that starts with us, a plan where we are the investors and therefore, we reap the rewards, a plan where the federal government reaps the rewards of our intellect and our knowledge. It reaps those rewards simply by staying out of the picture. We need to break back the EPA's powers. We need to de-fund all of these entities that presume to be the higher power in this world, those that would challenge the cycle of the planets and the earth's weather. Certainly, the moral high ground is always the starting place for these irrational people, but it is just to get acceptance. In the end, it is them getting their way and them having the power. This is not rational. Our system is collapsing. Don't give up hope; I have a plan.

CHAPTER 6

SUMMARIZING SOVEREIGNTY

As we've discussed in earlier chapters, sovereignty is the most important means of protecting rights and freedoms. The rights are given to us by our Creator: life, liberty, and the pursuit of happiness. We consider that a given. We also know that in order to enjoy or embrace that concept, we must be free. We've analyzed freedom and have come to the conclusion that as a word, freedom is a very abstract concept. The word on a piece of paper means literally nothing. The only thing that makes freedom a true non-abstract, workable concept is to be able to have actionable freedom. In other words, if I'm told that I'm free but am told no when I try to do something for myself or my family, that it's against the law, there is no actionable freedom. You will be punished if you try to act in that manner. In that case, there is no freedom. We have to go back to the very early days of the United States of America to understand exactly what we came here for, how we intended to live, and how these abstract concepts were provided for.

We know that when our first ancestors came to this country, it wasn't just curiosity. It wasn't necessarily, in many cases, to gain wealth. The reason that we came here was because the other countries around the world, mainly European and especially Western European countries, had a very high level of oppression. People meant nothing and were attached to whatever landowner would supply them with the means to survive. From the very beginning, it was always 'might makes right'. Even back in prehistoric times, it was the strongest, with the biggest club, that controlled that community. They were able to force other members of their community to go out and hunt and to supply food and shelter. It soon evolved into a system where wealth was defined by how much land anyone could possess. The land supplied for all of man's needs: food, water, shelter. The animals that were slaughtered, the trees that were burnt for fuel to sustain fire - they all came from the land. He who had the most land therefore had the most wealth. This is the basis of early economics. Land could be traded, land could be sold, and land could be forcibly accumulated by building a powerful army. The army was owned by those who owned the land. History shows hundreds and thousands of battles fought around the world because of land. Those were basic economics: simple but effective. If I had the land, I had the power.

As time went on and civilizations spread out, trading became a common way of life. There became a need for something of monetary value, something that one could put in his pocket and take with him. It would be considered wealth. You can't exactly take an acre of land and put it in your pocket.

Because of the many attractive elements of gold and silver and precious jewels, they (mostly gold) became the money of the time. This went on for several thousand years. Gold equals wealth. If you had enough gold, you could purchase land. If you had enough land, you could sell it for gold. This was the beginning of the economics of sovereignty. You see, what we found out in those times was the true meaning of sovereignty. A king was sovereign in those times; why was he sovereign? What does sovereignty mean?

Sovereignty means that he was independent from all others. He had the land, he had the gold, and he built armies that protected the land and gold, as well as anyone who was under the king's control. It was at this time that sovereignty became the number one prize for wealthy individuals. It was the ability to protect his wealth, the ability to protect his land, the ability to make any choice that he wanted - whether it was life or death over people, whether it was to go to war, whether it was to share or to conquer. He was sovereign. He made whatever choices he wanted, and no one could stop him. He was 100% sovereign.

This has expanded in detail, but the concept is the same. Wealth provides for sovereignty. It enables independence. Another ruler at any time cannot come to a sovereign king's doorstep and make demands. He would find himself tortured and killed. Perhaps his people would be taken into slavery, and his land and wealth would now be part of the sovereign king's wealth. As the years progressed, we find that over time in the modern day, sovereignty has become an abstract word. When sovereignty is an abstract word because you cannot protect yourself, and because you do not have independence, and because you do not have wealth, then freedom as well soon becomes an abstract word. What is freedom if it's not actionable? Let's take a quick look at society today. In America, as in many countries, the serf's peasants, and slaves have been given their freedom. Once again, though, are they free? Can they act on that freedom? Can they take their God-given rights by extension, act upon them in a free manner, and therefore have personal independence and be sovereign individuals? In some cases, the answer is yes, but in many cases no. The problem arises when the individual has no wealth. We know that wealth equals sovereignty. If you have no wealth, you can't be sovereign. Take the ghettos or the welfare recipients. Take anyone who survives because of government entitlements. They are required to do many things: live in areas they wouldn't want to live in and accept terms that they wouldn't want to accept. Because of their dependence on the government, they are forced to accept those terms. These people are not sovereign. They are not independent. They are chained to the government by invisible economic chains.

We have, over the course of our existence, come to realize that there must be rules. When these rules are implemented, there will be things that we are not permitted to do. We call this rational sovereignty. In other words, one who would prefer to just go around killing people and taking their wealth is not permitted to do so in our society. In a society where there is no rule of law or rule of law cannot be enforced, you have anarchy. It's every man for himself.

The weak will not survive. Through our Constitution, we have decided that certain laws will apply, that a certain form of government needs to be in place, that the rights of man must be adhered to, and that in all cases individual sovereignty must be the norm, not the exception. As far back as the early settlers, before there was even a government, the settlers got together and formed communities and made laws. They set down rules. As we got to the date of our Constitution, they saw that the foreign countries that they had escaped from to find actionable freedom and sovereignty, had taken over.

They started imposing taxes. They put in place governors and militia; they forced the people to do their will, the same way that they had done for thousands of years. If you take a look at the people that came here, and why they came (so that they could have individual sovereignty and liberty), this wasn't going over very well at all. A bunch of heroes got together. They first formed the Continental Congress. Then the day came when they took all the tea at the Boston Harbor and threw it in the water. The revolution was on; it was imminent and it was going to be bloody. Those who came here for sovereignty could not bear to live without their freedom. One of the things that helped America was that we had so many resources and such a diverse population that we were able to take on the British and demand our sovereignty. The Declaration of Independence. Independence Day.

Independence is the word. Independence equals sovereignty.

Even in those times, there were problems. You see, Britain had the wealth.

Therefore, Britain had an army. Britain had the navy. Britain was multi- powerful. We had our freedom. This was freedom we were willing to die for, but we had no wealth. The wealth of the United States had been drained by the foreign countries that occupied our land. We had to turn to France because of the French hatred for the Brits. They were willing to side with us, and they provided money. That was the key! Once we were able to amass the wealth to fight our war, we were unstoppable. It was economics that brought us our independence once and for all guaranteed us rights as human beings and afforded us the ability to extend those rights into everyday life. Because of the large size of the country, people settled in different areas and soon realized that they were going to have to draw boundaries. This enabled one group within the boundaries of what would be their colony, and later their state, the ability to make their own choices. One state may decide that slavery was wrong, while another state might decide that it's okay. When the founding fathers developed our system of government and wrote the Constitution, they made sure to put in there that it was the states that had the ultimate power to decide for their citizens what would be right and what would be wrong. There are some issues, like protecting the country from foreign invasion, since it involved every state, that would be the federal government's job. This is written in the Constitution as state sovereignty. The states had their own economies. The states paid their own bills. The states, other than having large militias, mostly had smaller militias that dealt more with civil unrest than fighting a war. However, the states were given that sovereignty. When you take the individual sovereignty of citizens of a particular state, combine them, and put them inside borders, you now have a system where the state sovereignty is governed by individual sovereignty. From day one it started with individuals. Unlike the European nations, which had evolved in a completely different manner, where land was wealth and 'might be made right', we came up with a different system. This one started with the individual, and moved onward to the state; then, when the states combined to be the United States of America, all of the states united and formed a federal government, which was there to be sovereign itself and protect the rights of all of its citizens.

That sounds simple at first, but as time went by, we found that the very same components that provided for the sovereignty of the king also provided for the sovereignty of our nation. This protected the sovereignty of the state. This protected the sovereignty of the individual. Those components were the same: Wealth. Whether that wealth came in the form of gold, silver, land,

or printed money, it was wealth that provided for our independence. This is why I find the issue of sovereignty, and its connection with the economics of the world, such an important issue. No country can be sovereign without its own wealth. It cannot depend on any other country for its wealth. Whether it is a number in a computer or bars of gold, it does not matter. The nation must supply its own wealth. There better be enough of it to provide military strength so that no one can come and take that wealth. The wealth is spread through the citizens. They work and they get paid for the job they do. This puts the money into the pockets of the people. When, as in our country, 300 million people come together - some with small amounts of wealth and some with large amounts of wealth - the nation as a whole can retain its sovereignty. This has been the concept for many, many years and is absolutely true. However, something has happened. We have found that in the new technological age, the ability to build and sustain wealth is directly tied, and even in some cases secondary to, our ability to produce energy. Now that we've entered into the industrial age, now that we're into the cyber age, now the economics of the world have interacted and, in some cases, united, we find that without a proper amount of energy, we simply cannot exist.

Because of the means provided by nature, which became evident in the early 1900s, there were huge pockets of a burnable commodity - namely crude oil. We found that oil can be refined and turned into gasoline. It opened the age of the automobile. We grew and grew as a nation. The world grew and flourished. The energy was abundant. We weren't thinking so much about how energy affected our economies and therefore our sovereignty. Those who had the largest supplies were willing to sell them to us for the lowest price.

We entered into an age of double dependence. Because we didn't create our own energy, the millions of jobs that would have been in place (and that at first were in place, when we did produce our own oil) would soon go by the wayside. The prices of oil continued to go up. The gasoline continued to go up. The economy goes into a nosedive. We had a Great Depression. Thousands and tens of thousands starved to death and died. We came out of that depression and said we would never let that happen again. From then on, we would take care of the people. We would create an entitlement class. You, for being an American, are entitled to certain benefits. If those benefits need to be monetary or food substance, then that's fine. The problem is that by doing so, we took away the sovereignty of the individual. The individual now is dependent on the government. The government's bills to supply all this entitlement for its people drain the reserves; the government, therefore, begins to borrow money. After several generations, we find ourselves where we are today. We are $15 trillion in debt. That's a trillion with a 'T'. In case you don't have a concept of what a trillion is, a trillion is a million millions. That's how much we owe, and it's going up by billions of dollars a day.

We look at our plan for sovereignty. First, we need a strong economy. We are trillions of dollars in debt, and the debt just keeps going up. Our energy needs increase every day, but those who have the supplies that we need have decided that they're just going to take every dime they can get from us. We can't say no. We have no alternative. We are dependent on our oil. We are dependent for our money. Our economy is trashed. The United States of America has one leg of the three legs of sovereignty. That is our military might. Now, because of the economy, we are forced to cut back on the money that it takes to keep the military strong. As we continue to cut back on the military, the last leg of sovereignty collapses. The United States has become a third-world country. This is the importance of the economics of sovereignty. If you wish to maintain your individual sovereignty, then we better protect the country's sovereignty. If you wish to live in a state where the roads are kept and the tunnels and bridges are maintained, then you better put some money towards it. Soon will be the end. Now, because the United States has so positioned itself in the global economy, the failure of this country will ultimately mean the failure of the world.

Now we sit and ponder what the answers are. What solutions can we implement to save ourselves? Let's take a look at some of the big numbered items. The first thing we must do is get rid of all waste and fraud in our federal governments and in our state governments, the way any good businessman would do if he wanted his business to succeed. Secondly, we bring the budget under control. By that, I mean no more than $2.5 trillion in any single year.

One of the ways is the big items that we will need to take care of: the entitlements. Medicare has run amok. Medicaid is out of control and so overbalanced that there is no single state that can pay its own Medicare bill. It has to be subsidized by the federal government or it will cease to exist. What of the millions that rely upon it and depend upon it? Dependency puts you at the mercy of others. What of the debt? We have to get rid of the debt. We eliminate the debt and keep our military strong, and there's only one thing left: energy independence. It is the effort to achieve energy independence that is the key. How do we take people out of welfare lines and food stamp lines?

We give them a job. Simple as that. Each person who is on welfare and receiving the entitlements takes out a bite of our revenues each month. Each person who works legitimately pays taxes, pays into the Social Security, and pays into the revenues. For every person we take off of welfare and put into a viable job, we get a double positive. If we can cut a half-billion dollars from the entitlement by taking people off and giving them jobs, we not only cut the half-trillion dollars from the budget but we add a similar amount back into the budget. It is a double positive. The way it stands now is a double negative. Instead of putting in, we take out.

It sounds simple. Let's just give everybody a job. If it was that simple, why is unemployment so high? We can't get back on track. Once again, I state the obvious: The effort to become energy-independent is the key. It is through that effort that we unleash the power of the people of the United States of America. Our abilities to create technologically advanced systems, our abilities to flex and bend in the wind without ever giving up. We as a people cannot be broken. Yet we teeter on the brink of disaster. I submit to you the reason that we can't be broken is because we don't sit around and do nothing about it. The reason we can't be broken is because when the time and situation merits, we get up and fight. In the effort to turn our paper economy into an energy economy - with trillions of dollars in assets, with a cyber-proof, efficient energy grid, north to south and east to west, for every state, every county, to every home - we take our need for oil and cut it by 70%. When I say cut it, I don't mean turn off all the motors and engines and cars in the country; I mean we replace it.

The chemistry now, and the technology that I've investigated, show me the most viable means of replacement for standard fuel, which would be mostly vehicles and transportation methods. It is a bio-methane. The power of methane gas is phenomenal. Our refined gasoline does not even come close to the efficiency of methane. We have billions and billions and trillions of barrels of liquid natural gas in this country that we can use. On top of that, we have the ability to take certain biological products, the kind that we grow and can be harvested and converted. If we were to put in place a fuel that is a mixture of biological fuels and methane, we would have a bio-methane replacement for gasoline which would be so much cleaner. All the plans to cap and trade and force industry to bring the levels down to what we've decided would be a legitimate level in the future, we could do just by putting in a bio-methane.

The other good thing is that we won't eliminate our standard gasoline. What we'll do is convert our vehicles to accept either fuel or a mixture of those fuels, therefore creating a huge competition between the oil-producing manufacturers of gasoline and the producers and manufacturers of bio- methane. This gives the people all of the advantages because the competition will keep the prices at a minimum. Through this effort, I claim to produce 10 million jobs in the first five years and an additional 5 million in the second five years. That's 15 million jobs in ten years, all based either directly or indirectly on a monumental effort to turn the United States' problems into success. Once we get energy independence back, that leg of sovereignty will be strong and remain strong.

The economic values attached to an economy, which, through this, will reach 10% growth or more within the first five years. This will strengthen the economy and therefore add hundreds of billions of dollars in revenue into our taxes by taking the 15 million people off of the unemployment line and out of the ghettos, off the welfare lines. We would cut our budget needs by hundreds of

billions of dollars. Therefore, the economy becomes strong. There is more money than we need. We have budgeted ourselves at $2.5 trillion. Now we're looking at surpluses of 0.6, 0.8, 1.2 trillion per year. It is that money that pays off the debt, keeps America strong, and gives us back the third leg of sovereignty, our wealth. At that point, we are once again 100% sovereign.

There are more people than ever working and relying on themselves; that means individual sovereignty. It takes a big boost. The revenues from the taxes prop up the states; the states can pay off their debts. Now the state once again becomes a sovereign entity. Sovereignty for the individual equals sovereignty for the state equals sovereignty for the federal government and the whole nation. That's what is going to be required to save us.

Now the other countries of the world; what will this do for them? When the bill passes Congress and is signed into law, the price of oil will go through the floor. When the whole world knows that the United States of America is checking out of the oil-buying market, there will be a panic. The ensuing panic will drop gasoline prices down, not just in the United States by $1.00 or $1.50, but by $2 or $3 in Europe, giving the people and governments amazing amounts of new capital and a great new market to invest it in. They can invest it in the technology of clean, efficient energy. Our actions will prop up the world. This all comes from a simple concept that I call the Economics of Sovereignty. As a concept, it sounds great. Many others have great ideas as well. Problem: One word. This word has been causing us to be stagnant when addressing these issues for decades. The word is *how?* How can we do this?

How do we pay for it? Who initiates the plan? Who will be in charge of the plan? How much will it cost? How long will it take? How? I believe that I have been endowed by the Creator as a messenger. I am about to enlighten all of those that read this book. It's time for Part II: The Answer to How.

PART II
THE PLAN

CHAPTER 1

INTRODUCTION

We have taken some time to look at sovereignty under a microscope.

Hopefully, by now, you have read the Constitution and the Bill of Rights and, along with my commentaries, you have come to realize just how important sovereignty is. We have defined it in very simple, understandable terms that came from a dictionary: "Independent of all others". No one - man, woman, or group - was ever so intent on finding that independence as the first Pilgrims and pioneers that ventured across the giant ocean just to escape oppression. Many different core values were at stake. Some had been deemed criminals or debtors. Certainly, most were poverty-stricken and faced a life of servitude.

Others had to hide in secret basements to worship in the manner that they felt was appropriate. So horrific were these oppressions that they were willing to risk all to escape it, willing to suffer incredible hardships which had the likelihood that their lives would be very short. In their hearts was a "live free or die" concept that overwhelmed them to the point of irrationality, to the point where an unreasonable thought process was what controlled them - in many senses of the word. Sovereignty meant "walking into hell for a heavenly cause" - a quote from *Man of La Mancha*. They were willing to do just that!

When we look at the psychology of the human mind, we find that the very strongest emotion is that of fear. It is the only emotion that animals have, and it comes from a deep, deep part of the cortex of the brain, a place where rational and analytical thought processes do not exist. The only things that exist are subconscious triggers that set off physical responses. We are all aware of the 'fight or flight' response to fear. Something comes over us when the adrenaline pours into our systems, and we just react. When the Pilgrims decided that they were going to endeavor on this journey, they had a very slim chance of ever seeing land again, once they left shore. Certainly, the strongest emotion that was present was fear! One of our greatest fears is that of the unknown. When we don't know or don't have a reasonable projection of an outcome, we tend to back away from it. Our minds start to take on a worst-case scenario and we begin to allude to pain, suffering, and loss of life. We even fear starting a new job, even though it may be something that we have been trained to do because we don't know exactly what's in store for us. Some peoples' fears become so overwhelming that they can't even face tomorrow because they don't know what tomorrow will bring. These fears bring on severe anxiety and depression. Yet these brave souls were so intent on making a new life for themselves, that they were willing to put away those fears.

I'll give you another quote, this time from Star Trek: "To boldly go where no one has gone before." It is their fortitude that not only eventually provided for the birth of the nation but was the basis from which all things in America came about. It is why the Founding Fathers struggled to get a full understanding of sovereignty and what it meant. Through diligence and determination, they put together a plan unlike any other in the history of the world. They fought for it. They fought over it. They nurtured it until it grew.

They started with the inalienable rights of the human being; now you know that came from the Pilgrims. It is what they were fighting for. They started with the individual because that's how the country started - with individuals. They moved up to a state representation primary government. The Federal Government was not the primary government. They gave most of the power to the state because people of like minds grouped together in mass and drew borders. They said, "If you believe in this, the way we do, then come live within our borders." This is how we see things. Different groups sectioned off and created different states. The state was the most important government because it had the most intimate relationship with the people. The people could have their voices heard in the capitals of their own states. They divided into districts and elected representatives to go to their state's capital and represent the individual groups. When the people of a state got together and complained, there was no way that the government could ignore them. The people were in control.

When we look at the individual and state sovereignty now, we see that the state, by various means, has had its sovereignty compromised by the Federal Government in such as manner as to make the Federal Government now the most powerful of all the governments. This is wrong! This is why we have to put this plan into place. This is why we have to start the movement towards giving people back their sovereignty and letting the states operate in the manner that is described in the Constitution. This is why we have to let the Federal Government go back to doing what the Founding Fathers intended for them to do, to protect our country! That was their job. It is why I am so saddened by the Civil War. It is because I do not believe that the Constitution, in any way, shape, or form, provided for the type of interference that the states received from the Federal Government that caused the loss of lives. In the end, the black man, rather than being free, was blamed for all the death and destruction. That is where the hatred and racism that we know today started. Before that, they were farm equipment. They were treated like farm equipment, and any farmer will tell you he doesn't want broken-down equipment. He takes care of his equipment. It was after the Emancipation Proclamation that the North and South both decided to blame the war on the black man. How much injustice can one country put up with? Especially the most righteous, generous, and caring country that has ever existed!

You see that whether you like it or not, you're programmed for racism. The wounds of that war have been carried on from generation to generation. Our children, without even understanding why, still feel hatred. We try to talk it away; we try to explain it away. If racism doesn't exist, then why are we still talking about it every day? If it didn't exist, there would be nothing to talk about. You'll see, as we go on, how our plan will provide opportunities not just for blacks, but for Hispanics, Native Americans, Whites, and Asian Americans. Everyone within the borders of this country will become a sovereign independent citizen capable of making their own choices and deciding for themselves what is rational sovereignty and what is not. That's just one of the goals that we have in a very multifaceted plan. I'm going to explain to you how this plan works, starting with the primary goal. Then we will have secondary goals and tertiary goals. We'll have policies, rules, and protocols that we set up for ourselves to operate efficiently while utilizing every opportunity that we get to move closer towards a better society - a wealthier, more prosperous society, a more unified society, without class warfare, with the same fervor and intensity that we showed in the second World War when our backs were to the walls and it took an entire nation to change this world. We once again are going to muster that intensity with one very different aspect. There will be no loss of life, there will be no loss of treasure, and this plan will be sustained forever. This plan will grow jobs. I will describe to you a positive growth scenario, one that is based on factual evidence, that is simple to understand, and that doesn't use fuzzy math to convince you of something that simply isn't true. The truth that we'll find in this plan will be self-evident. You won't have to put together an algebraic formula or get a team of accountants to verify it (although we will). Just by looking around at the quality of life that you have, you'll see the quality of life that so many others have achieved by being invested in this plan. That is our primary goal: Sovereignty - individual, state, and national.

Let me explain a concept. When I tell you this, you will undeniably agree.

When we look at sovereignty, we ask the question, how do you get it? How do you maintain it? Countries all around the world throw the word around. "We are sovereign. They are sovereign. We can't mess with them because they're sovereign." Let me explain something to you: Because you've drawn borderline, that does not make you sovereign. We can tell that simply by looking at the definition of sovereignty: Independent. Within that border are they independent? Can they sustain all facets of life within that border, as well as protect it physically from invaders? That is what you need for sovereignty. We look at the world in a macroeconomic sense. Remember, the book is called *The ECONOMICS of Sovereignty*.

Let me first say that sovereignty is a three-legged stool. That is one of the reasons it is so volatile and so precarious. The loss of one leg means it teeters. It takes nothing but a slight imbalance at that point to make it fall. With the loss of two legs, the country is in serious, serious trouble. When you lose two, the third will collapse under the weight. Let's look at the first leg of sovereignty. That would be the ability to defend our borders physically. That means our military. Right there, you look around the world and see that pretty much all of the countries in the world - other than the United States and several other countries that are close - have a broken military leg. You can't tell me that if we decided to go in and take over one of these countries, they could stop us. They may put up a hell of a fight, but if we wanted to get down and bloody, there would just be nothing they could do about it. They are not sovereign. They have a military that they use in concert with other military forces and forge alliances, most prolifically with the United States through NATO, so that they can utilize our military might along with their own and their friends', in case of a serious attack on their country. The leg is not completely broken off in some of these countries but certainly has structural damage to it. At that point, they are quasi-sovereign. Wait a minute! What does it take to build a military of such might and force, such high levels of technology, to provide such incredible training for its forces that the mere existence of that military provides leverage for that nation? Leverage is very important in maintaining sovereignty, not so much if you have it, but more important when you have it. This is critical. I'll explain why: In order to build that military, we need money and we need a lot of it. That means that we have to have a strong economy. Without a strong economy, we cannot sustain the military. Therefore, the economy now becomes the second leg of sovereignty.

As we look at the macroeconomic conditions, specifically in our own country, we find that the economic status is failing miserably. Recently we have even been downgraded as to our credit condition. Never before in history has America been seen as a bad risk. Yet because the economy is so bad, in order to sustain life, we have to go to those who would love to take over and utilize all of our resources, which we have so many of, to sustain their own societies. They know better than to go to all-out war with us because they saw what happened when the Japanese awoke that sleeping giant. They would prefer to manipulate us. They step up to the plate and say, "We will lend you the money that you need." Of course, they charge a nice interest rate, so right off the top, they make money, and a lot of it. That's not the basis for their generosity, though - no! It's because of their understanding of macroeconomics that they see the vulnerability of our country and know that if they put themselves in the position of being responsible for us (to carry out everyday aspects of life for us), they now have - I'm going to use that word that I told you was so critical - leverage. They have leverage over our economy, and, boy, are they using it! They charge us a fortune to import goods into their country, yet we let them import goods into our country for practically nothing. They keep their dollar low so that we pay more of their dollars to cover the same amount of a bill, when in actuality the value of their dollar is higher than it seems on the surface. This gives them a greater return on their investment. It grows their economy, giving them leverage. Now we look at this economic rock-and-a-hard place that we've put ourselves in, and we see that there is more to it than just that.

We must look at the backbone of our nation. What has made us great in the past, and what will return us to greatness, is industry. In the Second World War, we simply out-produced every other country in the world. The faster they would knock them down, the faster we would put two more in the air.

That industry spurred technology. When we added the power of the people to the backbone of the industry, combined with the genius of our innovation and our technology, we came out superior and sovereign! I ask you: What is at the core of the industry? Its very base core is energy. Because of the resources that we had, and the capability to supply the energy necessary to utilize the manpower and the industry, the technology, and the innovations, we were successful.

Now I offer this to you: What is the third leg of sovereignty? It is energy.

Where do we stand on energy today? Do you remember what I told you about fear of the unknown? Ask yourself: what is going to happen in the future if the countries that we are relying on – yes, we are dependent on, as opposed to independence, which is the essence of sovereignty – would decide that they can do better selling their energy somewhere else? What if our enemies conquered those countries and took over those sources of energy? How would we fight a war? That neutralized the military and it neutralized the industry.

The people can't go to work, the economy collapses. Like a house of cards, our sovereignty disappears. One leg, two legs, three legs, it's gone. I will submit to you that at this time in history, energy must be the strongest leg of our sovereignty. Without it, the other two legs will certainly collapse. The way that things look today, I will give you one more quote, from the captain of the sinking Titanic, when he said to the beautiful young lady, "Madam, it is a mathematical certainty, this ship will flounder." Are you scared? Fear does two things: Fight or Flight? I don't know about you, but I'm not running anywhere.

CHAPTER 2

HOW IT WORKS

I hope that by now I have sealed your interest and that you've committed yourself to reading all of this book. I hope that I have awakened the fear in you and have compelled you to stop the denial, open your eyes, and face the truth. I wouldn't instill that fear unless I had a plan that would take it away. Starting now, we're going to put the plan together, first with the biggest pieces, and then later with more detail. What I intend to do, and hope that I'm successful at, is to draw a picture for you. Let's look at it this way: Suppose this plan was a 5000-piece jigsaw puzzle. It's very complicated, very intricate, but when it's finished, it's one big picture. Now if you simply dump the pieces of the puzzle on the table, you immediately find yourself with the question, where do I start? Those who have done jigsaw puzzles know one thing for certain: You find the four corners and separate them, then you find all the pieces with a flat edge and separate them, and then you put the corner pieces together along with the flat edge pieces so you have the perimeter of the picture. This is a good place to start. It gives us our boundaries. It shows us where different colors integrate to form the whole picture. What about the rest of the puzzle? Many simply, by trial and error, try one piece at a time over and over again to find the one that fits exactly in that spot. However, the designers of the puzzle have done something for us that gives us a huge advantage. They have put the picture in its finished capacity on the lid of the box. It is by utilizing this lid that we're able to separate pieces by color, knowing that this basic color, which may be green, would fit in this part of the puzzle because that part is a green field.

What I'm trying to do in this book is give you the top of that box. I'm going to separate the colors, show you where they fit in generality, and then together we will take the individual pieces and find where they belong. To start our endeavor, we start with those four corners. We start by saying, "What are our goals?" Obviously, our primary goal is sovereignty. One word that, when broken down into individual pieces, becomes very complicated. All pieces must, in some way, enhance our progression toward that goal. Since we've decided that sovereignty is the single most important issue for any country that hopes to sustain its society over a long period of time, we're going back to the three legs of sovereignty and saying, "Where do we start?" I hope in my explanation that I made it clear that the single most important issue - the backbone of our nation, the most pertinent – of our time is energy. We are going to utilize a massive effort to secure that energy as the means to bring our economy back under our control. Therefore, the economics of sovereignty in this plan are based on energy. Our secondary goals, those you might con- sider to be the flat sides of our puzzle, are to supply energy, not only in an affordable way or an efficient way but in an environmentally friendly way. We're talking about clean energy. We're talking about a reduction in the use of dirty energy. Those are two different things.

Let me explain: When energy is efficient, it is automatically clean for one simple reason. It takes less of the source of the energy if that source produces high levels of energy. Therefore, rather than having to use a barrel of oil, we could come up with a new fuel that provides the same energy using half as much, therefore producing half as many toxic byproducts. This is how we utilize energy as a form of reduction. Of course, another way to do that is simply by turning out all the lights, turning off your air conditioners, and buying a bicycle; that will certainly reduce the need and therefore the volume of fuel. It will make that fuel that we still use more efficient. For now, we're going to abandon the idea that we're all going to start walking to work and let's stay on course with cleaner, more efficient sources of energy.

Some of the other obvious pieces would be those, again, on the perimeter of our puzzle; they obviously belong there. One of these would be affordability; this is where we get into trouble. At this point, there is a battle going on between politicians and within the home and workplace, over whether the government should get involved and either try to force us into cleaner means of producing energy, or take our hard-earned tax dollars and start pro- viding funds to companies that say they can produce energy more efficiently, in hopes that those funds will be utilized in a productive manner. Then we will usher in a new era, the other side shouting, "You must let private industry solve this problem." When private industry is involved, their motivation is profit. Therefore, to explore this huge market, they must be willing to put in tons of their own money, which means they are driven by profit to do it in a way that's affordable. I agree 100%. Problem: The amount of working capital that it would take to explore these new sources of energy, to build the facilities, and to distribute the energy, whether it be electricity or fuel, is so massive that there is no single company, nor even a group of large companies, the mega-corporations, that could possibly ever sustain this type of investment. The demand will always be there, but no one will ever take on this problem in a serious manner - no one but us! It's our lives that depend on it.

We're the ones that are going to fix it.

Step One: We are going to start our own corporation. You and I and every soul within the borders of this country are going to get together and make this happen. We will be a legitimate, viable, legal corporation. Our corporate position will be one of investors; this will be an investment company, one with massive, unheard-of amounts of working capital dedicated to one simple product, and that is energy. That will be the product. We're going to utilize many forms of this product. We're going to utilize different forms of this product in different areas of the country. What do you have in this area that can be utilized in the production of energy? We will invest in it! We will turn our money into assets, the assets being those facilities that produce energy.

One of the good things about this type of investment is that when the investment dollars are spent, you not only have better, cleaner, more efficient, and affordable forms of energy, but you own the assets that produce the energy. This is much different from big government methods of throwing money at different companies and asking them to produce energy for us. With the money that we give them, they produce the energy, they make a profit with the energy, and they still own the asset - the facilities that they have built with our money. This is ridiculous! This is why we're going to form our own company. This presents a number of hurdles. The first one is, what about the working capital that we have to come up with? How much is it? How do we collect it? How do we distribute it? How bad is this going to hurt? In our company, we're going to use sound economic principles, and it is going to be relatively painless. It is going to come with huge dividends, mostly in the form of cash. Because it's our corporation, that means we get to make the rules. We set policies and protocols. We design and structure our corporation to suit the needs of the investor, and that is us. Since the investor is also the customer, we can use our own money to make money in this business, while supplying ourselves with the product that we all need. It's a win/win.

The first thing we have to look at when we're talking about investment is something that the government doesn't seem to be able to comprehend.

Barack Obama tours the country, talking about it being time to invest in America. What nonsense! What he presents to us is not investing; it is tax- and-spend. He wants us to give him more of our money so that he can throw it at these companies, hoping that they'll survive, hoping that they'll come up with a product that we can use. As we all know, in the end, if there is any success, it is at a cost that is too exorbitant for us to swallow. The problem with tax-and-spend is this: He takes large amounts of money out of the pockets of businesses, corporations, and - yes- individuals. He spends it. At this point, we may or may not have something to show for it. He says he is creating jobs. If it takes a year or two to build the facility that provides these products, which will ultimately be a failure, then you have a few jobs for a short period of time, and then it's gone. The jobs go, the money is gone, and there is a new product out there that no one can afford. The company fails, and our tax dollars have been wasted - not to mention the suffering that it causes us when we have to hand the clothes down from one child to the next, drive that same car for ten years, eat cheap and unhealthy food, and give up vacations. What does all of this do to the economy in our country? In a macroeconomic picture, it is easy to see that this cannot work. In a true corporation, the big difference is we collect the money, and put it in as our working capital. We make the investments. Those investments build facilities in a much larger capacity, which enables us to mass produce items we need, thereby making the product cheaper and more affordable. The facility stays in business because it is profitable. At the end of the year, we get our money back. In some cases, some investors do lose money - certainly, especially in an economy like we have now. However, it is not the intention of the investor to lose money. It is the intention of the investor to not only get the money back but with interest and dividends. If we're going to truly invest in energy, we absolutely have to set ourselves up as an investment corporation that guarantees that we get our money back at the end of the year, with interest!

Yes, I say the word *guarantee*!

Suddenly, I can feel all of you nodding your heads affirmatively and saying, "Now you're talking. Let's do this in a way that we get our money back with interest." I'd like to describe this in a very simple concept that has been used for several generations by banks. If you take a little bit out of each of your paychecks and put it into a savings account, over the course of the year the principal amount grows. I, the bank, guarantee you a fixed rate of return; let's say it's 5%. Several weeks before Christmas, the money becomes available. In the meantime, I, the bank, have utilized this inflow of investment capital. I have lent the money to other companies, and I have built office buildings. This will return profit to me, the banker, and is greater than the amount of interest that I'm going to pay you for letting me use your money. The benefit to you is you're guaranteed your money back with a fixed rate of interest. Now our investment company is utilizing standard banking procedures to capture large sums of money to be used as the working capital for our endeavor. The first thing we say is, "How do we collect that money, and how much?"

At this point, I have to say that you must endure the next few sentences without losing hope. I'll explain exactly why this is the most efficient, the most prudent, and the most un-painful way of doing this. This involves some intervention of the Federal Government, but - believe me - this is the only part of this plan in which they will be involved. We are not giving one bit of control of this to any politician ever. I'll say it again: No politicians ever! We will raise the money, we will spend the money, we will get the benefits, we will recoup our investment costs, and we will do it with this one item that involves the government: The Federal Government must put a bill through Congress to levy an additional tax on gasoline. Please hear me out! We will utilize the IRS in this manner: We now have a means of collecting the investment revenues. When the IRS totals up its books at the end of the year - at the end of our economic fiscal year - they will be tasked with separating the amount that was raised from that additional gasoline tax and putting it in a separate escrow account for our use to invest. This money does not go into the Federal Government coffers ever! At the end of the year, we apply with the IRS to get our money back. This comes in a lump sum. The little bit that we've been putting in each time we go to fill our gas tanks will be there for us when we apply to get it back. Therefore, we utilize the IRS - which, by the way, we pay for - to absorb the huge expense of setting up our own accounting practice, as well as trying to find another means of collection, one that will utilize every single person in the country. Every person in the country - someway, somewhere, somehow - uses gasoline, or oil products, for energy. Even if it means that you're putting gasoline in your tank to take your kids to school events, or just to transport them back-and-forth to school, they, through you, are actually paying into that tax, and you, of course, get all of the money back. One suggestion that I have would be the following, and this will happen: Gas stations will offer you a deal. They will give you a card that you swipe each time you come in for gas; this card will be usable at any of their affiliate gas stations, anywhere in the country. We will charge you when you get your first card, $10; for that $10, you will be on the computer. Each time you swipe the card, it automatically keeps track of how much gasoline you've used and exactly what amount is due back to you on your refund. At the end of the year, they will provide a statement. Of course, if you find yourself in a position where you have to use one of their competitors' facilities and don't have a card, simply keep the receipt. This compels you to use the same product all the time. This does wonders for their business because they know, by looking at how many people are card-holders, just about how much gasoline they're going to sell, and it keeps you loyal. You, on the other hand, don't have to worry about anything. You can just wait for your statement at the end of the year. During the year, if you'd like to check up on how you're doing, you simply go to the website, punch in the number code on your card, and access your information. It's simple! This is one of the reasons why I chose gasoline as the medium by which we will collect the working capital. It's easy. It's efficient. The gasoline retailers already are set up to pay taxes. This will simply be one addition to that system, which automatically keeps track of what your investment pay-in, and therefore return, will be.

What we have to look at next is how much. How much working capital do we need to run our corporation and get the job done in as timely a manner as possible? This is the job of providing new clean sources of energy. I have run a number of scenarios, and what it comes down to are a number of variables that we do have control of and must decide which ones we want to use and at what level. In other words, do we want to put airplane fuel as one of those tax items? Should the airlines pay in as well, or should we just give them a pass? I don't mean higher prices. The major trucking industries - certainly I have them figured in - as well as railroads, boats, lawnmowers, weed whackers and the like. Rather than throw a number at you on a per-gallon or per-capita basis, we will try to average this out, since everybody is so much different. What I've decided to do is cut to the most important number of all: The amount of working capital we need to come up with per year is $200 billion. You should remember me telling you that no company will ever take on this endeavor because it's just too big. Now you know why. In order to pull this off, we can easily spend $200 billion per year, and every few years we upgrade that amount, either by using inflation or by statistical analysis of what we've accomplished so far. Even at $200 billion per year, this could easily take 15 years, which would be $3 trillion in investment. That is why we must make a corporation with 300,000,000 investors and must sustain this forever. By the time we are finished with this, we will have already started to replace old worn-out equipment with new technologies. There will be a constant need to expand and grow. One of our goals and one of our needs is to rebuild our entire energy grid, across the nation, top to bottom, end to end - which we will do. You see that not only do we save all the money that the government would have us pay in, so that they can throw away, but on our investment, we get our money back with interest. I'm going to explain the interesting part of this in just a short while.

First, let's address the benefit that this plan provides for us right off of the top. We are going to start the biggest corporation in the history of the world, and we are going to have it okayed through Congress. We are going to show the world that we are drop-dead serious about eliminating foreign oil from our shores. What do you think this is going to do to the price of oil? The day that bill is signed, and probably even before, when the investors start contemplating what is about to happen to the price of oil, they will already have started to abandon oil and roll their investments into what they know will be the replacement products: bio-fuels, methane gas, wind turbines, solar energy, hydroelectric turbines. They will begin to buy up huge farmlands and get them ready to start producing on a major scale. This is how private capital comes into the picture. Now they're willing to invest because it's a done deal. These sources of energy will be the new tomorrow. The oil is going down. I submit to you that in the first 24 hours, we will see oil prices below $40 a barrel. This means an average family could return $1000 or even more, into their bank accounts at the end of the year, just for this investment, all the while enjoying the incredible drop in the price of gasoline. This happens as we move ever steadily forward into creating a scenario where we have not eliminated conventional gasoline but instead have created a product to have competition with the standard gasoline. This is a huge inflationary factor. We know how the price of fuel affects inflation. Every product that is moved anywhere in this country, that utilizes fuel, sees an increase in overhead when fuel prices go up, and a decrease in overhead when fuel prices go down. These are always passed on to us, the consumer. In order to keep our new fuel from becoming totally dominant, and therefore volatile, as to speculators and the stock markets - who we know are such righteous people, LOL - we, through the competition between fuels, eliminate their ability to manipulate prices and gouge us. If you manipulate one, we will simply buy the other. This is but one of the advantages that our corporation will create, because this is the first step to putting the people, the customers, back in charge of the economy. Now standard supply and demand scenarios are predictable, and we're able to keep them within range.

The next thing I'm going to show you is how you're going to get your dividend. Stay tuned.

CHAPTER 3

HEALTHCARE AS A DIVIDEND

I promised you that we would build dividends into our plan. So far, we have written into the legislation a means by which we receive 100% of our investment capital back at the end of each cycle. In the first cycle, we get nothing, but that is because we have to take the first year to build the reserves. After that, 100% will be returned at the end of each cycle. As for the dividends, of course, we would like to have something that we can count on that gives us a guaranteed amount back in the way of cash. But we're going to try and take a little bit of a different course. Since we have many options, let's take a look at what would be the best for us as a nation. What is it exactly that we need the most? How do we turn that into cash?

One of the things that we know is very problematic in our society is the need for affordable healthcare. We have a great healthcare system, but the costs are just getting out of control. The costs get too high, and people start dropping out of the customer base. Then it starts to raise the cost even more. The less volume that an insurance company does, the higher percentage of profit they require. You can make a higher percentage of profit but still at the end of the year have less to show for it, if the volume drops significantly. We have millions of potential customers, but the issue of cost is holding us back. I propose this: Each person must incur, somewhere along the lines, some cost for healthcare, especially if they have no insurance. Even the cost of over-the- counter medications can be exorbitant. As our dividend, we write into the law that each individual - whether they supply their own insurance or have no insurance - must incur over-the-counter costs for things such as cold remedies, stomach antacids, or any number of items that we would deem to be for healthcare - they would, as their dividend, receive a rebate at the end of the cycle. This rebate would be determined by setting a cap of $100 billion per year. That is just a number that I'm putting up there which I believe we can afford and will be enough to do a lot of good. I believe this could put us up into the 15 or 20% return range. Whether I have healthcare through my employer and have to pay co-pays, pharmaceutical costs, or over-the-counter costs for medication, I would, at the end of the cycle, receive the percentage that we decided on in the form of cash. It will be added to the dollar amount that we'll get back for our investment capital. Therefore, we realize an increase in the amount of our return, which all comes back in the form of cash.

Now, if you're a business, you get to deduct as overhead 100% of any expenses you incur for providing healthcare to your employees. That doesn't mean you get 100% of the money back. What it means is this: If you're a business that runs on a 20% profit, after you deduct the cost of your healthcare, you will realize a 20% return. That still leaves 80% out-of-pocket expenses for that business. This is one of the things that makes it so difficult for businesses to continue to provide quality healthcare for their employees. We can't pay for everything. In fact, we know that a one-payer system does not work simply because the expense is too great. No one entity can afford the entire cost. In a few cases, some of the larger, more profitable companies come very close to that. There is still always some portion of it that comes out of the employee's pocket. Often, they have to pay additional amounts to ensure members of their family, and, of course, they usually have co-pays; depending on the policy, these can be quite exorbitant. That means that the employee and the employer share the expense. We're going to give each individual, whether employed or whether they pay for their own insurance, 20%, let's say. In order to help the employer, on top of their 100% tax deduction, we will give them a rebate of an additional 10%. What this means is the employer and the individual share the expense along with a third party; that third party is the government who, with our tax dollars, will give 20% back to the individual and an additional 10% rebate to the employer. Now this begins to look more affordable. We, in essence, have created a three-party paying system. The government pays part of it by giving us rebates, we pay part of it out of our pocket, and if our employer covers us, they pay the rest.

If an individual has no insurance, then they could certainly use a 20% rebate at the end of the year. A $500 expense per year would yield a $100 return to the individual; which would come included on their check. The people that slip through this crack are these: Those who are lucky enough to have such good health that they never pay anything towards healthcare and have no agreement with their employer pertaining to the provision of healthcare for them; they will actually receive nothing. So, what is their dividend? It's simple: Health! I, for one, would gladly forfeit any percentage of repayment to enjoy the benefit of great health. For them, I say, "Just be happy that you're so healthy." This can work out quite well in a number of ways.

There are a number of facets to creating affordable healthcare. Later in the book, I address healthcare in a comprehensive plan that keeps healthcare choices in the hands of the people, while providing a system that will bring down the cost dramatically. We will discuss that shortly.

As part of our plan, this certainly would be an opportunity. Rather than put it in the *Options and Opportunities* section of the book, I'm putting it in the general plan because it would have gone through Congress along with the rest of the plan, to make it law. In our plan, we have included health care as a dividend to supplement our return on our investment capital. Besides that, it gives us a solid base from which to explore a comprehensive plan that is not a government-issued, socialistic, one-payer system that, as we look around the world, we see does not work. This way, we provide quality healthcare that we do not have to ration. Doctors can be paid a fair amount for their services while at the same time, we assist the people in the business with the cost.

CHAPTER 4

A TAX-FREE CORPORATION

Now we have shown a basic structure of what our plan is, and have attempted to define some of the elements that are important to the plan. What we've been doing is showing the parts of the plan that are so important that they need to be incorporated into our bill that we would propose to Congress. The last but not least important of the things that need to be incorporated into our bill are those that pertain to profit.

Our corporation is going to have massive assets and incredible amounts of revenue. As per standard capitalistic values, we would expect that a corporation, whether it is by the people, for the people, or simply an endeavor by the wealthy to create more wealth, would be subject to taxes on revenues. This is one of the things that we address in our bill. You see **when we complete a project, that project's assets will be gifted to the people of the state wherein the assets exist.** The people of the state will decide what to do with them, but we, as a corporation, have given away those assets. The revenues that are generated, that end up in the hands of the federal government, will enhance our ability to balance budget and pay down debt.

Out of those revenues, in this bill, we require that we get paid back, that we get the full amount of our investment given back to us through application to the IRS, and therefore these should be considered investment rebates. They are tax rebates. These tax rebates also include a percentage of our healthcare expenses that we document and send to the IRS, along with our application to have our rebates sent to us for our investment amount.

These are considered to be rebates. They are not profitable. They are not dividends. They are not capital gains. They are tax rebates. This means that they are non-taxable. This is very important. The amount of assets generated in a single year from our corporation would be $200 billion, the amount of our investment. When we ask for repayment, it would be considered dividends, interest, or capital gains, any of which are valid items for taxation. As non-taxable rebates, we can enjoy all of the gratuities that we receive for our investment, as well as not have our corporation strapped with tax on investment, which those in Congress have increased to as much as 39%. Since we are giving away the assets and have the returns through the IRS put in as non-taxable rebates, our corporation now can assume the status of a charity organization. We build and we give away. There are no profits. Therefore, our corporation will assume the same status as any legal entity that is strictly charitable. For example: The Catholic Church. Any organization that operates under these rules is considered to be tax-exempt.

Now we have not only endeavored to create such massive growth through an entity that is funded by the people and is owned by the people, but the federal government cannot charge the people with any tax obligation. How does the government make out? The tax revenues generated by all of the contractors and their employees throughout the country will be so massive that they cannot only pay us back our investment amount as well as give us our healthcare rebates but there will also be hundreds of billions of dollars on top of that which comes into the coffers of the federal government for discretionary spending. I think that is enough to warrant their consideration to go ahead and pass this bill through Congress and get our new corporation up and running. The ultimate end is one of win, win, win. We win individually, America wins a nation, and the federal government wins in its endeavor to balance a budget and pay off debt.

CHAPTER 5

RULES, POLICIES, PROTOCOL AND BANKING

So far, our corporation is looking pretty good. We've found a way to collect massive revenues, we've found a way to build (to our specifications) new sources of energy and the facilities that are needed to produce them, and we've managed to bypass the Tax Man. Of course, it will take an act of Congress, but the plan is pretty simple. I think that if we get enough people shouting on the doorstep of Congress, we can pull this off with relative ease.

The previous chapters of Part II describe the plan and how it works; however, there are still some items that I would like to address, just for clarity and to show you, the reader, how it can be structured in much more detail.

The very first thing that I want to address is so important that it should be in the general plan, but since it wouldn't necessarily need Congressional approval, we're going to put it in this section, which is called *Rules, Policies, and Protocols*. That which I am speaking of is a plan to secure the banking industry by taking away billions and billions of dollars that would normally be put into escrow accounts in a large bank but instead will be distributed. Here's how it works: Since we are our own corporation, we get to make the rules.

This is Rule #1: When we are given from the IRS, which has collected the tax revenues from the people as they fill their gas tanks, we have upwards of $200 billion at our disposal; that is a lot of money! We have to decide what the best way to use this money is. Not just in our projects but even before. Remember, working capital is the key to all endeavors that plan to generate revenue.

Let's do this: At first, we will have the money transferred to a megabank. You know the ones, those ones we had to bail out, but this will be for a short period of time. What I plan to do is this: As we sign contracts with general contractors who we hire to do the work in the field, we have contractual obligations, both with us and with them. Since we write the contract, we put this in as an article in the contract; that is a must. In other words, if the contractor refuses to comply, then his contract will be null and void, and we will give it to the next highest bidder. Certainly, when we're talking about projects that are in the billions of dollars, this will be something that they will absolutely want to comply with. What we're going to do is this: When a contractor submits a proposal or a bid if you will, there is one requirement that must be adhered to. Somewhere in the area, within the state where the project will take place, he will be required to submit a number of banking entities. I would say six, and we would pick four. The requirements are this: First of all, they must be community banks. Small banks, as opposed to the scale of the much larger, too-big-to-fail banks. They must not be too big to fail. These could be credit unions, savings and loans, community banks, or whatever meets the criteria. The criteria are this: First of all, they must be solvent. They must have enough working capital to cover the amount that will be deposited. The project would start in May, let's say. Statistical analysis would have to be done prior. Let's take a look at a theoretical sample. Suppose we were to build a huge facility to process and mix a bio-methane fuel. We would have to first look at the needs of that state, or at least that portion of the state, and decide how big it must be. Let's say the cost will be $5 billion.

The schedule will be five years. (I'm picking these numbers because they make it easy to understand.) Before the project starts, once the contract is signed, the amount of $1 billion will be divided between four banks. Some banks may get more because they have more working capital, and some banks have less. That doesn't disqualify them. If we need to use all six banks, we can do that. Let's say four banks, $1 billion; that means $250 million cash injection into each of the four banks. Generally, it takes several months to get the project actually breaking dirt. In the meantime, each of those four banks, which are located in or near the communities where the work will take place, will have a sudden influx of cash that gives them the ability to lend $250 million to the people in the area.

Now let's look at what small banks do. Small banks supply school loans, small banks provide car loans, small banks provide single-dwelling housings, and small banks consolidate loans; in essence, small banks provide for all the needs of the community. This is a fantastic use of funds. Since mortgages handed out by small banks are also carried by small banks, rather than bundled and sold on the international market, it means that there is a very intimate relationship between the banker and the person who is borrowing the money for the mortgage. This is the way it's supposed to be. School loans are the same. Each one of the small business loans is strictly regulated, and the small banks make out, while the locals of the community are able to manipulate assets in order to grow their small businesses or consolidate their loans. This is the way the banking system was built. This is how the banking system needs to operate. Every small bank that has an intimate relationship with its depositors makes money, and it isn't until the small bank becomes so big that it becomes too big to fail. It then begins to bundle. It gives hundreds of loans, bundles the loans, and then sells them on the open market at a small percentage. A 2% gain of $2 billion is substantial. We need to return our economy to a small banking system, one that works within a community provides for the community, and is substantiated by the standard revenues that are gained from that community.

We can do this! If we were to put $200 billion a year into small banks, in ten years we could put $2 trillion into small banks, thus protecting our- selves from having to bail out the big banks who over-speculate, work on a 2 or 3% margin, and then, when they collapse, our economy collapses. This is just one more way that we can, through our corporation, feed America in the way that it needs to be fed, with small business loans, college loans, and individual mortgages. In this way, we have control of our banking system once again, rather than having four or five megabanks that, at any time, can burst their bubble and bring down our economy. It is the answer to banking. We could put 8000 banks in good standing, with a total of $2 trillion. This gives the banks one year to invest the money and get profitable returns before the money is exhausted on the progress payments to the general contractor.

Another batch of money will then be deposited into the bank to pay for the next year's work. Cash flow to the small banks enables them to offer affordable loans to the communities they serve.

CHAPTER 6

RULES, POLICIES AND PROTOCOL – GENERAL CONDITIONS

How did you like that last segment? It's one of my favorites. It's funny because I wrote that two days ago, and yesterday while I was watching the news, they were discussing the economy, European banks, and the American banking system. One of the points that came up that was agreed upon in the consensus of the panel is that much of our problem came because we allowed small banks to be gobbled up by the mega banks. The banks got too big to fail, and when the bubble burst it, all came tumbling down, costing us hundreds of billions of dollars - just in bailouts, not to mention that some have given the statistics as being $7 trillion in investments, pension funds, 401Ks lost because of the collapse. I was sitting there with a huge smile because we had just finished our discussion about that very thing, and we decided that we were going to create a large growth in small banking. We were going to do that by offering small banks huge injections of cash. Since we had it in the budget and were planning on spending it anyway, we might as well utilize it for the simple reason that if nothing else, it provides a means for small businesses and for average people to find ways to get loans, mortgages, car loans, school, small business and many other so gravely needed movements of cash through our society and therefore through our economy. We have decided that if the bank gets too big, we don't do business with them anymore; that is an incentive for the small banks to remain under the limit that we give them. Another thing that provides for what I had been thinking of is that when the small banks become prosperous, the same thing happens that has happened before. The big banks gobble them up, and then they become part of the problem, not of the solution. The beauty of our method is that once they become part of the big bank, they no longer get the incentives in hundreds of millions of dollars from our willingness to use them. Now the whole reason that the big banks would want to incorporate them, so that they could get in on these hundreds of billions of dollars every year, goes away. The very thing that made the small bank prosperous is gone. Therefore, where is the incentive for the big banks to buy them out? I love this plan.

As much as I love what we've done with banking, this next part is really, really sweet. I'm practically giddy. Are you ready? Get out the champagne; you're going to want to celebrate. You, being one of the primary investors, are responsible for what's about to happen. We see that $200 billion a year is going to be pumped into the economy. It's going to be pumped in by way of energy. We're going to expand domestic production of oil, we're going to massively increase the production of solar panels, we're going to massively increase the production of hydroelectric turbines as well as wind turbines.

This means billions and billions of machined parts, specialized equipment, and high-tech methods. Who is going to do it? With the government plans, one of the things that they never plug in – and maybe it is because they're not allowed to mess with business because of the United States Constitution; I believe that's probably the reason - is that they can't tell the builders and the owners and the manufacturers where to get their parts, where to get their materials, where to do the assembly work, and, mostly, what country to do it in. What labor force are you going to utilize? We can't, as a government, tell them. But guess what! We are our own corporation, our own entity. We have, because of the United States Constitution, the right to decide for ourselves.

This is why this is so important, that I'm not putting it in under Options and Opportunities; I'm putting it in as part of the Plan, an integral part that we absolutely cannot leave out. It will be under Rules, Policies and Protocol as follows:

Because we have the right to make policy, we will require that a minimum of 80% of all parts manufactured, all equipment, all assembly work, and everything that it takes to make these projects happen, will be done in the United States of America by American workers. Whether citizens or here on work permits from other countries, they will live and pay taxes in the United States. The companies will be based in and have their operations in the United States. They will pay taxes, and they will be under scrutiny as per our contractual obligations, to have to prove it. This is the system that I described, wherein we have a number of forms and a number of conditions that we require for anyone to be allowed to bid on these projects. They require things such as certificates of compliance, which they show every worker, whether it's in the construction field or in manufacturing, designing, building, or assembly. You name it; they will show certificates of compliance each month when they turn in their request for a progress draw. We will have a team onsite that will take these and double-check every one of them to make sure that everyone is in compliance. Anyone who fails to comply will be considered in breach of contract, and we have the right to eliminate them from the job. All materials that we have purchased from them on our Stored Materials Data Sheet are ours, and we keep them. We will have a tight rein on exactly who is getting the jobs.

When we ask for submittals or proposals, or when a proposal is sent to us through a gubernatorial body from any state, we require that these issues are addressed. We're not even going to waste our time doing all the statistical analysis, to double check all of your numbers, to make sure that the project is viable and worth our time and our money. Therefore, you will have to show us who the suppliers of the equipment are and who the vendors will be, what banks you're going to use as we require, what percentage, and how many jobs. Show us the viability of the plan statistically so that we know from the very beginning that the companies and the contractors have already been made aware of these requirements and can prove their capability in compliance with them. We're not going to wait until it becomes a contractual obligation, to find out that they were just throwing numbers at us, figuring that when the time came, if they got the job, they would set about the task of compliance. No! We want to know upfront how many American jobs you are going to need onsite. Who are your manufacturers? Who are your suppliers? Who are your vendors? Are you using giant earth-moving equipment made in the United States of America, or are you using stuff made in China? We can't tell the rest of the businesses in America what their protocol should be. The government can't tell them, but they can't tell us, and other businesses can't tell us. If it costs a little more to keep it American, then so be it. We're not going to give away millions and millions of jobs to foreign countries just to save a buck. We want guarantees that living wages are being paid, that prevailing wages when it comes to skilled and semi-skilled labor and even unskilled labor, are being met. This all comes down to our approval when we analyze the certificates of compliance each and every month. This doesn't mean that because a company does have its main operations in another country, it can't get it on the action. It simply means that they will have to build or buy a property in this country, equip it with American-made parts, and show us that they're willing and able to comply with our demands. Of course, if a company or manufacturer exists that has stocked their facility with foreign-made machinery, that's okay. We're not going to be ridiculous, but that's the beauty of being our own corporation. Since we make the rules, we can break the rules. We can bend the rules.

One of the things that I just put into this was an 80% minimum. Let's suppose we put up for a big $1 billion project. That means that on the value of that project, a minimum of 80% of it must be American. Since we make the rules, we can flex. Let's say some company that makes turbines imports some of their parts from another country that are crucial to making those turbines. We want them to set up their operation so that they can eliminate the foreign company and have it made in the United States. That could take a while; it could take years. In the meantime, we need those turbines. What do we do?

They show us that they can do 70% in the United States. While we have other companies that are doing 90 and 100% in this country, what we need is 80% overall. Therefore, although we require 80% from each vendor, an application for exemption can be made and must be made at the time of the proposal submittal. We can't wait until we've already dug the basin and are ready to put the turbines in before they let us know about the little glitch that they have, that they won't be able to comply with. We need to know that upfront so that when we put all the statistical analysis together, we reach our goal of 80%.

Let's take another look: Suppose we put this $1 billion up for bid and get three or four major bidders. All bidders are viable. All numbers are in the same ballpark with each other, as they should be. A bidder that's way too low is not what we're looking for, and a bidder that's way too high is not either.

We want the group somewhere in the middle. That cuts us down to one, two, or three viable bidders. We look at their proposals and see that this particular bidder can comply with all of our requirements, and when the bottom line is achieved it comes out 85% American, and 15% other. This could be because some of the major equipment needed is going to have to be purchased, and they can't get this in America, especially in time. We've given them a break because if they're using the equipment that they already have, and it's from out of the country, then that's fine. That's why we have the 20% buffer. They come in at 85%. Right here I'm looking at a proposal with basically the same prices, a viable company able to comply with all requirements. The bottom line is 92% American. To the 85% guy, we send them a Dear John letter, "Better luck next time. In the meantime, try to get your system better built to comply with what our goal is, which is 100%, but we will accept 80%." When we move into the States to do these projects, special considerations again come up at the top of the list when we talk about compliance. We utilize much of the same strategy that we use from the major bidders, in that not only do we want American but we want all of the parts - the piping, the wiring, the plumbing parts, as much as you can possibly give us - from that state. In other words, we're not going to stand by while some major companies that have giant manufacturing facilities in another state are getting all of the bids. Even though the project is located in, let's say, Pennsylvania, we find out that only 50% of the manufacturing is being done in Pennsylvania. We require that the submitter of the proposal has an obligation to use diligence to locate and have conversations with manufacturing plants in that state. Also, you can't bring your crews that were working on a project halfway across the country into this state; thereby much of the labor needed on the project site is not from Pennsylvania. What's wrong with this picture? This is meant to spread the projects around, provide employment opportunities and opportunities for prosperity and small businesses to grow. We require that the banks in that area be used. When a state gets approval for a project, it wants all of it. We, as our rule, as our protocol, have decided that, if at all possible, we will deliver.

Every state will get projects. Every state will get massive projects. We want to spread the wealth around. This is not a socialistic type of wealth distribution. It's common sense. Here is why:

Every person in this country will be an investor. Every person in this country will have a shared interest. Every person in this country, therefore, deserves their fair share. If you have a state, say Pennsylvania, that I believe has something like 12 or 13 million people, its share of the $200 billion could be billions of dollars itself. That's every single year. Therefore, we have the obligation to make sure that Pennsylvania gets its billions of dollars back in the way of projects. It works out fine. In most cases, the more people you have, the more projects you'll need. The bigger the projects, the more expensive.

Just take the energy grid, for example. As we cross Nevada, we don't see that the grid becomes that expensive or complicated. While we're in Pennsylvania, with its 13 million people, it's going to be a very expensive amount of work. If we take that work at its dollar value and supply that state with the amount of projects to balance what was put in by the investor, then it should work out well on a per capita basis. The bigger and the more populated the state, the more people need to be served. The projects are bigger. When we look at it on a per capita basis, it should even out pretty well. There are some cases where it won't. Even though the population is very small, we may have to cross a large expanse of land to get there. We may have to cross mountains. We, as the owners of the corporation, will, as a rule, take this into consideration.

However, when we need to set off an imbalance and take more money to put it into a lower populated area to make it work, then we have the right to do that. That will all be done by our Dream Team, our Board, our five superstars. They need to make the decisions.

Of course, as we look at this over time, we see that it will be a rather simple means to balance this, as time goes on. If your project is more than what your investment value is, we can still get it done for you. Since you're putting in these billions every year, perhaps next year you won't get as much. It may take several years before we recoup the difference in the value compared to the investment amount that you provided. So, Pennsylvania may sit. We may have a $5 billion investment value and only get $4 billion this year, maybe another $4 billion next year, but the year after we may get $8 billion. We will balance it out over a five-year period. Five years will be the length of the contract that we put our superstars under. We ask them to give us the five best years of their lives. At the end of the five years, we can ask them for another five. They can reapply for their job, or they can walk; it's totally up to them. We want to look at these in five-year increments. So many of these plans are so huge that it will take five years, even more, with thousands of people working on it, to complete it. We're taking on Hoover Dam-type projects in massive numbers, probably 100 or 200 of them just in the first few years. Tell me that's not going to put some people to work if we insist that everything is American.

CHAPTER 7

BACK TO SOVEREIGNTY

We have another problem; this one, too, comes with a simple and reasonable solution. What do we do when the projects are complete? They're ready to be occupied. We have already addressed this, but let's take a closer look. Let's look at it this way: Do we want to become the property managers of trillions of dollars in assets? I don't think so. Our corporation is going to be massive; we don't need to make it any bigger. That's when things start getting screwed up. What do we do? Since we are so brilliant and because we remember the Primary Goal in all of this - Sovereignty - we are able to come up with a solution. We know that sovereignty starts with the individual.

Somehow, we have to give the individuals control over this property. We already have it in one sense because we are all investors in this large corporation, and therefore any of its assets are our assets. These assets are tangible, intrinsic, and high dollar value. The value of any asset is equal to the cost that it takes to build that asset. Therefore, if we have a $5 billion project, and you want to replace it or duplicate it, you would need another $5 billion. If you wanted to buy it from us, the owners, our price would certainly start at $5 billion. That's what it would cost you to build your own, and then you've got years tied up with massive amounts of revenue. Why not take the one that we've already got ready?

Wait a minute. We not only have a responsibility of sovereignty to the individuals, but we have a responsibility of sovereignty to the state. In the Constitution, most power is given to the state: Why is that? When you draw the state border line, every single resident within that border becomes part- owner of that state. If there are state parks, everybody owns them. If it's a county park, everyone in that county owns it. Everyone who pays taxes in that area owns it. Yet the sovereignty of the state has been so diminished that they have little or no power left. Everything is subsided or paid for through the Federal Government. Believe me, it comes with strings attached. Every time a state tries to stand up for itself and what it thinks is right, the Federal Government says 'Comply or lose your funding'. So, the state complies. When we look at the structure of government, we see that it comes from the individual, through the state and up to the federal level. Yet because the state has been so diminished, we pretty much look at the thing from a macro government point of view. It is all of us in the country tied together by a central government. Our states are being pushed out. I truly believe that the far-left wing, socialist value liberals would love nothing more than to see the Federal Government simply erase all state boundaries. Cut the country up into districts and eliminate state government altogether. We cannot let this happen! For God's sake, it will mean the end of individual sovereignty, which protects individual liberty, which is an extension of the rights given to us by God - life, liberty, and the pursuit of happiness. It will become America for

the American government. We know what happens then. Take a look at Europe. It cannot sustain the weight of its own ineptitude. It takes over everything. You think that there will be four or five giant banks and one or two little banks left - forget it! There will be one bank. One! It will be the Bank of America, not necessarily the one that exists today. It will probably be called something like 'The People's Bank of America.' Oh yeah, the people.

In order to stop this, we have to provide for the sovereignty of the state. We have to wrestle the Federal Government to the ground and force it to take away the chokehold that they have on states, and therefore the people businesses, and banking in those states. We, as citizens of the state, are supposed to make the decisions as per the needs of our particular state. Why can't we? Why is this happening? The states cannot print money. The Federal Government came in and said things like this: "We are going to provide for everyone in your state to get Medicaid. We're going to subsidize it, except you are going to pay 60%." What? I didn't hear any of the citizens in this state calling out for Medicaid. We supply what we can supply through the means that we have to supply it. You can't come in here and tell us what to do? They make a national mandate that goes through Congress: All states will comply. "But you can't do that! The Federal Government does not have that power." They claim they are providing for the general welfare of the people. I'll tell you what: It doesn't do my welfare any damn good. Now the state, with that burden, has to borrow money. It has to raise taxes. The taxes get too high, so the people, companies, and industry leave, leaving the state in worse shape than before. It puts more people on welfare, which the state now has to pay a certain percentage of in order to get its subsidy from the Federal Government. The state now is broke. They are billions of billions of dollars in debt. They can't raise taxes anymore. Businesses are closing their doors or moving out of town. How do we turn this around? That is one of the primary reasons that we, the people of the United States, have now decided that the Federal Government has to go. It has a purpose. It has a place. It is enumerated by the Constitution, and it needs to be put in that place and it needs to follow those enumerated powers. There are constant screams of compliance,

compliance, compliance. What about them? When are they going to comply? When are they going to comply with the rule of law that we have all decided to make our Constitution? They must be forced to give up some of their power. That's why we're building this corporation the way we are, with our own money, with our own investment, with our own corporation, with our own rules and regulations. We are going to eliminate that heavy thumb of the Federal Government. I'll get more into regulations at a later date because they have got to go!

Just a bit ago I was saying that we must start with the individual. We've already discussed that a state, by its collective investment, should get the number of projects done in their state to equal the value of the investment dollar that is realized from the investments through the gasoline tax.

Therefore, it should be considered that those projects done in that state, and the intrinsic value of the assets produced in that state, should therefore belong to the people of that state. How do you like it now? Now we're getting somewhere. Not only have we created the jobs and gotten the small banking system up and running, but we are selling homes like there is no tomorrow. The values are going sky high on those properties that used to be called toxic assets. Manufacturing is booming. Tax revenues are coming in hand over fist. We're getting ready to tell the Federal Government, "Take your Medicaid program and shove it." We'll set up our own and pay for it ourselves. We're out of debt and we have money. We're cutting away from the illegal forces that you used to control us. We, the collective owners of that property that is inside the state of Pennsylvania, will draw up the legal documents and will gift those properties and those assets to the people of that state. Not to the state government, but to the people of that state. It gives the people control over what they want to do with this huge asset that has just been handed to them. How do they want to utilize it? The way you do this is this, as many states do: When it comes time to have large tax increases or many different issues, even down to deciding whether they would allow gay marriage in the state, what the government does, along with the people - different groups and different entities of civilian people - is put together proposals. These proposals are then made transparent through the internet by TV ads, newspapers, and different media sources. There are people arguing for; there are people arguing against. Then, after a few months, it comes time for a vote. We like to utilize that system. Have a bunch of people, different groups as well as the government put together proposals on what we should do with our property.

Let me just throw a couple of these at you. Suppose we put in a huge hydroelectric system coming down the Allegheny River north of Pittsburgh, dumping into the Ohio River right at Pittsburgh, and following the Ohio River out of state. It's a huge project, billions and billions of dollars. Someone has to operate it. Someone has to maintain it. Someone has to be responsible for everyday operations, and security. There will be huge grid work projects attaching it to the general grid that we are going to build across this nation.

Computer operators with trained special software, you name it, get involved. Do we, the citizens, want to give control of it to our state government?

Perhaps we do. If we do that, then we eliminate the middle man and can do this: From now on, our energy bills to use that electricity will be decided on by what the cost to maintain the facilities is. Therefore, we could expect to see energy costs for electricity drop in amazing increments. There will be times, however, when maintenance will need to be done, and there will be sacrifice required in terms of money, and we will have to raise the electric bill. In the meantime, we're getting our electricity for peanuts. One of the promises we make when we gift that property is that when it comes time to renovate when it comes time to expand, these projects will be undertaken by our corporation. Proposals will be accepted. Everybody knows the rules. Many of the same companies that built the first one will be involved in renovation and expansion, which really means that these projects pretty much never end. As the population expands, we have to add on. New technologies are made available that are much more efficient. It's going to be a lot of cost, but over the long run, we don't want a decaying system. That's what got us into this problem in the first place - a refusal to maintain and upgrade. Why? Because we needed the Federal Government to give us that money. Even though they are so generous with the entitlements, when it comes to maintaining this country, they don't want to spend the money. Look at our infrastructure.

Where is the providing for the welfare of the people now? Our country is falling apart, literally. We will assume the burden of keeping the renovations and expansions within our grasp. As the corporation that built it, we know best.

Let's take a look at another point of view: This one I particularly love.

Maybe we bring a company in. In Pittsburgh, I believe it's Consol Energy or something like that. We say, "We have built the facility. You don't have to put in a single penny, but we need somebody to run it. We need somebody to maintain it. When things break down, even though it may be piping or whatever, we need somebody who will prudently handle this. Would you like to lease the property and the business from the people of this state?" I tell you what we'll do. We expect 10, 15, maximum of 20 years on any property before it has to be renovated. Let's say we pick the middle number. Of course, statistical analysis always needs to be done on every item, every issue. It can't just be a matter of, "I like that idea." We have to prove statistically the viability of the plan. In this case, it's a $5 billion facility. Suppose we enter into a contract with you where you will pay us, out of your revenues, $250 million per year over 20 years. That covers the $5 billion. Consol Energy doesn't have to put up a penny of upfront money. They take the business, they create the product, mark it up, and sell it to us consumers. We're close to watching that they're not counting their $250 million as overhead and then marking it up, therefore getting us to pay their overhead plus market markup, when it's us that built the property. That has to be separate. They have 20 years to get it paid. Look at this side of it: If they were to do it themselves, they would either have to spend unbelievable capital, which they probably don't have, which means they would have to borrow it from a bank for 20 or 30 years with interest. A $5 billion property could easily cost them $10 billion, maybe 7 or 8. We're not asking for interest. We don't want to over-burden and therefore see our energy costs go up, because they just can't afford to keep the thing running. We have to do our due diligence and our statistical analysis. We put it on the web; we put it in the newspapers. We let the people know what the real numbers are. We just want our $250 million a year, and here's why.

That would be the value of one property. Remember we in Pennsylvania were using generic numbers, but we said we put in $5 billion a year. That's one $5 billion project. We, from that single project, are receiving back $250 million a year into our state revenue. Because we're so smart, we earmark that money for a specific task. What is that? You remember I just told you about our crumbling America. It's coming to pieces. States can't fix it; they don't have the money. Government can't fix it; they don't have the money or the will. Let private enterprise intercede. Where are they going to get the money? Not that type of dough. Look at this single project alone: We are receiving $250 million a year for the next 20 years. I think we can rebuild some bridges, put in some new water systems, resurface some roads, widen, expand, and make them safer - with $250 million a year. Remember, that's one year's worth of revenue. Over ten years, if that revenue stays the same, you'll have $50 billion paid in, plus the balance owed.

Your payback will be $2.5 billion per year. Do you think maybe we could do some infrastructure projects with that? Remember that as we're building these facilities, anything that's in the way or anything that we have to tear up, or anything that has a part in the efficiency of this new property, we will deal with as we go. Much, much of our piping and our grid will be part of it. We may have to put in a couple of new bridges, whatever it takes. Much of the infrastructure is going to be fixed as we endeavor to bring our country back to sovereignty.

All of this prosperity eventually trickles upwards as revenue to the Federal Government. We of course are going to require that they pay off our debt.

There's going to be hundreds of billions, even over a trillion some years, in additional revenue into the Federal Government's treasury, and we don't want it wasted. You get the money if you use it to pay off the debt, and that's the bottom line. In America, by this time, we are going to realize that we are the ones who have control, that we're the ones who have the brains, that we're the ones who know how to make things work. We're going to get up and we're going to stand at the bottom of their beds until they return to the good old- fashioned notion of 'by the people and for the people.'

CHAPTER 8

THE DREAM TEAM

Wow! Are you as excited as I am? That was a great section. The plan is re- ally starting to come together. How sweet that is when a plan comes together. We've done everything from fixing banking to creating a minimum of 15 million jobs in the first 10 years. There's something that I want to remind you that I think should be an integral part of our plan; that is the DRIP factor. That is the Downside Risk Involvement Percentage. I mentioned earlier a 25% DRIP factor. I believe this is a prudent way of preventing risk, or at least covering the risk when it does happen. And it will happen! Everything has a downside. It is up to us to plan for it. When I make my calculations, I say I can provide 15 million new jobs in 10 years. Well, my calculations actually show more like 20 million, but if I set my plan up with 20 million and it makes 15, then I've opened myself up for failure. The downside risk in these types of endeavors always comes out to a monetary value. After all, it is the macroeconomics and its relationship to sovereignty that we're talking about. I talk about revenues versus investment capital going out. In order to compensate for any risk, I apply a 25% DRIP factor. Therefore, when I claim 15 million jobs, I can pretty much guarantee that we will get 15 million jobs. I believe that we can get 20 million. Either way, the plan works exceptionally well, even at 15 million. Therefore, its viability (and the basic concept) is sound. I recommend when we're doing bid proposals, that we have a large labor force for doing statistical analysis on all proposals that are generated within or without our system. Of course, those doing the bid proposals will want to keep their numbers tight. They will put in a small DRIP factor.

Being in the business for 35 years, I always plugged in according to the value of the job and, of course, how badly I wanted it. When you're talking about that kind of money, the desire to get a job is extremely high. The estimators have a tendency to lowball the job, hoping that, through sheer performance, they're going to be able to meet the numbers that they've proposed. Generally, I would put in a large job at 5 or 6%. I would pay 2 2% on performance bond. That would be added to the price as well. The performance bond protects me from lawsuits, as well as my corporate status protects me from personal lawsuits. It's the DRIP factor that protects the job from going too far under. When we're talking about 15 and 20% profit margins, a 5% hit on the gross value of the job is devastating. If we plug in the 5%, that pretty much covers us, and if we hit 6 or 7%, we're still good. We put in a 20% markup, hoping to get 17 18, or even 16. Without the 5% DRIP factor, my bid proposals were dangerous; with the DRIP factor, I always made money. And I always needed that 5%. There was always something that came up. On a half- million-dollar bid that I would put out, that would give me a $25,000 buffer.

That was critical. Now I'm looking at 25%, enough to cover just about any downside that we could imagine. Of course, since we're going to do hundreds of multi-billion-dollar projects, some could reach 10 or 15%, while others come in on budget. Therefore, of the $200 billion per year that we have as working capital, we can actually stand to take a $50 billion-a-year hit and still maintain our DRIP factor. Along with the few percentages that the construction company plugs in, that gives us an actual buffer of 30% or more. Everybody makes their money.

Of course, we want everybody to make decent money because it's our brothers and sisters and relatives and friends and ourselves who are going to be working on those jobs. We'll be in the factories that manufacture the products. We'll be in the field pouring the concrete or digging the earth. We want, for ourselves and our friends, a living wage - nothing ridiculous, just a decent living wage. We want some decent benefits along with that wage.

What's wrong with that? If it costs us a little bit more, that's fine because we have that calculated in. On top of that, we put in a DRIP factor. Suppose some of the companies working on the project face a large pay increase for their people. This could easily happen, since the great prosperity that is going to come to this country is, by its own nature, inflationary. Since it will become more and more difficult to supply quality labor, those in the labor force have an upper hand. Prices of goods and services will go up; the people demand an increase in wages to compensate. This is natural and it is one of the most important items in a positive growth economy.

What I would like to see, therefore, is a huge department that will work not under any one board member's team, but as a general department to be used by all board members. What they'll be tasked with is doublechecking all the statistics so that when we get these large proposals, we have not only the general contractors giving us their estimates, which they are extremely good at, but we also have our own team making sure that we're within an operable range. Many of our projects will be duplicates. Once we put in a system one time, it may be just a matter of reproducing the process over and over again. This gives us another great advantage. Even though we may take a hit on the first several tries, we will fine-tune the process, streamline it, bring manufacturing to a peak of efficiency, and bring assembly and production in the field to a peak of productivity; the numbers will settle down. My suggestion would be to maintain the 25% DRIP factor through all of our statistical analyses. Therefore, when our board members evaluate the project for approval, they know that we should have a 20-25% bigger number than those who gave us a proposal. If it comes down to a few percent, then they're wiping out our DRIP factor. We may have to reassess the validity of that project. Of course, this is always an everyday occurrence in big construction. It happens every day; it is not a big deal. People reevaluate and see how much they can shave off to get it down to a working number.

When I say there is no downside to this plan, it's because of that DRIP factor and one other point: There is nothing in this plan that we haven't done before. We have dug giant basins in strip mining, we know how to move massive amounts of earth, and we know how to build a grid. Our problem is making it cyber-proof. We handle large construction projects like a football stadium with ease. We even can put a dome that has no center support over the top of that football stadium. We're that good. What makes this proposal scary is the vastness of it. We're talking, over time, trillions of dollars. We're talking about facing problems that nobody thought were there. It's nothing that we haven't faced before, though. I don't care if we run into a giant piece of rock the size of Mount Everest. We'll dig through the middle of it if we have to.

Look what we do with our tunnel-building machines. We can put a six-lane highway right through the middle of the baddest mountain in the land with these boring machines. Preformed concrete slabs that are brought in and interlocked can take the force of the entire mountain on top. Through structural engineering genius, we can displace the weight around the tunnel. There is nothing we can't accomplish.

We're going to have to enlist our chemists. We need better fuel. We need a means to clean our coal. We're not throwing coal out of the mix. It is too abundant and it is domestic. We're going to figure out a cheap way to make it valuable, as well as clean. We're going to enlist an entire team that operates separately from the rest of the team and monitors and checks for any environmental concerns. On top of that, we will have the advantage of hundreds of environmental groups that you know are going to be watching over us on a day-by-day basis. We will work with them. We'll have our team work with their team. We will find ways to make it as environmentally friendly as possible.

What we aren't going to do is bow to the EPA. Their days are numbered.

One of the things that will be needed as we go through Congress is to have in our Bill a clause that says that we will be responsible for environmental concerns but we will not be under the thumb of the EPA. This plan is 'by the People' and 'for the People', and I'll be damned if we're going to let them ruin our projects, and cost us tens or hundreds of billions of dollars, just so they can pat themselves on the backs and pretend they're so incredibly needed. As we go along, we will have statistical analysis to back up our decisions, to utilize a regulation, to ignore the regulation, or to modify the regulation. Then we put it into the basic structure of our corporation and we go with that.

When we find out how many of these regulations are absolutely ridiculous and unnecessary, we have to take it back to Congress and tell them it should be an across-the-board decision to eliminate these regulations for all businesses, so that they can flourish as well. The ones needed; we keep. It's fine, but somebody has to put a handle on this and get the true analysis, the analysis that comes from everyday working with these conditions, so that we can rely on statistics, not idealism or the philosophy of an agency that has to hurt American businesses in order for it to survive.

We're going to have a large amount of statistical analysis. We're going to have to have the best that there is in the field, watching all operations. We're going to have to have people out in the field that can read these blueprints, understand them inside-out and upside-down. We need people who value their positions and take responsibility for making sure that we don't end up with substandard concrete so that another company can make a bundle and in a couple of years the whole thing breaks apart and the system fails. Those are the kinds of things that will kill a major project and could actually overrun our 25% DRIP factor. It costs a lot more to tear it back out and then re-install a new system than it does to build the system right the first time. In the meantime, between now and the day that we vote on whether to implement this plan, we need to get a statistical analysis of future projections. Test everything, I say. Check out my DRIP factor. Check out my claim of 15 or 20 million jobs. Check out how much money it will need; is $200 billion adequate? I picked $200 billion because we're looking at an optimum number. If we try to pour a half trillion dollars into this in a year, we will have massive failures. We can't do it that fast. We would need a team of 15 or 20 board members, making it so much more difficult to get projects okayed. At the same time, since we The People are going to be the investors, we can't make the number so large that it's going to break our backs trying to get that much revenue up.

Remember: We're going to get that revenue from a gas tax. We know that because - and this is something that needs to be checked - the strength that we show as a people and the determination that we present as a people to break this extortion ring that we call OPEC and put them back on earth to reality, will bring the gas prices down immensely. I say that even with our added tax, we will see gas prices at $3.50 or lower. What will happen is other countries will see our success and begin to implement some of their own measures. As the demand for oil decreases, the OPEC countries that now are thicker than thieves, which is what they are - thieves, will start to panic. Countries will start to break away from OPEC, figuring they can make their own deals and do a better job of it. Iran will get into bed with China in a big way, promising all their fuel to China. Of course, China, being a smart buyer, will say, "Of course, we will take that deal but under these conditions: This much per barrel. Take it or leave it, because Venezuela is knocking on our door as well. So is Syria.

We're getting offers from all over. Who is going to give us the best deal? We'll take a long-term contract, 5-10 years." The countries will start to compete with each other. OPEC will crumble. Once this competition comes up, as the demand goes down, you will see oil prices that are incredible. What we're going to do to really stick it in is create another fuel, one that's better, one that's cleaner, one that's available right here in our country. It will compete with the oil and therefore in this country - where we won't be buying oil from other countries - we will still have a very competitive market. When our new fuel price gets higher, we can switch back to standard conventional gasoline. That will drive the gas prices up since demand will go up. As the demand goes up for that gasoline, the price will come down on our new fuel, in order to compete. We can switch over to the new fuel, which then drives the gasoline down again. It will be a scale that we will have control over. Supply and Demand, which are the basic principles of economics, will rule the day, not what we have now. Basically, OPEC is a monopoly. Because it's international and because we need the product so badly, there is not much we can do about it. Besides that, they have so much power that they have many of our politicians in their pockets. This too will end!

The concept of fuel that is driven by supply and demand values, as that which decides market price, is something that we haven't seen in 50 years in that industry. Well, I'm here to tell you: We're getting it back. Since we don't, or will not, need foreign countries, we excuse ourselves from the volatility of that market.

Our markets will be stable and solid. The country will continue to grow not only in prosperity but in number. As more people are in the country, more energy is required, more cars need to be built, and more fuel needs to be created to run the car.

Let's take one last point here about fuel: Please, America, I beg you. Stop with the nonsense of electric cars. It is pure insanity. It cannot work, it does not work, it will never work! It won't work to put this country in a position where, at minimum, the passenger personal transportation vehicles - which total at this point approximately 256 million - rely on electricity for those vehicles. Where will we get it? It's insane. Even if we could produce it, we have to get it to the homes. Gas stations will go out of business. You have the weight of the battery, plus you have to have a gas tank full of gas. It's counter- productive. The price of electricity will make the price of gasoline look like a pittance. If you get 20 miles to the gallon and it costs $4 a gallon, that's $4 for every 20 miles. If you go to electricity, it could cost you $50 for 20 miles. You'll end up just dragging dead batteries around with you while you utilize the gas tank part of your vehicle because gas will be so much cheaper. It's stupid. Do you know this number? I think I mentioned this before. A $40,000 electric car actually costs close to $300,000. The rest is subsidized by the government, and that means us. It's insanity on steroids.

I'm going to get ready to wrap up this section, and I'm going to tell you I'm practically giddy. Just look at the last chapter. We have taken our prosperity and gifted it back to the people. Hopefully, that generates new revenues from whatever the people decide to do with those assets. If those revenues are put back into infrastructure projects in that state, it now creates a whole new set of jobs. So far, we haven't borrowed one single penny. We've given massive amounts of sovereignty back to the individual. They've uploaded this power to the states; now we've created state sovereignty. We're enabling the states and the people that live within them to walk away from the Federal Government and all the strings that are attached to their so-called gifts. We've strengthened the safety net because we've taken the weight off of it.

Sovereignty - that's what our goal is. I'm here to tell you at this point we have achieved a major breakthrough in returning sovereignty to the people, where it belongs. I hope that there will be a movement that comes out of this. As we see the value of individual sovereignty - and the liberty that it presents - with a constitution designed to protect that, we will have much more concern about what is happening in Washington and in our state capitals. We will become more involved. We will become enlightened as to what's going on around us. We will demand to have our say. Anyone who thinks otherwise is gone. When you have an entire country involved, you'll see much less need for radical groups to storm Wall Street, to storm the White House, to picket businesses, and so on. As the people speak, so shall it be. Of course, there will be radicals always, but their value will be so diminished that they'll be lucky if they can even get any media airtime. Who will care about them? They'll have to start blowing things up and murdering people in order to get any attention, and that would be their downfall.

As we try to wrap up this section on what the plan is, - what it looks like, its functions, its policies, its protocol, everything from how we accept bids to how we handle environmental issues - there is one more thing that I want to address. I call it my Dream Team. We've talked about this great plan. We have come to realize that it is us. It's all us and no one but us. This is the plan of The People. It will be implemented by The People. Yet we have to have a team of leaders. We have discussed how the leaders will operate and function, and in what capacities, but let's take a few more details, put them in there, and then let's decide who we want to be our saviors. Remember, these people will be responsible for what I call the re-founding of America. They won't make foreign policy, they won't dabble in healthcare or immigration issues, education, or any of that, but they will be the backbone of this economy. They are going to take us through generations, into the 22nd Century and beyond. What would we pay someone with that kind of responsibility? I say one-half of one million dollars per year, with a very nice expense account. Why that amount? It actually is very, very cheap. It's almost free. These people can make hundreds of millions of dollars in a single year. These people don't need the job. The $500,000 is a token value. It's a nice round number, and the main thing is it is greater than the amount that we pay the President of the United States. Whoa! What a slap in the face to our President. Make no mistake about it: Our President is the most important man on the planet, but he or she can only do so much. With a divided Congress, it's very little. These people on our team will have an incredible amount of power. We are building it that way. We are leaving most items for debate. They have total anonymity and total flexibility. What else do we see in our Dream Team? Wealth. Massive amounts of wealth. We want people who have built that wealth on hard work, a good value system, and an understanding of economics and business. After all, we're going to ask them to run the largest corporation ever conceived on this planet. We need people with know-how. One of the most important functions, especially early on, is that they know how to set up a team. They need to know how to create the system by which we will function. They know who to hire and they know who to fire, and they have no problem with it. They will set up a pyramid of power under each of them that will go from their group of direct assistants down through the channels to those that implement in the field.

Engineers, mathematicians, environmental consultants, statistical analysts. Upper management, middle management, and lower management. A spider web of connection is much like we see in the World Wide Web.

Interconnecting forces that all lead back to a single group that makes the decisions. At first, setting up this corporation is going to be a chore, one heck of a mighty chore. We're going to take the first year to let them begin setting up the system while we gather our first year's working capital of $200 billion. That gives time for those who would be potential bidders, those who would wish to inject their ideas and their proposals, and the time to put things together.

This means from the very first day you'll see great changes in the economic activities in this country. Draftsmen who are standing around hoping for a job will be in such high demand that they'll walk into the job making 20% more money than they were making when they walked out a few years ago. Colleges and tech schools will be flooded with high school graduates wanting to get a degree in these areas because four years down the road they're going to be starving for that kind of talent. They go in with hopes of coming out to a starting position with decent money; in over a few years, with hard diligence, they can work up into six figures. Now that's putting quite a burden on five people, but, remember, they've done it before. They've done it in their everyday lives. They are experts at it. One more reason why we cannot give this to the politicians! They simply do not know how. Massive failure would be on the horizon. These failures could take what was going to save this country and spin it around, as we would see monumental drops on Wall Street and in banking, inability to loan money. We cannot let it happen! Partisanship cannot be an issue.

That's why Rule #1 is No Politicians. We're not taking somebody out of Washington. We're not taking somebody out of state positions. The best we can do would be someone who was in the business before, who has taken a term or two in Congress, and then has returned to their business life. We may entertain that person if we believe that what they do suits our needs. Let's look at my Dream Team.

We start with a man who I believe is a seriously patriotic individual. This man cares for this country more than 99% of the politicians in Washington. He understands the needs of this country. He is a multi-billionaire. He doesn't need the money. If he were to take this job, I could even see him taking the money, the $500,000 a year, and giving it to his foundation. This man likes to help people. This man knows business, not just on a local level but on a global level. He has negotiated some of the biggest contracts in history. His empire spreads the globe. This man faced bankruptcy at one time. This man learned and he brought it back from the abyss. He now is one of the most powerful men in this country, perhaps the world. He does not need the money. This will be the labor of love. I speak of the incomparable business genius, land acquisition professional, none other than Mr. Donald Trump. He made a short run for President because he sees what's going on in this country. He is the one who screams all the time, "We have to break OPEC. We must break OPEC. This country will flounder. It is a mathematical certainty. We have to take the bull by the horns. We have to work a fair deal with China." He knows it, and he knows how to do it. At this point in American history, this job is probably the most important job on the planet, and I think he can do it. Let's have some applause. Hope and pray that if this plan comes to fruition, he would be kind enough to join our team as one of the Re-Founding Fathers.

Let's move down the list. My second choice: I was going to write a special thank you in the preface of the book to this man, but I will just tell you right now since I have your attention. This man is responsible for this plan. He was the man that inspired this plan. This man came out in 2008, before the election, and tried everything, using his own money - millions and millions of dollars spent - to make energy independence a key issue in that electoral race. People were so enamored with Barack Obama that they wouldn't listen. He talked and he talked. He put up statistics. It's where I get the number $700 billion dollars a year going to foreign oil. It's where I realized that energy independence wasn't just good business, that the sovereignty of this country and the national security of this country were teetering on a barrel of oil. This man has more money than he could ever spend. This man has run mega business for decades, always with success. He is as righteous as the day is long, and he loves this country as much as he loves life itself. He is not in this to make a buck. If he were in it to make money, why would he put millions of dollars into commercial ads trying to talk us into breaking away from foreign-interest oil-producing nations, to become self-sufficient by using any and all methods of energy production that are clean, safe, and affordable? Why would he do that if he was interested in making money? He had made his money in - guess what! - oil. I bring to you a man who has five very special years that he can give us and help save this nation. I give you the second Re-Founding Father, Mr. T. Boone Pickens. You started this, Boone; get on board and help us finish it. God bless you.

My third choice is a beautiful, beautiful woman. This woman has a heart so big that when Katrina hit, she personally put in $20 million and took the responsibility to have homes built. She gave those homes to those who had been displaced by that terrible tragedy. She started out humble. She started out with very, very little. She has been named, several times over, as the most powerful woman in the world. She knows how to build a giant enterprise. She knows how to put together a team. She is a patriot as much as George Washington was a patriot. She loves this country and she loves her people.

Yes, she is a black woman and she takes care of many, many underprivileged black children. I want the black inner-city impoverished people to get educated, trained, and find their way out of the ghetto by taking these jobs.

There will be so many jobs that without their help, we may not be able to meet the requirements for how many jobs there will be. Who else could I be talking about? The First Lady of Talk Shows, my favorite, Oprah Winfrey. I want her on my team. I want her to engage herself in projects where she can utilize black contractors who hire people from inner-city projects. I want to make those people sovereign. I want them to be able to look to the future, see a goal, and embrace the American dream. I am sick and tired of throwing crumbs on their doorstep and then pushing them somewhere that we don't have to look at them. Then we stand around and pat ourselves on the backs for our righteousness. Give me a break! Go, Oprah! Join the team!

Number Four: We're narrowing it down. Let's take a look at one of the biggest, most difficult, most expensive parts of our plan. That is to create a brand-new energy grid. Top to bottom, end to end with everything built in, with the ability to easily expand. I believe we may want to build it underground. Protect it from weather; protect it from invaders trying to take out our power grid with bombs. Utilize flexible materials and sections put together with flexible couplings so that even earthquakes can't put us out of business. The main component of this is cyber security. Absolutely! Have you been watching the news? The bugs are infesting our system, while we turn around and put the bugs in their systems. This thing is going to get more and more powerful. It's going to become more and more unstoppable. This is perhaps, at this time, the biggest issue of all for national security. It is contained within our plan for energy independence. If they can knock out our grid, then it doesn't matter how much energy we can produce if we cannot utilize it. This man has wealth beyond imagination. This man has a giant heart. He has a foundation that spends hundreds of millions of dollars on charity projects. This man may be the smartest man on the planet. This man knows how to put together a winning team. This man knows computer software. This man could give us five years and become Number Four on my list of Re- Founding Fathers. This man is William Gates. We need you, Bill. I know you love your country. I know you love people. Five years, buddy. We know that your name is already in the history books. Let's put an exclamation mark after it and an asterisk before it, and let's put it in bold print and underline it. We need you.

Now, who's left? In my Number Five position, I'm running to a point where I have a number of people that I would like but only one job left. I've struggled with this. I know of a man who certainly passes the wealth test. He passes the patriotic test with an A+. His life and his family are built around his love of country. He has a son who's a senator but has refused to enter into politics himself. This man can build a team that will rival any team on the planet. He has five good years left in him; I guarantee you. If he would answer the call and become the fifth Founding Father, I would be so thrilled, as now we have our team. This man's name is John Huntsman, Sr. - a man of faith, a man of character, a man of know-how, a man of dedication, a man that I see as one of the most valuable assets this country has. Mr. Huntsman, would you apply for this job?

Of course, the application is not limited. Those who wish to become one of the re-founding Fathers will throw their hats in the ring publicly, on the media, and on the web. They will not campaign. They will use the web to present their credentials. Media will ask them for interviews; certainly, they can accept. All of their finances must be revealed, and their qualifications.

Perhaps the CEO of a multibillion-dollar corporation may decide that his time there, and his usefulness, has passed, and he is looking for the ultimate challenge, to save a nation. We will take three months, at which point all 50 states will offer as a proposal to the people their list of applicants. These applicants come from all over the country. They must be citizens and they must reside here. The people choose five out of the group. All 50 states comply. Everybody gets a vote. A state counts for one vote, period. We're not going to build an electoral college. None of this nonsense. Your state gets one vote, and five choices, regardless of how many people live there. It's simple to tally this up. At the end of the day, we have the contracts ready and ask those who would accept our invitation to please sign on. We don't want people backing out and screwing up the process. If you want in, be darn sure you want in. If not, if some better offer comes along, then you do not have the commitment that we are looking for.

That ties up this section of the book. I feel exhausted but in such a good way. We have done so much incredibly good work, you and I. I think we should give ourselves a night out. We need a rest, for we're about to get down and dirty. I'm going to show you options and opportunities. Some of these might blow your mind, but it's all doable. Get some rest. I'll see you in a couple of days.

PART II
SUMMARY

In this part of the book, I've laid out the dynamics of a plan that is guaranteed to bring economic stability along with incredible growth to our nation. This will enable us to regain sovereignty. The sovereignty, as designed by our founding fathers, will start with us, the individuals. It will move upward to the state. Again, the founding fathers guaranteed state sovereignty. When each and every state is sovereign, we then combine our efforts to create a nation that is sovereign. In previous parts of the book, we've discussed what sovereignty means. Independence: That is the synonym for sovereignty. This sovereignty requires that we have control over three critical elements. These elements are energy, economy, and military. This book is designed to put forth to you, the reader, a plan that will achieve economic sovereignty by an endeavor to move forward in energy production. This energy production must be clean and efficient. It doesn't mean that there will be zero pollutants created by it, but that it will reduce the amount of pollutants to levels that are far beyond the goals that we have actually set for ourselves. It will also produce energy independence. There again is the word that is the key to the entire book: Independence. At the same time, it will produce tens of millions of jobs, making the individual independent and giving the individual the ability to seek a path to prosperity and well-being because of the liberty that is produced when the individual has economic independence.

In this chapter, I'm going to summarize exactly how this plan works in a very simple, logical, step-by-step progression. In the previous chapters of this part, we've looked at a lot of detail and have tried to put the pieces of the puzzle together so that we can all achieve an understanding of our goals and how we plan to achieve them. I feel now that it is time to put forth the plan in the simplest manner that I know how. In that way, we can carry the knowledge of this concept with us and be able to communicate the basics and how they work to others who have not read this book. It is imperative that we spread this concept throughout the country. It is going to take a massive effort to get those who control our destiny to realize that this is the best course of action. Because we work through a system where we elect the officials to serve us, we must make it clear to them exactly what we want them to do. We know that these are the politicians and that politicians operate on popularity. Therefore, in order to convince them that this is the way we want them to move, we need large numbers of people to be involved. That means the communication between individuals, which will drive the politicians to do what we expect them to do, must be simple and clear. That is the purpose of this chapter. I'm going to attempt to put together a step-by-step simple and clear proposal that we can all understand and that is easy to communicate to others.

Let's start where we should always start, at the beginning. The first thing we need to do is to put together a bill that can be passed through Congress by our elected officials. It needs to have powerful logic as well as backing from the American people. Let's take a look at what this bill must contain:

Number one: Our goal must be clearly defined. The goal is sovereignty through economic strength, achieved by an endeavor to become an energy- independent nation. Since energy is one of the key elements in sovereignty, sovereignty can't exist without being energy-independent. As we discussed earlier, we now realize that we are not a sovereign nation because we are not energy-independent. Since energy is the backbone of manufacturing as well as all other sectors of the economy, pretty much anything that uses fuel or electricity is dependent on energy, and the economy is dependent on those things. Therefore, the economy cannot be strong and sovereignty cannot exist while we are dependent on other nations for not only our sources of energy but also money because our economy is collapsing. Our goal then is to achieve energy independence.

If we're going to be investing in energy, we certainly want it to be clean energy. We want it to be as clean as what our technology can deliver. We have the technology to deliver massive amounts of energy that are basically clean. The problem is how to finance such an endeavor. We've seen over the last few years a Green Energy agenda put forth by the administration of what is now the President of the United States and his administration. It fell flat on its face. The idea of clean energy is one we all would embrace. The question is how to achieve the goal and how to pay for it. That's where our efforts have hit a brick wall. I believe I have the answer to this problem. It's not complicated, though it may be rather complex. Complexity simply means there are a number of variables that have to be dealt with, but in a complex scenario, we have the ability to figure out the values of each of those variables and therefore formulate an equation that takes us to where we want to go. In a complicated scenario, we simply have no means to figure out what those variables are.

Therefore, we move forward by trial and error, a hit-or-miss agenda that we find does not work after we've invested billions of dollars in it. This is how our politicians have been moving us forward: Trial and error, hit-or-miss, throw money at it and hope it works. What we're going to do is go back to the simple basics of economics that we know work. We're talking macro-economics.

We're talking about putting together quite a large number of variables. Once again, we know that the equation that we use is one that's been proven to be effective.

Let's start now, since we have defined our goal, with the first part of the equation. What we can do - and it is quite simple - is to create an investment corporation. This corporation will have 300,000,000 investors. The investors will be required by law to put a little bit of their paycheck into the investment fund. The way we do that is to have Congress pass a bill that utilizes a tax system to collect the funds. The taxes should be equal for everyone, and it should be a tax on something that we all use. In that way, we ensure a fair amount is paid. It will be paid in by virtually everyone. This tax, therefore, will be a tax on gasoline and other oil products because that is what creates the fuel and energy that every single one of us uses. In that way, we arc all part of this new corporation that we're about to start for the purpose of investing in new, renewable, and clean sources of energy. Because we have an entity at our disposal known as the IRS that already collects taxes on gasoline and oil products, we can utilize them to collect this additional tax, separate this additional tax amount from the general revenues, and make it available in the form of a grant that will be given to our corporation for the specific purpose that I have described. The target amount for the revenue we need will be $200 billion per year. I have calculated this is the amount needed to make this plan work at its optimum efficiency. Even then, it will take 15 to 20 years to make the transition from how we operate today to how we will operate in the future. The beauty of this comes in job creation. Job creation means more tax revenues. The tax revenues will be adequate to pay for many of the other things contained in this plan.

Let's move to this step: Since we will be investors, this will not simply be a tax and spend policy. The one thing that investors look for is to, at the very least, get their money back. This is normally done by corporations quarterly, semi-annually, and annually. The investor is also looking for a return that is above the investment amount. We want interest on our money. We want earnings gathered by the corporation to come back to us in the form of cash. We also seek out dividends. Our corporation will be no different. Therefore, in the plan, as we put the bill through Congress, certain guarantees will be installed in the bill, and they are this: Number one, at the end of a fiscal year we will get a check in the mail for the amount of every penny that we put into this gas tax. We will get our money back 100% guaranteed. It will come in a lump sum, therefore making it a valuable asset for us, the investors. A few dollars a week doesn't mean a lot, but hundreds or even thousands at the end of the year in one lump sum can be of extreme value, not only to the individual but to the economy as a whole. This is in itself a super stimulus. We recently spent $1 trillion on a stimulus package that didn't work. Having this kind of money come back into the public, spread out amongst every resident in this country, will create prosperity and jobs. On top of that, we are going to have a dividend. This will be, again, built into the structure of the bill that we put into Congress.

As I explained previously, we will use the one thing that everyone needs, that everyone is concerned about, and that is getting more and more difficult to provide. That would be healthcare. Because the healthcare dividend will come back as a tax rebate, it can be deemed non-taxable. The same goes for the return on our investment dollars. When we get our check at the end of the year, we will not only get every penny of our investment but all of the money that comes from our rebates on healthcare. They will not be taxable income.

Now we're talking approximately $300 billion per year back into the hands of the people, with no taxes taken out, in a lump sum that can be spent by the individual on whatever they see fit. In a future chapter, we're going to look at healthcare in depth to see exactly how this can work and what the benefits are. For now, let's just say we'll follow the guidelines that I've laid out so far and make sure that the bill in Congress covers us not only for the return on our investment but for those tax rebates that will make healthcare more available and more affordable. In order to implement this plan, there are some criteria that we must lay out and absolutely adhere to.

The next thing is this: We're building a corporation. Corporations are subject to laws that have been decided upon by our politicians. It stops there. The beauty of we, the people, having our own corporation is that we get to make rules, policies, and protocols. We just finished talking about that in detail. Still, there must be a governing body. As in any corporation, there is a hierarchy. There are those that we, the investors, have approved for their position to run the corporation for us. In this case, since there are so many of us, and there will be so many applicants for those jobs, we must have the means to decide who we want to hire. Again, I've laid out the means to do that, a way for us to state by state put in our two cents as to who we wish to hire to run our corporation. I've put together a list of what I call 'The Dream Team', those who are qualified and have proven successful in the past so we know we can rely on them. Right now, I'd like to add two more names to that list: Herman Cain, a superstar businessman who knows how to set up a major corporation. The other would-be Mitt Romney, again a man has proven successful year after year. As I've described earlier, each of these fits the criteria of not being interested in money but being interested in saving our country. They are patriots. Let's add them to the list that I've already given you as viable applicants if they would be so kind as to be willing to give up five years of their lives to save this nation. Once we have the hierarchy in place, they will do what they do best. They will build us a team of superstars. From the top of the echelon right down to the workers in the field, they will have control. This is why we cannot let the bill be twisted in a manner that gives the power to the President or to Congress to approve their idea of what would be our Dream Team. I said earlier: No incumbent politicians. Those who have run for office, or have been in office can apply, but we cannot let the politics and divisiveness that exist in Washington be a deciding factor on how our corporation will proceed. We need businesspeople. We need the best and the brightest and those who are willing to sacrifice for the good of the country. I would submit to you that in the future our Dream Team will be remembered in history with the same fervor and respect that we give to our founding fathers. It is up to them to save us. We're giving them the funding and the power. The beauty of having a corporate scenario is that those in power in the corporation have a great amount of flexibility.

You see when we talk about rules, policies, and protocols, you notice that I don't use the word law. The problem with Congress is when they seek to embark on an endeavor, they make laws. Laws are not flexible. Laws must be adhered to, right down to the very letters and the language that is used in the law. In a corporate scenario, there are no laws. There will be rules that will be very strict but not written in stone. There will be policies that will have greater flexibility, and decisions can be made at intermediate levels. There will be protocols, which will mostly be commonsense means of dealing with everyday issues. These can be very flexible. This makes our corporation a very fluid yet powerful force. We can roll with the punches and move on the run.

When we see something that isn't working, we can fix it. We're not bound by law. The other facet of our corporation is that we will have our own system of checks and balances. One of the biggest and most important will be the environmental concerns. We will have our own team of environmentalists who are always looking for anomalies that could occur that are detrimental to the environment and therefore negate our general objective of getting energy in an environmentally safe manner. We would ask Congress to give us special consideration and eliminate or diminish the power of the EPA. Private watchdogs of the environment will always be engaged. They will work with our environmental team so that we can foresee environmental issues and fix them before we've invested billions of dollars, and then have to turn back and rip those facilities out (undo the work we've done). We need to stay ahead on that. In our corporation, we will have a system where there will be, if I have my way, five leaders each with their own team. Their teams can interact, though. In a situation where one project needs more attention, one team can enlist the aid of another team. Therefore, we have five full-fledged teams that can interact and help each other when it's necessary, again the kind of flexibility that you cannot possibly get from those in Washington. When those in Washington put together a committee, that's it; the committee has to deal with the problem. They have no system for interacting with each other. It's too rigid and it makes no sense. For a project to move forward in our system, it must be voted on by all five members. Since we have the odd number of five, there can be no ties. Majority rules. If three members see the plan as a viable plan, then it's a done deal.

From where do these plans come? The first thing we want to do is enlist the aid of each individual state. After all, the revenues that will be gathered will be gathered from each state. We will use those numbers, the numbers that tell us how much money a particular state gathered and put into the fund. We cannot promise a to-the-penny accounting, but we can promise that (within reason) if a state puts in $2 billion, then it should get $2 billion worth of projects.

Therefore, we give the state the ability to look at its own needs, solicit proposals from within that state, decide which ones they feel are valid and submit them to the corporation for approval. Certainly, we don't want to be flooded by hundreds of proposals from each state. We will have to limit the number of proposals per year that they can put in. They must look at a number of variables. I explained those variables earlier as well: how many jobs will be created, and how much does it cost? Since we have incredible flexibility, we can also solicit bids for projects that those in charge believe would be useful and helpful to our endeavor. The reason this is important is because there are projects that could traverse through a number of states.

Take something of a keystone pipeline that's going to go through a number of states. Each state would have to build its section. Of course, we would supply the money and we would need to see proposals from each of those states as per the documentation that we would provide them so that we can put together a multi-state package. Between the solicitation from the corporation and the proposals from each state, we will have a number of viable projects that we can work on. We know from previous discussions that it will be required that all of the labor will be from here in the United States. The manufacturing will be done in the United States. The companies under contract will be based in the United States. Suppliers will be based in the United States. Their materials will come from the United States. We're not giving away any jobs. This is for us. This is what is known as protectionism. Let's face it:

Any family, state, or country must make protection a number one priority. Those that will call this isolationism are flat-out wrong. It will actually open up trade and investments from other countries going in and from us going out. It will provide for economic sovereignty in this country while boosting the economies of other countries. That issue we haven't discussed yet, but it is a valid part of this plan. I'm going to show you how a strong United States economy perpetuates strong economies around the world. That's what we want. In a perfect world, all countries would be sovereign. That would mean that they all have their own resources and a lot of money to be spent around the world. We buy from them and they buy from us. Prosperity would grow.

There are several issues that will be put into effect by setting up our rules, policies, and protocols. First, as we discussed, we're going to use our funds to prop up small banks, thereby giving small business entrepreneurs-people who need home loans, school loans, consolidation loans, and more - a means to acquire these loans at low interest rates. The reason the interest rates will be low is because we have given them access to free money. They don't need to borrow from the Federal Reserve. This is important. When a bank has all of its revenues invested but still has opportunities to loan more money, and therefore get greater returns, they go to the Federal Reserve. They borrow money from the Federal Reserve at what we call prime interest rates. The money they borrow has to be paid back and with interest. Then they lend the money to a small businessman or whomever. They not only have to charge that person the amount of interest that they have to pay back to the Federal Reserve, but they also have to add on to that in order to make a profit. If the prime interest rate is at 4% and the bank needs to make 5% to make their investment viable, they must charge the customer 9%. Because we're giving them huge influxes of cash, they don't need to borrow from the Federal Reserve. That eliminates the 4% prime interest that they have to pay. That means they can now lend you money for your business or home at 5% and still realize the same profit. Do you see how great this is? By putting $200 billion a year into small banks that serve communities, we enable individuals and small business entrepreneurs to get super good rates, and that helps to grow their business or to get that home, which creates jobs and prosperity for that community. This is one of my favorite parts of the plan, and it doesn't need to go through Congress. It will simply be part of our policies.

Here's the final point that I would like to make in this chapter. Again, it is reiterating what we've already discussed. Again, it will be policy and, in fact, one of our most stringent rules. It is one of our most critical rules which enables our corporation to be tax-exempt. As we travel through the states doing projects, creating facilities and infrastructure, supplying water to farmland, and having refineries to create our bio-methane fuel, (which I will explain in Part IV of this book) we cannot make a profit. The investors' money comes back through the IRS. It incorporates the investment amount on the tax, which is generally considered a tax rebate, as well as money returned for personal expenses on healthcare, which again would be a nontaxable tax rebate. Since we as the corporation own all of these assets, we have to figure out what we're going to do with them. Whether we sell them, lease them, or whatever, we will not show profit. We cannot have that. Since this entire endeavor is meant to generate sovereignty from the individual on up, the logical solution would be this: We simply give the assets to the people of the state wherein the assets exist. Every penny that we have spent is now accounted for either in overhead to run the corporation or in the gifts that we give away to the people. This gives the people control of those assets. The people then can vote on what they want to do with those assets. I gave you several ideas on how they can use them. Either way, the assets and their values are transferred upwards into the state coffers. This now means the people are in control, giving them greater sovereignty. They then pass that sovereignty along to the state government, giving the state more sovereignty. All of this sovereignty is based on economic prosperity, which is why this book is called *The Economics of Sovereignty*. When the states have control of this and are following the demands of the people, they can pay off debt, use the money for infrastructure development, lease the facilities... whatever they want, they can do. There isn't a damn thing that the federal government can do about it. It belongs to the states, and it is at their disposal. I truly love this part.

I ask you now to please stand with me and push our politicians to consider this plan as I know in my heart it will be the answer to all the problems in this country. You know what I mean when I say all of the problems. You must read Part III. When we have prosperity, we have the ability to solve a list of problems that are plaguing us. How about immigration? Giving people jobs can help. How about entitlements? Giving people jobs can get them off of Wel- fare. What about education? Another area where prosperity can help solve the problem. The list goes on. These are all addressed in Part III of the book. I'm going to give you one last item, and this is what we call a tease. There is one detail that I've left out in this part of the book. It is so logical and so powerful that you will not be able to contain your enthusiasm when I give you this bit of information. This part needs to be in the bill, but you're going to have to wait for it. The purpose of the tease is to keep you reading. I expect that this tease will compel you to complete this book. Goodnight and God bless you.

PART III
MISCELLANEOUS OPTIONS AND OPPORTUNITIES

CHAPTER 1

EDUCATION AND THE GHETTO

Hello, my fellow investors. I hope you've been able to get some rest. I know that the concepts that we've talked about can keep a person awake at night.

One of the reasons for that is that we built into our initial basic plan the ability to create opportunities. The opportunities are so vast that it's hard to stop coming up with new ideas. That's why this section may be my favorite. This is the part where we just turn our brains loose, remembering that because of who we are and what we are, all things are possible. Whoever thought that we would have come up with a way to make the phrase "Made in the USA" a common phrase and one to be proud of, just like the good old days? Since we are a corporation, we get to make the rules. We decided that at very minimum 80% of every item that is attached to any of these projects will be American- born, American-made right here in the good old United States of America.

Now we're going to take the time to think about how many more options and opportunities are available. How do we implement them? Mostly we want to have them directly attached to our business and our projects, but there is always this: If we do this, then can we do that? How has our new prosperity brought us to a point where there are subtle details, but nevertheless very important ones, that we can look at to see if there is more opportunity lying within them? I'm here to tell you: There are plenty. In this section, I'm taking my personal ideas and I'm putting them out there for your approval or disapproval. Please don't be a bystander, watching this parade go by. Jump in! Join the parade. Come up with some ideas. Talk about it. Put it on the web.

Who knows, one of your ideas may turn into a proposal that is accepted and utilized to make America strong and sovereign again. After all, you own part of the company. I'm going to ease into this. I'm going to try to save my best stuff for last, but I am submitting this for your approval.

We know that we want to create opportunities for those who are in the inner cities. Why do we want to do that? Number One: Because it's the right thing to do. It's good for America. It's good for those who are living in poverty and, in my opinion, we owe them. It is through the creation of these job opportunities that we can lift those who so desperately deserve a way out to a more prosperous, fulfilling, and satisfying life. The opportunities for employment are opportunities for sovereignty. We've already discussed how economic status goes hand-in-hand with sovereignty. If you are dependent on the government for your subsistence, then you cannot be sovereign. You cannot be independent. You must follow their rules. One of the rules that they preach to us as true is that you should be satisfied with the crumbs that you get. They go around pretending like you are. I know better. You know better. That life sucks! There is nothing satisfying about it. A child steps out into the streets of the inner-city, looks around, and his first thought is, "There is no hope. There is no way out. Why do I even have to go to school? It means nothing." We're going to talk a little bit more about education. Now we've already talked about building an army of qualified teachers, and I would be surprised if any of you out there thought this a bad idea. Teachers can only do so much. Without some tangible reasons to have hope, hope becomes a very rare commodity. Even if there is hope in the beginning, it will eventually be crushed under the weight of despair.

Let's start at the beginning and work our way to a successful conclusion.

That is not handing out jobs, for who would be in charge of deciding who gets what job? That would be a governmental approach. It doesn't work. What we want to do is create jobs, and we have done that, at least 15 million in the first ten years. You might be thinking, "15 million! That's great! That knocks our unemployment numbers down to a few percent, and that would be fantastic, but where are we going to get the other millions of jobs that we'll need to pull the people from poverty?" Let me give you one statistic, one that absolutely no one is talking about in earnest, and I watch a lot of news. I have emailed repeatedly different members of the media and asked them, "Why don't you address this?" No response.

I'm going to do it again right here and now. There are 10,000 people retiring every day. Now that is approximately 3.6 million jobs per year that are opening up for America. In normal circumstances, a person who is retiring will have pretty much reached the maximum pay potential at the job that they are doing. This leaves an opportunity for a subordinate in that same job field the opportunity to be moved up, either through a promotion or in some cases just an increase in responsibilities. For the most part, you would believe that the person most qualified - sometimes this even is done on a seniority basis - will take over that slot, and this may well mean an increase in pay. As we follow this backward down the ladder, we reach the beginning of what may be a career for someone looking for a job. Perhaps this person is just graduating from high school or college. In some cases, it will be someone who is already employed but wants to make a step up. It helps someone who is underemployed with a part-time job to get full-time employment; in any case, it is an opportunity. Opportunity is what we're after. If we total up jobs over the course of the next 10 years, we're getting the 15 million that we're creating with our plan, plus we're getting the opportunities left behind by the retirees. I'm going to use the number for 10 years at 30 million. Some years may slow down, and towards the end, I think that the numbers will decrease, but all in all we should have a total of about 45 million jobs opening up or being passed down. If you look at the numbers that we have of unemployed, they are massive. At first glance, someone would perceive this as an insurmountable task. However, with the help of the baby boomers, of which I am one, we can utilize this to enhance our position even more. What we need for this to happen is a positive growth economy. I know you're wondering what Nico's perception of a positive growth economy is.

We know that our President, Barack Obama, has a perception, at least while he's making his speeches, that at this time we are in a positive growth economy simply because there are fewer people that are applying for unemployment this month than there were last month, and therefore we are in a positive direction and the economy is growing. So, he calls this positive growth and claims that all of the people who are coming off of unemployment are doing so because of his economic brilliance. Wake up, America! This man is not our leader. Let's just look at this: Two months ago, the numbers said 115,000 fewer people applied for unemployment. He claims that is because there are 115,000 new jobs that his economic plan has created. He refuses to give the true statistics that show incredible losses of job opportunities for that month. First of all, all of the kids graduating from high school and college are coming out to a jobless market. They are unemployed. They are seeking to be employed. Therefore, I say that puts them in the category of 'I Need a Job', and they should be added to the list of the unemployed. Many have had their unemployment run out. They, too, are removed from the list of unemployed.

They are much of the reason that the unemployment percentage numbers seem to be coming down. They are the reason that our President can claim that he has created jobs. Let me submit to you, since apparently you know more than our President about economics, and you do have the ability to add and subtract, that if the retiring baby boomers are leaving behind 10,000 jobs per day, then that is a total of 300,000 jobs per month. This has been going on for a while, for several years. If the economy was dead flat, it wasn't growing but it wasn't shrinking. If we consider those who are coming out of school, as well as those whose unemployment has run out and they've given up on finding a job, we still have this: If nothing was done, absolutely nothing, and the economy was zero flat, we would still have 300,000 job openings per month, yet the best that the President can claim is that 115,000 fewer people applied for unemployment. When I do the math, I come out with 185,000 jobs lost. The math is simple: Where did the 300,000 jobs go? They just disappeared in a puff of smoke. Apparently, business owners were holding on just for that last bit to let the person reach retirement. In reality, they don't need anyone in that position anymore, or the job would have opened up.

Someone would have come off the unemployment rolls, or come off of the partial employment that they don't want because they want full-time employment, or we would have put another kid to work.

How is this a positive growth economy? We are still bleeding 1-200,000 jobs and more every month. Don't be fooled by these fake numbers! Look at this problem from the realistic standpoint of the need for a positive growth economy. I'm going to give you the criteria that are required for a positive growth economy. First of all, as we look at unemployment, we must take into account ALL unemployment. Anyone who wants a job should have a job out there that they can take. You would still show percentages of unemployment because there are always people moving out of a job and onto unemployment because the company happens to be slow that year; this is what we call a reduction in force. They will show up as in the unemployment line. At the same time, when we take a look at available jobs, the number of available jobs must be equal to or greater than the number of people looking for a job. That is a positive growth scenario. We are actually creating more jobs than we are losing. A large company could move to China and drop 10,000 jobs overnight. Yet in a couple of months around it, job creation was up 10,001. We have grown faster than what the unemployment numbers actually show. This is a scary thought, in that what happens when you don't have enough people to take all the jobs? That is why, in our capitalistic society, it is necessary that the available workforce grows at an equal pace to job opportunity growth. That number will fluctuate. We want to keep it as close to zero as possible. If we grow too fast, we can't supply the labor. If we grow too slowly, the labor pool starts to back up. We are always better to stay just a little bit under, and then bounce a little bit over for a couple of months, to stay within a couple of percentage points.

This is important because an overabundance of jobs without enough of a workforce to carry them will definitely cause a negative growth scenario. It sounds strange because what is wrong with prosperity? We look at that company that just left America to go to China, and we wonder why. Maybe it's not because they can do better on their taxes, maybe it's not because the labor over there is cheaper; maybe it's because they can't get enough qualified people. I know from my experience of being a businessman for a number of years that the worst time I ever had was when the growth of the area that I contracted was so fast that I got stuck with contracts that I had signed and promised to fulfill those obligations, and I could not do it. I could not find an adequate workforce. I ended up hiring 25 people for every 15 jobs, just trying to meet deadlines, trying to find the 15 that I could use to grow my business and meet my obligations. Soon after, I was filing for bankruptcy. Terrible things happened such as - a small businessman - losing $60,000 in six weeks, because of the lack of response by the labor force. I was actually trying to solicit workers from other states, and it just wasn't happening. That's our first goal towards a positive growth economy. Balance the labor force. Let's look at point Number Two.

Point Number Two is GDP. As you know, GDP stands for Gross Domestic Product. It is the value of all goods and services produced in any particular year by the entirety of our nation. It is directly linked to the stock market.

When you have growth in the GDP, it means several things: The value of those goods and services is going up, and/or the number of businesses offering these goods and services versus the number of people that are in the demand pool - that are looking for these goods and services - is increasing. Therefore, the labor force needed is increasing. Therefore, there is money in the pockets of people. Therefore, investments do well. This drives the investors to take money and invest in whatever they think is going to make them profit. We have a dollar value assessment in our GDP that directly reflects the confidence of the investor and therefore drives the stock market upward. On any given day, the stock market is volatile; it doesn't really know what it's going to do.

We look at it month by month and year by year. This number must increase over time. The funny thing about it is that we can show positive growth by looking at this number, but it's only one of several factors. Besides growth in jobs, we have the growth in the GDP which shows in the ups and downs of the stock market. Yet we haven't reached a true positive growth scenario. The next thing we have to do is take a look at GDP versus spendable income and how it relates to inflation. You see, GDP can grow. The stock markets will show growth, as well. The fact that the

GDP is growing does not necessarily mean that the average person has more money to spend. One of the things that we're looking at in our current economy is the fact that little by little the GDP is going up, and I mean very little. Certainly, by less than 2%, and by some accounting methods it shows less than 1%. Yet the average person has less money left over after they pay their bills now than they even had five years ago. It has not grown one bit; it has gone backward. We always point to taxes and say any increase in taxes eats into that spendable income and - in many cases - is responsible for that spendable income shrinking. This is true. It's why we fight the battle over taxes all the time. You need the money to pay the bills, but if you take more taxes from the people, there is less money for them to spend on services and commodities. Therefore, you will see the GDP increase because there are more people working. Companies are producing more goods and services, and the demand for them is increasing. Yet the spendable income of the average person is diminishing. This is not a positive growth scenario. In a positive growth, we see that the spendable income of the individual increases. As far as taxation is concerned, if we decrease the amount of taxes we require, the amount of spendable income will increase.

That increases the demand, which means more people have to be employed, which shows a positive increase in the GDP and will show positive increases on Wall Street without building a bubble such as the one we're building now. Yet some politicians refuse to accept this as a logical means to stimulate job growth.

When we look at the numbers, we try to decide how much back taxes will yield new jobs, what effect will those new jobs have on demand, and therefore have on the GDP, and therefore on investment values shown in the stock market. We try to strike an optimum cord. Of course, one of the main culprits to decreased spendable income - therefore decreasing the demand, the need for jobs, GDP, and stocks - is that nasty thing that we call inflation. Inflation must, absolutely must exist to have a positive growth economy, for the simple fact that when people have more money, they spend it. When they spend it, the producers of the goods and services show an increase in demand, and therefore, by good old-fashioned supply and demand knowledge, we know that the product is now worth a little bit more. Therefore, they raise the prices. That's inflation. That is good inflation. It comes from a positive growth scenario. Here's bad inflation: Iran threatens to block the Strait of Hormuz.

Syria is in the middle of a civil war. Yemen teeters on the brink while terrorist forces inhabit much of their land. The situation in the Middle East is volatile. What does that mean? It means that the single most powerful, most demanded source of energy on the planet is at risk of being lost. That is, of course, oil. The speculators on Wall Street see this as an opportunity to raise the price of oil since the demand is still there and grows every day, while the supply shrinks every day, and the ability to get it out of the ground and to us here in the United States, or anywhere in the world, is getting more and more difficult.

When the price of oil increases, the price of gasoline increases. When the price of gasoline increases, all means of transportation, every one of them, feels the pain. A truck that used to be able to deliver 80,000 pounds of product for X amount of dollars in fuel to put in his truck now has to face the fact that the cost of that fuel has doubled. And it has! Just in the last three-and-a-half years. Every item that goes on that truck shares the increase in the overhead that the owner feels from the high gasoline prices, which he then adds to the price for his delivery service, which then means a higher sticker price when it reaches the shelves of the retail supplier. That's where we, the people, get burnt.

Inflation can wipe out a positive growth scenario. What we're looking for is an increase in GDP, along with the spendable income of the average person, to increase at a rate greater than the rate of inflation. That is a positive growth scenario. If inflation wins, even by a small amount, it starts the chain reaction that comes from less spendable income, which means less demand, which means a lowering of production rates, a laying off of the labor force, and a slowdown in the GDP. Let's not forget how all of this affects the banks. The banks simply cannot exist in a negative growth scenario. Of course, when they do not have the money to lend or do not have the will to lend because the interest rates that they can get back have shrunk along with the demand, there is no incentive for them to take any new loans, especially long-term fixed loans like that of a mortgage. When it comes in at 3 1/2% over 30 years, they're cutting their own throats. We need this investment capital, and they have some but it is quickly going into the Red. Even small banks are struggling, and they don't get a bailout. We thought about that, though, didn't we? We put into our primary plan a way to get hundreds of billions of dollars into the hands of the small bankers, and we're going to turn this thing around.

Let's look at what we've done. With our plan, we are breaking that dependency on oil; that is the key. That is the one thing that is killing us on every front. It is driving that inflation through the roof, and it is bad inflation because it's not coming from an increase in spendable income. We know that starts the chain reaction that I've just described, about three times. It's why we can't get this economy turned around. Yet with our plan, we demand prevailing wages for our people. We demand that every item, if possible, must be created in the United States of America. That guarantees us a positive growth in jobs. Prevailing wages help set the levels for living wages. That helps us to get more money into the hands of the people. That is a positive growth scenario.

Not only do we move away from foreign oil - and I say 'foreign' because we will continue to produce domestically and utilize our own rich resources - but as we break away from foreign oil, we find something interesting happening. No longer do we panic every time somebody flinches in the Middle East. It's bad for the world, but it doesn't harm us much, other than when the rest of

America: Return to Independence

the world is in turmoil and inflated oil prices are tearing holes in their economies, our exports go down. So, we want them to do well. Another thing that we've accomplished is to have job creation and job opportunities at a rate that's growing faster than the population growth, and therefore growing faster than the number of people looking for work. I'm here to tell you from personal experience that when a company has jobs that need to be filled and a shrinking job market makes it more difficult for them to find qualified people, they will pay more. This is the essence of the relationship of all of these items combined to put us in a positive growth scenario. Remember, we look at the positive growth scenario from a distance and over time. We count it by the day, analyze it by the month, and set our goals and future by the year.

What of these jobs that are being created? How do we fill those positions? Remember when I tried to fill those positions with untrained labor, it killed me. It took a million-dollar-a-year business and squashed it, and it didn't take long. That's going to bring us now to the basic point of this chapter: Education. Education and training! Remember now, we are building an army of qualified teachers to go into these high-poverty areas and try to work with those kids and instill hope in them, in order to prevent them from falling into the pit that poverty creates. There is so much more we can do. We look at the job market and we can tell what the future is going to hold. Our plan creates the need for every type of career. We have giant construction jobs and we need all kinds of skilled labor on those jobs. Many of these jobs are unskilled, and that's good because there will always be an unskilled labor force, and there has to be a place for them. We want to create as much wealth as possible. We're utilizing our power to demand prevailing wages, living wages. How about this? This is something that is unrelated to our plan yet has a thread that connects us. Of all of these jobs that we're creating, the majority of them will be semi-skilled.

What we're talking about are construction trades, as well as a host of other jobs that are created by the related industries. For example, who is going to supply the paint? Somewhere there is a paint manufacturer that we will use, someone who is going to need to supply tens and hundreds of thousands of gallons of paint. They need people on the floor doing the mixing, they need people managing those departments, and they need accounting departments, receivables, payables, and upper-level management. They even utilize some form of chemistry; they have representatives in the field, and on and on. All of those jobs, many of them highly skilled, are mostly jobs that you can't do without training. It doesn't necessarily mean a four-year degree from Harvard. There will be millions and millions of these intermediate-level jobs. That's where we're going to get hurt. Right now, we have a great need for engineers. When we look at the future, as soon as high school kids graduate and look for options, many of them will say, "I'm going into the engineering field." Years down the road, we have enough engineers. Many of them will "I'm going into agriculture," because we're going to need a lot of a special product we call ethanol. I will talk, in an upcoming chapter, about exactly how we're going to utilize our ability to produce this substance, and how it's going to fit into our plan in such a beautiful way.

What about this? Suppose the teachers are doing the best they can to build hope in our young students. When the students go through their schooling, they are required a certain number of credits in certain areas. Early on, we must focus on those areas. We must get those credits accounted for. When we get to the junior and senior years, we're going to do something that was slightly attempted in the past but simply wasn't expansive enough. We're going to teach these kids a trade. We're going to teach them some type of skill that will guarantee them a good-paying job, a living wage, and a way out of the ghetto. The first thing we have to do is supply all of these schools with tools and equipment. We start with the underprivileged, of course. We don't say we're going to do this in every high school in the country, though it may grow to that. We want to get into the ghettos and bring the tools and equipment needed to give these kids a taste of what a career in that field may be like. We not only want people from those fields to come in and talk about it, we want hands-on training. We want to take a journeyman electrician and make him a teacher. We take these kids in their junior and senior years, we do what we must to fill any requirement that they haven't yet, and we give them options on a couple of different things. But we require much of their later years. Of course, their senior year will be the biggest, since they will have fulfilled enough of their primary credits to be able to move into this new method of teaching, which is teaching by hands-on experience. We want to give them a number of options: All of the construction trades, technical school-type primary training. We want them to know how to work a motherboard. We want them to have a taste of what it would be like to be in the field of electronics. We want them to know what it would be like to be a carpenter or a cabinetmaker, an electrician or painter, a drywall finisher or a concrete finisher. We should have a way of giving them at least a few weeks of hands-on training. If they find something that they like, they can stay in that training and continue to hone that skill.

Here's the beauty of our plan: If the jobs aren't there, what good is it? All of the people - politicians and the super-righteous know-it-alls that keep screaming to put more money into education because 'education is the key' - are fruitcakes! They obviously don't have a clue about what it takes to survive in this world. They want us to pour hundreds of billions of dollars into giving everyone a college education. Give me a break, please! Not that many people have the ability to go to college and be successful and to take it to a career.

Most people want to have wives and children. They would like to have a house, some creature comforts, and a little money in the bank for retirement. That can be achieved on a mass scale if we just take a logical approach to this. If a kid goes into his junior year, tries out a half-dozen different trades and skills, and decides that he or she would like to be, let's say, an electrician. They find out that electricians make very decent money. They're one of the higher paid in the construction trades. That alone may be appealing. They run some wire and string some wire bend some conduit and make some connections.

They turn the power switch on and make the lights come on, and they throw the switch and the motor starts running, and they say, "Wow, I can do this. I have a knack for this. It interests me." Of course, we know that to be an electrician you have to learn a lot more than just how to string some wire and trim out receptacles. You've got to be able to read incredibly complex diagrams. You have to be very thorough and very cautious in your work because you could burn down a $50 million building. You have to learn about circuit breakers and ground fault interrupter circuits, and how 440, 220, single, double, and triple phase motors and equipment operate. For now, we have a candidate. We know that he or she is interested in this job. They've had some hands-on. In their senior year, maybe they try out a few other things.

Maybe they decide to try and get some additional mathematics or science to help them in the future. They also decide to take some of their credit time and learn more about being an electrician. We, through our plan, have created millions of jobs. All the kid needs are to graduate from high school and to have taken a number of credits in different trades or technical skills. We'll say, "You've earned a voucher up to so much money, to enter into and complete any trade school or technical school that you want." Oh boy! That could be a few thousand dollars per person, just to get a few months of hands-on training by some experts. I submit this: Would you rather have them on Welfare for the rest of their lives? Would you rather have them face-down in the gutter with a bullet in their heads from a rival gang? We set them up in high school. We give them the knowledge that if they stick it out and apply themselves; they will graduate and will be able to go to a trade or tech school of their choice. We will pay for most or all of it, depending on how extensive the training is. This gives them the ability to walk out and get an entry-level position. There are thousands of people who want that entry-level job, and they know nothing. As an employer, I'm telling you: It's a nightmare! You spend incredible amounts of time and wealth trying to find the one kid who has the knack, the basic skills, the interest, and the determination. They are so hard to find that it's incredible. When this kid comes out of that trade school and says, "Yes, I took this in high school, I have this many hours, I went to this trade school and I want a job. Make me an apprentice. I don't claim to be as skilled as a journeyman would be, but from the first day on the job I can contribute. I can be part of the crew, and a valuable part of the crew. You need not waste your time and money trying to find me, because I'm here." This is the way out of the ghetto. I believe we need to reel back the Department of Education and perhaps defund it altogether. Take the money and set up these training programs. Give these kids some hope. Give them a teacher who knows what they're going through, who understands, who has been specially trained to deal with these problems. Through the positive growth scenario that we have created, the kids know that there will be a job for them if they only try. I'm telling you, America, when we re-instill the hope when that hope is not a false hope - the way we try to convince them now that anyone can work their way out of the ghetto by just applying yourself, and we know that is a bunch of bullshit! Some do; most can't. Most can't because they don't have hope. Their older brother graduates from tech school and goes right into a starting position with a big electronic producing company, comes home with a pocketful of cash every payday, and finally says, "I'm moving out of the ghetto. I got an apartment on the other side of town." Then those kids will sit up and take notice!

It is the hope. Hope only springs eternal if we have an eternal spring, meaning the flow from that spring must be self-sustaining, and this is. It takes some maneuvering, and some injection of cash, but just look at the value.

Millions of people coming off of Welfare - do you think that might save us a little bit of money? Unemployment Compensation is at an all-time low; do you think that might save us a little money? The average grades of our students are rivaled with some of the highest in the world. Why? Because we don't have all of the low scores to drag down our high scores, those high scores will still be there. Those that can go to college, those that have the aptitude, will be going to college and will be successful in their endeavors. That's what we want. Think about this Department of Education. I think we need to take a good look at this. It is all part of our plan that we call The Economics of Sovereignty.

CHAPTER 2

IMMIGRATION

How about that last chapter? When we look at that picture on the top of the box, it contains the thousands of pieces to the puzzle that is the future of America. We see up in the corner part of the picture that shows giant bulldozers demolishing what was tenement housing in the slums. Because of our new intellectual and spiritual enlightenment, we have finally decided that it's time that we get at the root of the problem and get this thing solved. We decided to create jobs through our plan and, as a result of these jobs, take the opportunity to school and train the people that live in these Projects through no fault of their own. Staying on that train of thought, let's look around at some other opportunities. Again, this opportunity is not directly related to energy, but as a result of our plan, this door has opened for us. It is one that is critical to the future of our country. It is the problem of immigration.

The system we have now is so broken that no one can even agree on where to start, other than some consensus that we need to secure the border between the United States and Mexico. That is absolutely true! How is that going to solve the problem of people sneaking into the country and then draining our assets by utilizing our Welfare system, by undermining employment opportunities, and by creating all of the problems that come with poverty, just as you see in the ghettos? There are now ghettos that are strictly Hispanic. Now the problems of crime and cost to the people are growing rather than shrinking. We saw how the 45 million jobs that will be opening up over the next decade require that we seek out and prepare viable candidates for those jobs. We need to make sure that they get their high school education, that they get their basic training, and that the job opportunities are there. Our plan, along with a little help from the Baby Boomers, guarantees that the jobs will be there. As I look at how many jobs can be absorbed by our efforts to get into the ghettos and get the people ready for those jobs, I see that it's not enough. The job market is simply going to outrun the labor force. We've already discussed the downside of that. We know that if we're going to take action, we cannot let any unintended consequences stop the progress after we've spent hundreds of billions of dollars in getting this thing going.

What does that mean for immigration? Immigration has nothing to do with our energy; that is why no money will be put in from our fund, out of our working capital, from our corporation, to try and fix these problems. Money that will be used in the inner-cities needs to come from state, federal, and private funds. Donations would be fantastic. Later in the book, I'm going to show you a means to enhance revenues for the projects that will ultimately train our new workforce. As far as immigration, we don't have to put in one penny. If taxes are used to finish securing the border, that's fine. That's where we invest through our taxes. The problem that we see with immigration is that all of the millions of people that come here illegally are just hoping to get some kind of relief from their poverty, and the crime that they're living in among other parts of the world, and to hopefully somehow get a chance at the American Dream. There is so much confusion and so much arguing about just letting them in and giving them amnesty. Should we deport all of them? Those who think that the illegal aliens are stealing their jobs want them removed.

The more compassionate souls understand what it's like to suffer in poverty and want to give them a shot. The problem comes back down to the same old thing: Where are the jobs?

We've solved that problem. The jobs will be there. Now, by proxy, we are looking at an open door of opportunity to actually solve the immigration problem. The jobs will be there, and as a matter of fact, we need this labor force desperately, and it will happen fast. Jobs will grow by 10 million in the first five years, and there will be nearly 15 million jobs left behind by retirees. That's only five years away. We have to get started now, or we're going to get caught with our pants down.

This is true in both our plan to shrink the ghettos as well as in our new plan to fix immigration. I know you're starting to get excited by now because we've got a good bit of this puzzle figured out. We recognize how the parts are coming together. With the help of this picture that I'm trying to paint, we will be successful in our endeavor to create a new America.

Let's start at the beginning. What about those that are here and are illegal, and they work undercover? They're not on anyone's payroll, yet they exist and they absorb a lot of jobs; however, there are still way too many that are crowded into small areas. They try to keep 10 or 15 people in one apartment so that they can survive. I ask that perhaps we put some cameras on this and go through a couple months in the life of an illegal alien family. I think we would be appalled. I think the compassion would override common sense and we would just start pouring tax money into it, to help them stay alive. No matter how you look at it, it's crumbs. This is not a life. In fact, in many cases, it is a death sentence. They come to our hospitals hurt, injured, diseased, or whatever and we don't turn them away. The cost is passed along to insurance companies, who raise our rates in order to pay the enormous fees of the hospitals, which need the revenue to keep their doors open. In the next chapter, I'm going to bring you a means to fix the healthcare issue, after I show you how to utilize this labor force to help us get healthcare costs under control.

The key to this is people having jobs that are on the books, jobs where Social Security and other taxes are taken out by the employer, as well as the taxes that the employer has to cover: unemployment insurance, state insurance, a share of Social Security, and, as they gain wealth, income taxes and capital gains. All of these items come from employing people and having them recognized by the state and federal governments as being a resident in this country, and as being a tax-paying resident as well. First of all, we have to incentivize the employer. They like the system the way it is, especially in a time when the economy is so bad. Many will say that it is critical to their businesses that they maintain an under-the-table labor force, thereby saving them money. This is bunk! In a positive growth economy such as we've described, the needs for qualified labor exceeds what the savings will be by using unqualified labor under-the-table. It's as simple as that. When there is this positive growth, the demand for that labor expands, and the demand for those who are in the country illegally expands, and then the people that are here illegally begin to rally. They stand up and say, "Look, we want on the books. We want recognized as residents of this country. We want a path to citizenship. We're tired of being used and abused by these companies. We want in!" When we look at it today, we say no can do. "There are too many of you and not enough jobs." The unemployment is through the roof. It's probably double what the government officials would have you believe. We discussed that, and we understand now. We have been enlightened. We know that's a load of crap! What about what happens when we initiate our plan for energy? Suddenly the argument that there are too many of them and that they will just take our jobs is null and void. In fact, it reverses. Soon employers will be begging them, "please come work for me. I will put you on the books." That's one of the ways that our plan affects immigration.

There's another event that will occur. That is: The people working for a company that still wants to abuse them and remain an under-the-table operation, will be targeted. Those who want to be legal, to get on the books and enter into a pathway to citizenship, need only to drop a call to a specific government agency that we will have dealt with this, and that employer is busted. Right there we've taken a huge step to get these people on the books. It not only takes them off of the welfare rolls but has them productive and paying into the revenue that we need to operate this country. That will be a huge improvement. On one hand, they stop taking out; on this hand, they're putting in. It's a double positive. We save the money from this one, plus we gain the money from this one. In order to make this stick, we have to address the employer. Employers must comply - Period! There is no alternative. There is no loophole; there are no exceptions. We set the system up with an agency that follows through on all complaints, as well as statistically takes a look at the different businesses and how their labor costs match up to their gross sales. When they're under-the-table, they can't be shown on the books. They have to fudge the books; that's a fraud! It's tax evasion! It's serious business.

The red flag is this: If you gross $1 million and only have $10,000 in labor on the books, who the hell is doing all the work? Red Flag on it! First offense: You put everyone working for you on the books, and you're on probation for the next five years. You will be audited every year, and you will pay a stiff penalty, let's say $5000, or maybe even $10,000, per worker. That'll get their attention - that, combined with the knowledge that these workers amongst them have at least one person that's willing to drop a call on you. I believe the employers will straighten up their acts.

If they try again, the second time is possible jail time, increased penalties, increased probation, and they now have two strikes. Strike three: You're done. We pull your EIN numbers; we pull any licensing that you have. You are not allowed to have insurance, Workman's Compensation. Even if you want to get on the books at that point, it's too late. You're finished, and we might put you in jail for a while, just for good measure. This is what has to be done.

When the employers read this book, they're going to say, "You're killing me here!" That's nonsense! The market share will adjust. I believe that you'll get more qualified workers, and I believe these workers will work hard for you.

When you're picking them up off a street corner, it may be a day's wages, or it may be two. You know they want to make it two. They're going to be there for two days but give you one day's work; that is the standard operating procedure when you're an illegal alien. When you're trying to get a job off of a street corner, you do not want to work yourself out of a job. If you do and try to show that you're worthy of being kept on the crew, the other members certainly have something to say about it. Very often, they will corner that worker and explain to him or her how things are done. If I can get one day's work for one day's pay, and it's quality work, I'm a happy camper. I can build a crew and sustain that crew. I get a crew of good workers and I keep them. I take care of them. They are on the books. They're now on the way to citizenship.

What is this path to citizenship? How is it going to work? We have all kinds of ideas, including one that's bouncing around now called The Dream Act. I like half of it. There is no amnesty. There are criteria that if a person complies, he can get the pathway to citizenship. Let's take a look at what options we have. As always, you're part of this deal - you're a big part of it. It's your money that produces the jobs that create this opportunity. Feel free to jump in at any time, get on the web, get in touch with other people, and throw around some ideas. My ideas aren't set in stone. I'm sure you can find a lot of flaws. In many cases, you'll see that the plan opens up another door that I missed, and you can add on. Remember: The more doors of opportunity that open, the more we get for our money. I'd love to hear from you, shouting out from the rooftops or bouncing around the web or standing at a rally, calling on politicians to listen to the people for a change.

The first thing we're going to do, since we have the problem between employer and worker handled and we have the border secured, is use what is right now a fantastic opportunity to create that pathway to citizenship. There are actually more people leaving the country right now than are coming in; that's how bad our economy is! Even though they will work for peanuts and crumbs, there simply are no jobs. We're fixing that problem here really quick. In the meantime, since the herd has been thinned out, and the run on illegal entry has slowed down, now is the time to act. If we create the pathway to citizenship, those that have hunkered down in this country and are more than likely collecting welfare, those that have fled the country and those that want an opportunity to get in, will see our plan and hopefully want to comply. We have to make the plan reasonable. We have to make the rules simple. We have to make it so that it covers everyone.

I suggest this: Number One is we give those people that are here illegally one year to get on the books somewhere. If they're here just to suck off the system and don't want to get a job - it was different when they couldn't get a job, but now we're providing the jobs - there is no excuse. One year after we start, we begin deporting. We mean business. We show them we mean business. We start slamming employers. If we find an employer that is using illegal labor, we will hit that employer. Now we know everyone that's there, and we put them on our computer file. For each one, there must be an employer that acts as a sponsor. Simple matter: All you have to do is fill out the W-2s that we all fill out when we go to work for someone. Add an extra form with a few lines that says, "I sponsor this person." Have your signature notarized and send it in with the W-2s. That person is on the books. Now we know who that person is. We know who he's working for. We know whether or not taxes are being paid. The W-2s tell us that. All of a sudden, revenues for things like Social Security come pouring in. I think we could use a little help in that arena.

For those that are out of the country and wish to come into the country, we will set up a website where they can either put in generic resumes, telling who they are and what they're qualified for - to just leave on file - or they can scan a file created by employers that are looking for workers. We will have to coordinate this with the government of Mexico, but I don't see a problem.

There will be some costs setting up, but once we're set up, it's not very expensive. If it is, we can ask potential employers for whatever amount to list their jobs. Remember: They'll be hungry and will need people. When we hook up the migrant workers, or the would-be migrant workers, with an employer, they can go to a number of different agencies set up by us and run by us in America or in a number of other countries; mostly we're looking at Mexico.

They get their paper stamped and get a card that has all their information on the card; now they are legal to come into the country. It's a great deal for them; all of the ones that are here hiding under tables, wondering if they're ever going to get a job or if the Man's going to come and take them away. We have problems with people that are here illegally, but their children were born here. They're trying to use them as what we call 'anchor babies.' "You can't throw me out of the country. I stay with my son, the citizen." That citizen might be one, two, three, four, whatever years old. Everybody is arguing the constitutionality of citizenship and what we should do about it. We can say this: A household needs to have one qualified worker, but in order to comply, that worker is on the books and must give us a list of everyone in his household that he takes care of. If we look at this, we can take those names and assign them a number as a co-applicant for citizenship. Now they're in the computer, so we immediately take a look and see whether they're collecting welfare. If they're cheating the system, they're gone. If the head of that household, the money earner, whether there are two or even three, is complicit, then he's gone - simple as that. Once an employee hooks up with an employer and gets that card, enters into this country or shows himself to be in this country, they immediately begin their path to citizenship. This path needs to be workable.

Let's face it: They're going to have us over a barrel because we're going to need their labor. They're going to make the difference between whether we can balance our labor against this phenomenal growth we're expecting. If we outgrow our labor force and send ourselves back into a negative growth scenario - which will systematically take our economy apart again - our one ace in the hole is our continuing effort in our energy programs. That should be able to sustain us for periods where we enter into a negative growth economy because of whatever problem - I believe labor is the one that is most formidable. We say this: Once you enter into a contract with America, in order to sustain that contract, you must work 960 hours per year. Why 960? It is less than half of what you would work if you worked 40 hours a week 50 weeks out of the year. There are two weeks that you won't work because of personal days, illness, holidays, etc. All you need to do is work less than half of that year. The good thing about this is we're going to watch it in six-month increments. Once you have reached the 960, you're covered for the year.

Anything that you work above that is in the bank for you. You can draw off of those hours next year if things slow down for you. Between two years, you only need 1920 hours. With 960 hours of work in the first year, you actually have bought yourself two years of opportunity. There are some other good things that come with that. Once you've reached your 960 hours, you are now eligible for Unemployment Compensation, Welfare, for Food Stamps. If you can show that your position has been terminated and you have no work, of course we're going to make sure that you're down there in the offices applying for jobs on the internet with other companies. This is how we control the cost. Every time someone slips through the crack and collects welfare illegally, we all pay. If your hours run out - in other words, you're in a year where you have no leftover hours, and you have no hours for that year - you have until the end of the year. Here's the thing: There becomes a point in time when it is mathematically impossible for someone to recuperate the needed hours by the end of that year. We are compassionate, generous people. You can still stay for the rest of the year. In fact, we'll give you six months into the next year to do - what? To get on the books again! To be sponsored and show that you are here legally, you're looking for work, you're working as much as you can, and that you want to be part of this country. I have no problem with that. At this point, you can string this out 2 1/2 years before, finally, you're just out of luck. You've got to go. We know where you are, we know who you are. You have a temporary number that the employer plugs in for you. We keep a database on you; we keep track. Any time you move, the next employer you hook up with will provide information to go into the system, and we'll keep track of where you are. Do you think that's unfair? No! It's what we have to do if we're going to provide a path to citizenship. Here's the overriding rule: In order to move on from Phase One of your application for citizenship, you must be able to show, at the end of five years, that you have compiled 960 hours times five. I believe that's 4800. You have five years to do it - five full years! If you don't make it but are in a scenario where we're giving you an extra six months into the following year, then you can continue on until you do get that number of hours. I believe that we should put a stop to it if you keep juggling your hours around for seven or eight years. There has to be a point where we say, "You're just not cutting it." I don't care! It's up to us, and what our Congress decides. If we need their labor the way we will, we may decide to just slack off and let them take their time, as long as they're putting in an effort. You break your chance for citizenship at a certain point; we say, "You have to start over. You have to comply with these rules." You have five years; that's the best way.

We've given opportunities to juggle hours around. We're asking for less than half of a work year. We're getting the tax revenues. The employers are involved. They're sending out their lists of jobs they need to fill. They can come from anyone; you don't have to be illegal, but we want to make this open and free for our friends in other countries.

Once you've secured your five-year compliance, things get sweet. You are now considered a permanent resident. You can now enjoy all of the benefits of citizenship, except one. You cannot vote in federal elections. You cannot vote for the President or the Vice President. Senators, Congressman – you can't.

This lasts for five years. There are no requirements on how many hours you work. If you're considered to be indigent, you can get Welfare and Food Stamps. If you're laid off, you can get Unemployment. You're still eligible to get on that database and find yourself a job. It's all in your favor. It's easy. It's five years of coaching. Just don't get any felonies! A felony negates your contract.

That is considered a breach of contract, and you blew it! During those five years, we're going to ask one more thing. Although you're not allowed to vote in a federal election, you will be required to vote in local elections. You're required to vote for state representatives. You can vote in a gubernatorial race. You can vote in county races. You must vote for something at least once every year. If there are years where there simply aren't any races going on - which I don't think ever happens, but I guess it could - as long as you have a total of five voting experiences in the next five years, you have qualified for citizenship. The reason I bring this in is because if we want a path to citizenship, then one of the things that we're most concerned about is that this person will be a good citizen. That's why we put the felony rule in there, and that's why we ask them to vote. We want them to understand the voting process. We want them to understand what campaign laws are all about. Since they're on the books, they're on the registry. All they have to do is show their card, and they get a vote. You're going to have some people screaming bloody murder about this one, but I think it's in our best interest. We don't want to be turning out millions of people - who are going to have tens of millions of children - into our country, who have no clue of how the political and government system works.

In fact, even when they do comply, they have to take a test. On that test will be questions about the voting experience, and they better know them.

Something else about the test: It will be done in English. I'm sorry. You've had ten years to learn our language. In fact, I believe there will be organizations that will set up websites that will have something like a Rosetta Stone program, where they can even learn the language online, along with the interaction. We do want interaction between the migrant workers that are now considered permanent residents, to enhance the process of Americanization. At the end of those ten years, you've met these simple requirements. You go down and take the test. If you pass the test - and it's not going to be that hard - then you are a citizen. I suggest that we go about the country and test random citizens around the country, try to be proportionate, and create a test that is reasonable. We're not asking them to know any more than an average citizen who was born here and grew up here would know. We want to know: Do they know the voting process? Do they know how the judicial systems work? That's very important! These people go around committing crimes and then get into the judicial system, and they don't have a clue what their rights are. They sit there like bobbleheads because they can't speak the language, not having any idea what's going on. If we're going to do this, let's do it right. That's what Americans do. We do it once and we do it right.

This crap that goes on in Washington is a joke. They have to continue to add on to rules and legislation and regulations constantly - so that they have something to do so that they can justify their jobs. If we were to set up logical systems and force them to do the will of the people, they could spend half of their time at home talking to the people and finding out what it is that their constituents want them to do in Washington. They are totally disengaged.

They don't know what their constituents want. All they know is what their party tells them. It's not about them and us anymore. It's about them and their relationship to their particular party. We have been cut out of the mix. The only time we get to say anything is through the election process, and that's one of the reasons that we need to have the applicants for citizenship learn how this works in their second five years. At the same time, I'm hoping that through this plan, and our involvement in it, we're going to start a new movement. Once we see how efficiently this is going to work - while we're at the helm and we're calling the shots - we're going to want more. We're going to want to be more involved. We want our Senators and congressmen back here talking to us. We do this state by state because - remember - states have the ultimate power. The power comes from the people that live in the state. The Constitution guarantees that sovereignty. We're going to finally start getting really involved. Our generation, my generation, the Baby Boomers have slipped away. Now that we're getting up there in age, we're looking at the mess and wondering what the hell happened. We weren't engaged in the process. We let it slip by. So many people have lost faith in the government that they don't even care to pay attention anymore. They say

"Don't turn on Fox News! My God, you might get enlightened. You might find out the truth." Then what do you do? I'm telling you: It starts now Picture the United States of America with us in control once again. Liberty or death. I love you, America.

CHAPTER 3

HEALTHCARE REVISITED

How about us? We've managed, somehow, to take immigration and come up with some good ideas. Though it is indirectly attached to our plan, and could easily be left out of the plan completely, we figured that there is a need for some type of labor force coming across the border, in an organized manner, that we can utilize to keep our plan on target. As before, I ask that you use your giant brains and the internet, or whatever means you prefer, to complement the plan that I put forth on immigration, by coming up with ideas of your own that can complement our plan or give it more substantive detail. This is what we're all about now. We're about a team, a team of 300 million Americans with their eyes on the prize and their heads on straight.

That leads us to another issue that I addressed earlier, and I told you that we would be coming back to this issue later in the book. That time is now. It is time to revisit healthcare. Let's refresh our memories. We started with the basic premise that investment in new cleaner and renewable sources of energy is paramount. It is paramount for the security of the United States, and it is the answer to our economic problems. Because we are investors, we demand that we get returns on our investments. The basic plan says that we get back every penny of our investments, and there are no ifs, ands or buts about it. It is part of the deal, and we have set up a means to ensure that return comes back every year. We also decided that we should get some dividends for our investment as well. If you lend money or deposit money in a bank, they guarantee you a certain rate of interest. At the end of the year, you are guar- anteed that you can go take your money back out - every penny - and also get that interest on top of it. You get a return on that investment. In our wisdom, we decided to take on the healthcare issue and utilize that in a way that we can assure ourselves that we are getting a dividend on our investment. That dividend would come in the form of rebates on our healthcare. It's part of the basic plan. It is one of the biggest parts of our strategy because healthcare is one of the biggest problems.

We're faced with Obama Care which everyone knows is a bad idea. Putting Obama Care on the backs of businesses and individuals at this time in our history, and because of the bad economy, would be like putting another giant hole in an already sinking ship. It's just a bad idea. Since we've decided to engage healthcare by tying it to our plan, we have sort of opened the door for a deeper look at the problem, to see if we can build on our basic healthcare idea, where we get rebates. Therefore, we come up with a comprehensive plan, one that starts with the rebates and grows into the real deal. We're pretty darn sure at this point that Obama Care will be repealed. Many of you, by the time you read this book, will have realized that it's gone. Very soon now, the Supreme Court will make a decision on this. At this point, it's probably a week away. What do we do if it's repealed? We have no contingency plan. We don't have anything to replace it with. A lot of the problems are accepted by some people because there is nothing else in the works to replace it.

Let's get to work on it right now. Let's start with borders. We all know that the backbone of capitalism is competition. Competition is anti-inflationary.

Competition is what spurs innovation. It pushes manufacturers or deliveries of any service to get better and more efficient. This is passed along to the consumer by way of price reduction. That's what makes it tick. One of the problems that we know with healthcare is that so many states have closed their borders. You cannot go into that state and solicit customers unless you are in and of that state. This was fought for many times by the insurance companies. They like to protect their turf. They have that particular state sewed up, they have millions of customers and very little competition. The few competitors that they have got together and decided amongst themselves what the going rates should be, thereby eliminating the competitive factor and securing their future. However, when we open up this new market, and everyone is getting these rebates - not just the individuals, but the businesses as well - suddenly the market expands to a point where it's not logical to keep your borders closed anymore. You want to be able to get out and solicit customers from states all around the country. The potential for growth outweighs the logic of isolationism, keeping your borders closed in order to protect your turf. I believe that insurance companies will change their tunes. They're going to want to get into your state and solicit your business. In order to do that, they have to open the doors for someone in your state to come into my state to solicit my business. Suddenly the floodgates are open. These are state issues, but I believe the states will fall like dominoes. As soon as the insurance companies realize the potential for growth, they will begin to lobby on the state level for the opening of borders. This is a win for us.

Now we have put the machine to work for us. Competition becomes stiff. Prices come down. We're not just going to stop there. One of the beautiful things about this is that we can now join together en masse by going around to all the different states and offering them a chance to come in with us so that we have a huge customer base. When you have a million or two people in your customer base, I guarantee that you're going to get a better deal. Because the borders are open, we can go all around the country and ask the different insurance companies what kind of deal they can give us if we give them a million customers. It's a beautiful thing. If we put together the small business owners, the ones that can't afford the healthcare at this point, we give them their 10% rebate and combine them with our customer base. We now put many of the labor force that don't have insurance onto the list of workers that do. Why is it important to have them join our customer base? The answer is simple: Employer-paid healthcare is the bread and butter of the industry. Why is that? The giant consumer bases like Medicare and Medicaid have gotten to the point where they simply can't sustain themselves. They're collapsing under their own weight. They have gotten together and, because they are federal plans - you say Medicaid is a state plan, but it is funded in part by the federal government - they have much power in that area, as well as in Medi- care. They have told the insurance companies, "This is how much we will pay." It's breaking the back of medicine. Many doctors already refuse to take Medic- aid and Medicare patients. There simply isn't enough money to be made to justify the trouble, especially since Medicare people are elderly or disabled.

This is a losing proposition for the insurance companies. Therefore, the employer-based customers are the best. If you are employed and are working, then you can't be very ill. You may have some problems or you may get hurt in a skiing accident, but these aren't the big-ticket items. If you have an incurable disease, one that has to be dealt with on a daily and weekly basis, you certainly aren't working. If you get hurt at work, then you're paid by Workman's Compensation. The incidents of giant payouts by the insurance companies to the workforce are very limited, since those workers come in bulk batches. Just look at McDonald's or General Motors; some of the big banks have hundreds of thousands of employees. This is nothing more than gravy for the insurance companies. They depend on it; they need it.

As we go about putting together our groups that are looking for health- care, the fact that we incorporate a large number of the working force makes the deal better than ever for the insurance companies. This gives us leverage to negotiate a better price - simple as that! The engine of competition will drive prices down. At this point in our lives, we would just be happy if we could stop the bleeding - that's a pun- and get the insurance rates to settle in to a growth that is equal to inflation. That would be very significant for our country. I believe we can do better. The competition is just one way to utilize our plan - to battle against the ever-rising healthcare premiums.

The next thing that we want to do is stop the insanity of what has become the most litigious country on the planet. We sue everybody. We sue for any reason at all. We know that because of the costs involved in fighting a lawsuit, if we ask for a little bit less, the insurance companies will rather pay it than fight it. This is insane! How dare they bend us over like that! Many of you out there have utilized this method to put money in your own pockets. You have to be honest with yourself: Are you really that injured? Was this lawsuit the righteous thing to do, or did you just see an opportunity? Did some attorney convince you that you're just too sick or too badly injured to not sue? Folks, you have to be honest with yourself. If you're back working and you're fine, but you have 20, 30, 40 thousand dollars (or even more) for a claim that you know in your heart was bogus, then you must repent. You must join forces with the rest of us and get to your state officials and tell them that when the insurance companies are doing business in this state, we will not allow attorneys to draw up litigation for a bogus claim. It's done by the state, it is within the state's powers, it is within their responsibility to address these issues. We know that the lobbying force of the lawyer's association is so powerful that this will be difficult. Remember: We have a strength of 300 million. With- out us, they're nothing.

What should be a logical way of doing this? Certainly not all lawsuits are unwarranted. Many people have been injured by a doctor or surgeon who probably shouldn't be practicing medicine, or just had a really bad day. Either way, the doctor caused that suffering and that pain, so she should pay. What have some of the states come up with? California right now is seeking to put in place a cap. No matter how badly you're hurt, or what the circumstances, you can only get $250,000. You have people out there getting more than that for stubbing their toe. That is not fair! It is up to a judge and/or a jury to decide what punitive damages the defendant should have to pay, as required by the damages that can be proven to have occurred. Several states are talking about something that I absolutely love. It's called 'the loser pays' system. If you choose to challenge me in a court of law and I choose not to pay "the ransom", as it would be - not to pay the extortion that is going on - then you must be able to absolutely prove your case. I, the defendant, have to prove that you're wrong. Here's where the going gets good: If you lose, then you have to pay all of my legal fees for having to defend myself against what is obviously - since you've lost the case - a bogus accusation. Let's turn the tables. Those that would seek compensation for no good reason - when they lose - will have to cough up incredible amounts of money to the one that they accused. If they win, the defendant not only has to cover their own legal expenses but will have to comply with the court order for whatever means of compensation have been declared. If you're one of these, what we call, 'ambulance chasers', when a potential client comes to your door and says, "This is what happened. I think we should sue them." The first thing we would do is try to get medical tests and deposition that would prove that the case is valid. If that attorney thinks that the case is too weak, that you're asking them to put all of their money up front to try to win a case that they know they can't win if the defendant chooses to take them to court, they simply will not waste their time. They may take a one-time shot at calling the accused and saying, "We're going to sue you unless you give us this much money", and they may get lucky.

However, I believe that the majority of those who know they're being extorted - that they're the victims of fraud - will simply say, "I'll see you in court." At that point, the attorney calls the plaintiff in and says, "Sorry, we can't take the case. You don't have the medical papers to prove the injuries that you claim." People are tired of hearing, "I'm so stressed out because of this that I need a hundred thousand or a million dollars." It's just not going to fly anymore.

These types of attorneys will have to play a whole different game. They will actually have to become attorneys, not negotiators for a settlement that their client doesn't even deserve. Anybody can file the basic paperwork; it's done by the paralegals. The attorney doesn't even have to lift a finger. When it comes time to present a case in court, now it's on. They're going to have to do their job. I submit to you that most of them are incapable, or they would have been in a different business. They saw easy money and they went after it!

We call this tort reform, and I love that. Because of all the studies done to figure out approximately what these costs the insurance companies every year, some have come up with the number $100 billion. One hundred billion dol- lars! Every penny of that is recuperated by the insurance company by raising our rates. It's a simple as that. We have to stop the insanity. That is the second point of our healthcare plan.

We've given small businesses back a nice boost, a good rebate that helps make it more affordable. We've given the individual back 20% rebate on all of their out-of-pocket expenses, making it even more affordable. We put $100 billion a year back in the coffers of the insurance companies, which we can expect or demand some of that back off of our premiums. Since we've opened the floodgates of competition, somewhere out there is an insurance company that will comply with our demands, in order to get that huge volume. It has a number of the gravy policies wrapped up in it. Their ability to seek and solicit has made all of this a worthwhile endeavor for them, as well as for us. In fact, I believe that insurance companies will go to the point of actually setting up these huge group policies. They will advertise on television. If you are an employed worker and you have no healthcare, call this number. We're giving away smoking deals as long as we get a million or more. It's going to be a bid- ding war, along with a feeding frenzy. We win, win, win!

At this point we've realized that we really got it going on. We're coming up with answers left and right. So far, they haven't cost us a penny, but it is at this point of the plan where I must ask you for a slight donation. I'll show you how this donation fits into our plan and how it too will come back directly to you, into your pocket with benefits. We've decided that the best way to come up with the working capital we need is to instigate our plan of building a new corporate entity, designed to take energy into the 21st century in a big way, and provide us with sovereignty and security. We then look at another opportunity that it presents, and I ask you: Since we have a mechanism in place to collect massive amounts of money, and to have that money paid back at the end of the year in a nice fat check, then what if we decide to increase the amount of our investment capital that we pay at the pump by another 8 or 10 cents? The goal is to accumulate an additional $30 billion that we are going to instruct our government to use to subsidize hospitals. There are some subsidies out there; there are some state and county, as well as charity organizations that try to help, but we need more.

Here's the logic: We, being compassionate and generous as we are, make sure that no one is turned away when they come into a hospital. We take anything from a life-threatening disease or traumatic injury down to the point where many uninsured uses our emergency wards as their primary care. They do this because they don't have their own healthcare plan. The hospitals face a dilemma. Even with the help they get, how do they remain profitable? How do they keep from closing their doors because of a lack of cash flow? What they do is raise the prices for those of us who do have insurance. Then, they can make enough profit off us to cover the losses of all those that come in uninsured. The $30 billion goes to shore up the hospitals so that they can realize a good cash flow and a means to cover part of their losses. I say part of their losses because even $30 billion is not going to be enough. However, if the system is altered, it can be. First of all, the hospital goes to the charity organizations and the state and county funding apparatuses that subsidize these hospitals; that pays for part of it. We look at the bill and say that over time anyone should be able to pay this amount - let's say $10,000. That $10,000 will be billed to the person who received the care. It will be set up on a payment system depending on the economic status of that person. Most of the people who are very indigent and very poverty-stricken get welfare and therefore get Medicaid. Those who do well and have a job, or are ultra- wealthy, have insurance plans. Many of the middle class have insurance plans through their work as well. There are millions in this category who have no insurance, primarily because they work for a small employer that can't afford it. We've already addressed that in a big way. We're going to make it easy and affordable for employers to get coverage for their people. That's going to shrink that number. That helps all of us all around every day. What we have to deal with is what's left. Many of these people have a job; it just doesn't provide insurance. We can ask them to supply $50, $75 or $100 a month - whatever is deemed a proper amount after considering their economic status. This is a fantastic thing. It provides immense cash flow.

A hospital may have five or 10,000 people that can't pay. When you send someone a bill for $50,000, they throw their hands up in the air and say, "Can't do it! No way! Why even try?" However, a $50 a month payment that - by the way - shows on their credit report that they pay their bills, can be acceptable to a lot of these people. At $100 a month - and you have 1000 of these - then you have $100,000 a month in cash flow coming into the hospital. That's not all that much when you consider the cost of running a hospital, but those payments come in year after year after year. Each year you add another $1000, $2000, $5000, or whatever it may be, onto that. It's paying $100 a month. You've stretched their payments out over 10, 12, or more years. You even set up plans where you can have it removed directly from their paycheck or their banking account. The people don't even notice that much; it's kind of like a basic cable bill. Now you start seeing millions of dollars a month coming into the hospitals, who then can lower their prices for those of us who do pay insurance. The insurance companies realize those profits, and when we take our group of 1 million customers and start soliciting insurance carriers across the nation, the deals that they give us can be even sweeter because their profits are up. Their profits are up because we've broken this tort insanity, we've given the hospitals a means to cover their losses, and we've enabled ourselves to be part of a large bulk group of consumers.

Now we're really kicking it. All of this brings down prices, which means that more employers and individuals can afford to get their own healthcare. This means that the lines are not so long at the emergency room, that the hospitals realize better profits, and that they take down our prices to the insurance companies. The insurance companies then rebate all of their good fortune to us through lower premiums. Here's the beauty: All of the dividends that you receive come back to you on the same check as the other investment money.

How's that for making money work for us? This all comes because we've instigated a plan that gives us opportunities that can be used in so many ways. That is why I ask you to put your thinking caps on. Let's communicate. There are more and better ideas. We can add on to the ones we have, we can create new ones, we can adjust, and we can modify. Until we become engaged as a nation, this will not happen. This ship will sink. I believe that after a couple of years - when things are really kicking into gear - we not only will have stopped the growth, but we could realize as much as a 25% drop in the cost of healthcare. At this point, the market stabilizes and the cost grows at the rate of inflation, the way it's supposed to. They force the country to pay obscene amounts of money for healthcare. We know we will never get the quality that we have now, while the cost is so far estimated at $1 trillion. Most of us know those are government numbers, and it would probably be at least twice that.

Over ten years, that makes our investment in a gallon of gas worth its weight in gold, especially since we get it back. This is capitalism. It doesn't work unless you put money into the system. You can't just expect the system to drop golden eggs, like the proverbial goose, without putting anything in.

Once we join together as a nation and attack these problems, it's simply a matter of sticking to the plan and they will be fixed.

CHAPTER 4

MISCELLANEOUS OPTIONS AND OPPORTUNITIES - INVESTMENT, INFLATION, POSITIVE GROWTH

Look what we've just done! We took what was an integral part of our plan, the part involving healthcare, as a dividend for our investment. Rather than just putting a dollar amount or a percentage of interest, we've come up with a better way. Everybody needs healthcare; everybody pays in one form or another. The young and healthy have the good luck of getting very little back as a dividend on their investment. I say they have good luck because what would you rather have: 20% back on a large number that you've paid in because your health is not good, or getting little to nothing back because you're perfectly healthy? I will take the health any day of the week. I would say if you're one of those that receive their investment money back, but no dividend, your health is your dividend. You're in a very good place. We've taken the opportunity to use the tax system to return significant amounts of money to individuals as well as businesses. We're smart enough to know that a comprehensive plan needs to be put in place. We've decided to utilize what we have as a base to grow into a much larger and more efficient healthcare system. We're utilizing both state and federal government because by donating at the pump, that money will be distributed by the federal government, while issues like borders and tort reform will be dealt with by the state. The dividends from our investment come back to the individual through the federal government, through the IRS, which is an agency that works for us and is paid for by us. Look what we've got now: A comprehensive system that leaves the basic choices up to the people, another victory for individual and state sovereignty. Let's give ourselves a round of applause.

As we look around, we still see more options and opportunities that we want to explore. Here's one that I like a lot: It is the opportunity of investment. We've got in place a positive growth scenario. That opens a lot of doors for investment. Along the lines of energy, though we will be dragging down the value of investing in oil, we will be uplifting the value of investments in many other energy-related fields. The positive growth scenario, therefore, remains strong. Even though we've lost a lot of ground on the oil, the stock market will still show strong growth. Here's why: In a negative growth scenario, or in an anemic growth, if you had ten companies to choose from for investment, less than half would be losing value. Not a good thing if you're an investor. Re- member, investors want, at the very least, to get their money back and make enough to compensate for inflation. That would be considered lucky in a negative growth scenario. If the majority of investments are losing money, then certainly the confidence factor comes into play and people simply hoard their money. They take it out of the market. They may invest in gold or precious metals as a hedge against inflation so that at least their money makes enough to cover inflation and therefore they aren't going backward, even though in many cases they aren't going forward.

We see right now a run on gold. Because we're in a negative growth economy, more and more people want to at least make back their money plus inflation, which is always doable when you invest in gold. It just so happens that in the bear market which we have now, the run on gold drives the price upwards. Those who got into the gold early in the recession are showing substantial gains. This can go on for quite a while, but substantial gains in gold mean that the other markets are dying. We don't want to see that. Gold should be part of a portfolio so that it is solid - so that it is always worth what you put in and grows at least with inflation. When we turn this into a positive growth economy, what we're going to have been numerous opportunities. Rather than an economy where the odds are your investment will lose money or go nowhere, you will have a situation where 6, 7, 8, or 9 out of 10 investments are showing returns above that of inflation and therefore they add to the wealth of the country. Remember there are some entities that control billions of dollars: Pension funds, mutual funds, and a number of investments that utilize many investors bundled into one package. In the positive growth scenario, all of the investment dollars out there will be making a profit - let's say 80%. There are always going to be a few losers. Of course, that's why we want to diversify our portfolios, to cover for that. The investors that are sitting on large amounts of cash, as well as the small investors that individually don't have a lot of cash (but there are a lot of them), will all run as fast as they can to get vested.

When you take all of that money that's sitting and waiting for an opportunity - which could be several trillion dollars - and slam it into the markets all at the same time, you create a feeding frenzy. You will see 8 to 12% growth. All economic factors will be showing large growth and growth potential. On top of that, you will see a spike in small business startups like we haven't seen in decades. That too is investment, but it doesn't show in the stock market return. That is why I predict in the first five or six years an 8 to 12% growth rate in our economy. Remember: That is not the only criteria for positive growth. Sure enough, when you see one, you will see the others. They all work off of each other.

Confidence in the markets, confidence in the ability to start a new business, confidence to go ahead and expand - all this, along with the knowledge that we know where healthcare is and what its costs are going to be. We're aware that as we put into place the things we've talked about, the cost will go down, not up. It all adds up to a feeding frenzy.

I would submit that the 8-12% growth prediction is based on a number of different statistics that are factored in as a means to assess the growth.

However, it can be somewhat misleading. You see, when we factor in stock market values with GDP, we have to be careful not to put too much value on those stock market numbers. The GDP and unemployment rates are more important. When we factor in the stock market, we get a higher percentage of growth rate. Why is that? In the first years, all of that money that we're talking about - which people are sitting on - floods into the stock market as investment capital. If we look at jobs and GDP, we see that it isn't naturally moving up as fast as we think. Although the investment opportunities are going to be major, we have to be careful not to over-speculate. Yet in a positive-growth scenario, we can be pretty sure that the growth will catch up with the stock market. Here's why: Eventually a feeding frenzy must slow down, for the simple fact that everyone is nearly 100% vested. Simply stated, they've run out of investment capital. They have everything that they can put into the investment community already in the investment community.

Therefore, the stock market then settles down to a realistic growth number.

That's because it can only grow as fast as investment capital grows. If you get a pay raise and you have more spendable income, you will add that to your portfolio and invest. As your investments return dividends, you will want to roll those dividends over, back into your portfolio to utilize this growth in the market. That means there will be more money injected into the stock market.

The big banks, the big hedge funds, and the big players make substantial gains. They always want their money to keep working. They always take it and invest it right back in. Therefore, we see another means to grow the investment numbers. They will only grow as fast as the economy grows. They can only use what the economy provides. It is at that time we can really get an accurate reading on what the growth rate is.

In the beginning, we pretty much want to ignore Wall Street, other than making sure we get in as fast as we can - especially on energy products because we know they're going right through the roof. For every dollar of oil we lose, we'll put in two in order to grow our capability of clean energy.

I predict this will take five to six years. I use five years for a lot of things. I use it for that. I also use it for a term of contract for one of our Dream Team members. I use it as the time for reevaluation so that we can adjust how much we collect due to inflation, project what our needs will be, and make sure that our plan is on schedule. Every five years we should revamp the system, see where there is anything that could be better, and move to enhance the efficiency of our plan. I predict in the first five years an average of 8-12% growth with an inflation rate that could hit 4%. That's a lot! There will actually be people who, in the short term, lose out because their pay increases aren't that much. If they get into the investment, though, they'll be fine. As the long- term projections come true - with the need for a bigger labor force - the pay rate will catch up. One of the good sides of that is that the drop in spending capital will retard the growth of inflation. We're also going to set up several other means to stop the growth of inflation. One will be that the fuel costs are going to drop significantly. That's because we are going to create a new fuel that will compete with the old fuel.

When companies compete, the consumers win. Fuel is maybe the largest contributor to inflation. Everything that moves in this country, everything that is manufactured and must be distributed, and everything that is grown must find their ways to marketplace. People have to travel to get to work. The increase in fuel costs inflates all other items that are associated with it, and that is just about everything. Even though we may realize a spike in inflation for a period of time, the growth rate will double or triple that. You cannot have a positive growth without inflation. One of the other terrible things that we do to create inflation is to print money. Money should only be printed as it is needed to pay off all of the labor force and the companies that do the hiring.

Most of this is done electronically anyways, so we should rarely find a need to print money. What the government is doing now is called quantitative easing, which is simply printing money and putting it out into the country, thinking that people will take the money and spend it, and that will spur growth. They are wrong! The people take the money to pay back the bills that they owe.

They don't go out and buy any new products. The quantitative easing causes more inflation because it's just adding dollars with no product to back it up. If you have ten products and ten dollars, each product would be worth a dollar. If you print ten more dollars and put them out there, now each of those ten dollars are worth two dollars. In the meantime, you're either out of work or you're taking a pay cut or you're not getting any pay raises. The inflation along with the problems caused by the high fuel costs drive us deeper into a negative growth scenario.

Therefore, if we reach 8-12% and hit a 4% inflation rate, it's actually a good thing. In a couple years, when the fuel costs are at their minimum and we've quit printing money, the inflation will even out. The numbers on the growth - because we have vetted all of our cash - come down to a reasonable, more viable, more accurate growth scenario, which I believe will be 6 to 2 or 6 to 3 (6% growth with a 2-3% inflation). That's still high but is proportioned to the growth rate. It's easily dealt with. I don't care if the prices go up a little, as long as I'm getting increases in my pay and my investments are showing good returns. That's what is important. It's that ratio.

Let's go one step deeper into our positive growth economy. In this scenario, the retiring baby-boomers are absolutely the best part of this, which is why we do not want to tell them that they have to work more years. You can't outrun the problem like that. We have to outrun the problem of Social Security and Medicare. We've already shown that we can drop the Medicare costs significantly. When we put all these people to work, we have more people on the books paying in. With a little bit of fiscal prudence, we can meet our obligations. Why is it so important for the baby-boomers to retire on time, or even sooner if they feel that their financial situation is good enough to do so? This is because of the way that our business plans work. You figure that the ones that are retiring have been in the business for 35-40 years or more and are well qualified and well paid at their jobs. You can't take them out and go out to a workforce that has just graduated from college, and then expect that person to come in and fill those shoes. That's not how it's going to work. That's not how the plan works. The business model shows a progressive march up the ladder to whatever level a person can achieve. Therefore, when someone retires, generally it is the one just below them, a subordinate that by now has equal talents and skills, moves up to take that place. Their subordinate moves up a notch, and on down the ladder it goes. This leaves the job to fill at the very bottom of the ladder. Why is that important? Where do high school and college graduates start? They start at the bottom and work their way up. This system is perfect. In the end, it's the bottom level job that opens up, which is perfect to give someone just coming into their career a good place to begin. Let me tell you why that is so important: Let's just take the college students. Right now, the amount of school loans that are owed to whatever entity produced that loan totals just over $1 trillion. Rather than paying it back, these kids have no means to even survive, let alone pay back their debt. The President talks about just skipping that: "We'll defer that. We'll give you zero interest. We'll give you smaller payments." That doesn't solve the problem; it makes it worse. What we need is those kids coming out of school to get straight into a job so they can pay back the $1 trillion they owe us. The business model is each person moving up a step on the ladder as others retire; this opens up that opportunity. That's why I'm addressing this in the Options and Opportunities section of the book. It's a fantastic opportunity. With the growth of jobs that we have in our positive-growth economy, and the opening of these low-level jobs because of the retirement of the baby- boomers, the opportunity is there for every one of these kids who graduates from college to come out and get a job in their field, to start their career where they will be paying taxes. They will become investors. They will invest in homes and businesses. Most of all, they will pay us back our $1 trillion. If we got that $1 trillion, we could slam it on the debt. Just like that, in five years we could knock off $1 trillion from the debt, simply by getting paid back for the loans. Some of this money will take the long way around. It'll go through different hands. In the end, it comes out as capital, as revenue that comes into state and federal budgets.

Since we're talking about debt, let's take a look at what our plan provides.

Medicaid and Medicare drop significantly. The people on Welfare, who are there because they just can't find a job, are going to come off Welfare. We're going to make sure they apply for jobs. If they need to learn some kind of a skill, we'll provide for that. It's better than keeping them on the Welfare line forever. We save hundreds of billions of dollars across the country, with our plan. We've already put together $1 trillion from paybacks on loans. The Obama administration has spent a ridiculous amount of money fixing the housing bubble that burst. They have spent hundreds of billions bailing out banks and investment insurance companies, such as AIG. They have spent billions of dollars bailing out car manufacturers. All of that money is owed to us. You could be looking at a few trillion dollars by the time it all comes down. The key is to balance the budget.

The term 'balance the budget' doesn't tell us anything. What do we want to balance it at: Four trillion dollars, the way our current administration is pushing us, or something reasonable? I say 2.5 trillion is the budget amount. We cut and slash wherever we can. Much of this is paid for simply by getting rid of duplicate subsidies, where we pay two different entities for the same problem (estimates over $100 billion a year). We quit doing stupid things like paying farmers not to grow. Since we're going to new forms of energy, bio- fuels are going to be a major part of that. Through our company, we will assist in setting up farms with necessary equipment, with irrigation and whatever else they need to get the production level that we require into place. Instead of the billions that we're paying now, we put out a little bit and get them profitable by growing, not by sitting on their hands. They're actually asking now for more. They want to double and triple the amount of subsidies. Forget that! We're going to make them grow and make them prosperous. We're not going to give away money for no reason. If you take that with the money, we can save by defunding the EPA, the Board of Education, other unnecessary or overfunded entities, we can save tons of money. On top of that, look what we're going to save on unemployment insurance. We will drop unemployment to 2%, maybe 3 over the next 5-10 years. Each year it gets better and better.

Here's the big item: With the kind of growth that we're talking about, the tax revenues will be substantially increased to a point where we'll be able to balance a budget at 2.5T, 0.33 of that going back to the investors at the end of the year for what we are invested in as well as our dividends for healthcare, leaving over $2.1 trillion in the budget. Remember, we've just slashed the budget by a trillion dollars while increasing revenues by 0.8-1.2 trillion. These are my numbers. We need more statistical analysis. I am only one man, and that's a lot of numbers to put into play. I simply don't have the resources.

One look at the growth: As we take a percentage of GDP as our revenue that goes into the tax system (and therefore into the Treasury), the numbers look very doable. Again, it is key that we balance the budget at 2.5T. If we do that, the $800 billion a year can be put down on the debt. Are you with me now?

Eight hundred billion a year on the debt! As inflation rises, that number increases. Also, as inflation rise, the value of that debt shrinks. What is $16 trillion now will be a much smaller percentage compared to our GDP, as we get closer and closer to paying it off. Not only does the value shrink, but our ability to generate the funds to pay it off in huge amounts increases also. I know that if we follow this plan, we can pay the debt off in a single generation. At the very least, we get it to a couple of trillion dollars and maybe we go ahead and pay some interest payments to keep relationships good between us and the lenders. At that point, we will have such a high credit rating that we could actually borrow money and lend it to other countries that need the money, at a higher rate of interest and actually make profit on it. The government is not supposed to make profit. It's not really like they're stuffing their pockets with it (although some will try); it's just that now we have a means to maintain that balance in our budget. There's one more way that we can balance the budget. It's down the road, but it's going to be there as a part of our plan. We might as well take the opportunity.

I'll show you how we can turn the world around, not by giving them money through the IMF but by creating environment so that they can grow and realize their own prosperity. There are other several miscellaneous items that I want to talk to you about. Remember, it all comes because we've created a positive-growth economy, and therefore we have options and opportunities.

Some of these aren't even connected to energy, or just in a small way. The investment opportunities are only connected to energy because the transition from investments in oil and the pullback from the investments in gold and precious metals will find their way in a large amount to investments in clean energy. I'm going to show you how investments in solar panels are going to be fantastic. Turbines - wind, hydroelectric - great! Fuel - fantastic! Hang on; it's going to get even juicier. The things that I'm going to tell you next are exciting. If they don't excite you, then you might as well just get in your car, drive to the nearest morgue, walk in the door and crawl into a coffin because you're dead. That's how good it is!

CHAPTER 5

TAXES AND EARMARKS

E arlier, we said that we would look for all open doors that stem from our basic plan and attempt to utilize them. We had to stretch our imaginations on that one, but it is doable. In this chapter, we're going to turn in another direction altogether. Our plan means that we have to put a bill through Congress allowing the taxation on gasoline to be increased by X amount. That amount will be separated from all other tax revenues and given to several specific entities, with specific purposes. It cannot be general revenue that the government decides how to use. It has to have a specific purpose that is outlined. We know that the biggest part of it is in our plan to become sovereign through the effort of becoming energy independent. When we put forth our plan in the form of a bill to Congress, there are several things that we must be sure to include. The first is that $200 billion be handed over to a team of experts that we hire to run our energy corporation. Then there is the issue of returning investment dollars to us - the investors - in a check once each year. All money is returned. All the tax revenues and benefits from the plan stay in the system. It goes to the people, the states, tax revenues, business revenues, capital gains taxes - all the stuff that makes the government treasury strong.

We also have to put in there the tax rebates for healthcare. We have to look and see exactly what amounts and what percentages we want to use, but I suggest 20% return to individuals for every dime that they put into their healthcare needs. We're going to include the over-the-counter products that are deemed useful as medical pharmaceutical products. For example, if you have acid reflux disease and choose to buy Prilosec over-the-counter, that would be considered an out-of-pocket expense for your healthcare, then you should get your 20% back on that.

We want to help small businesses and make healthcare affordable across the board; therefore, we put into our tax bill 10% return for all businesses that provide healthcare for their employees. We also mandate that the 100% tax deduction that they get currently remains in place as well. They're going to get everything that they got before, plus an additional 10%. These have to be put into the bill. This bill is at its essence a tax bill. We're going to create the corporation; the bill has nothing to do with the creation of the corporation, or any rules and regulations it wants to impose on that corporation. It simply comes down to this: We're going to put in a lot of money and we want $200 billion of it put into an account for us (the people) to use. We decide exactly what we use it for. According to my plan, that would be strictly for the purpose of energy independence to provide sovereignty.

Here's where we look at this effort to get this rather simple bill passed, and what do we see? Of course we see opportunity. This is another opportunity that is right in front of us. We've decided that in the bill an additional $30 billion should be collected and distributed to a committee in charge of helping hospitals pay for people that don't have insurance but need medical help.

We're not done yet. Here's a new opportunity that I'm very excited about.

This opportunity has virtually nothing to do with energy. It has to do with fixing a part of Congress that is an absolute mess. That is the part where Congressmen and women hold legislation up for ransom every chance they get. When the vote comes down to one or two votes either way, they hold out until the end and then say, "What's in it for me? I want to have something to bring back my constituents so I can get reelected." They make some kind of irrational demand for something that has nothing to do with that particular bill. After filibustering away the time to a point where someone has to give, they usually end up with some kind of kickback to their state in the form of what is known as an earmark. These earmarks hold up the process, as well as cost money. What we usually see is many of the other Congressmen and women come out and ask why others got something and they didn't. They want something as well. In the end, what should have taken a month to deliberate and either pass or reject has now taken six, 10, or even 12 months. The bill is being picked apart because everywhere you turn there is something that has been compromised in order to make a particular Congressperson happy, so that they will vote for the bill. This is insane! We could get five times the work done in a single year if we would just expedite our methods by disallowing anyone from using earmarks to hold a bill for ransom.

Currently because of the condition of the economy, we have taken a sabbatical on earmarks. Here's my position: I understand the need to bring something back to the constituents of your state and your district in order to show them that you are working for them. I have absolutely no problem with that at all. However, there is a way to do this that is logical and has many benefits. What I think we should do is put into this tax bill a clause that says this: We will allocate X amount of dollars for earmarks. I'm not exactly sure what the average is for earmarks in a year, but they can change drastically. We don't need that. We need to put down a specific amount. I think that $20 billion between 50 states is a fair amount. We say we're going to put $20 billion into a fund for earmarks, but those earmarks can never come through legislation that is not designed to provide those earmarks. In other words, you can't get $100 million allocated for a new bridge when we're talking about a military budget. They don't belong in the same bill. That's what happens.

That's what drives the cost of the bills up and takes all the time in Congress. We'll do it this way: In the Congressional fiscal year, we will run 11 months taking care of the business of this country. Legislation moves forward without the hindrance of the filibustering to hold out for some type of an earmark.

That way we can get things done in an efficient manner. In this plan, all of those in Congress will be working, along with their constituents in their states, to figure out what the state needs the most and therefore what to ask for from Congress when it comes times to decide on which earmarks we want to approve or disapprove. During that year, they will come up with numerous ideas. They will do statistical analysis and cost analysis, show the urgency of getting this done, and put it together in a proposal. That proposal must be in by the end of nine months into the fiscal year. It can go in any time during that year, but if it isn't in by the end of the ninth month, then it doesn't get a vote in the 12th month. We're going to work 11 months taking care of the business of this country, and we're going to take the last month when all we will do is vote on earmark projects. We can't debate, we can't filibuster. We have one month to decide on what could be over 500 proposals. That's why you want to get the proposals in early. If you don't have it in by the end of the ninth month, then you're out of luck and have to wait until next year. If you get it in earlier that year you have all of that time to study the different proposals. When we get into that last month, we will simply be saying, "Proposal number such- and- such presented by so-and-so for the state of whatever: Those that approve say aye, and those that disapprove say nay." Count it up: Whatever way it goes, that's the way it goes. That fast, that simple. You've had all this time to study the proposals. One of the things that you're going to be looking for is whether a particular proposal involves an amount of money that is considered overreaching for what they deserve. In other words, the very first proposals submitted will be the first ones voted on. The voting ends either when all of the budgeted money is gone or when all the proposals have been voted on.

That is the end of the process for that year. I don't want to vote for your proposal if it's a $1 billion proposal; there may be no money left for my proposal by the time we get there. This will cause the Congress people to look at all of the proposals and see what they're for and how much they're asking for money-wise. Those that get too greedy simply won't get their proposal approved.

What will happen next is something very, very extraordinary. It's one of the best reasons for doing this. If you don't want to vote on any proposal, you simply don't have to. However, many votes there are will be taken into consideration, and the majority rules. If I have a proposal that I want to bring to my people and think it's a good idea, I manage to put it in dollars and cents that are within reasonable parameters, and I go around to all of my party allies in Congress. I ask them to please take a look at my proposal and see if they can find a way to be a yes vote for me. Of course, the people that I'm talking to are going to say, "I've got my own proposals; do you think you can vote for mine?" A camaraderie begins to happen. Still there is the possibility that you could get voted down. After talking to his people and hashing out which ones will vote yes and which ones will vote no, the person who has submitted the bill asks those who are not entirely on board to simply not vote at all. An uncast vote is the same as a yes vote. You're looking at a situation: "I can still vote for yours, but you don't have to vote for mine; just don't vote at all." Once you've done that, the next thing to happen is both sides will cross party lines and ask members of the other party, "Would you vote for my proposal if I vote for yours? If you don't want to have your name attached as a yes vote because it may be unpopular in your state, would you simply not vote at all?" What have we done here? All of a sudden, we have true bipartisan compromising. A guy on the other side of the aisle helped me get mine through, so I could bring it to my constituents and hopefully get myself reelected, while I did the same for him. Everybody knows what the dollar amount is at the cutoff point. Some come together and say, "I can do yours, but my proposal got in at the end of the cycle and I'm worried that there won't be enough money left by the time they get to me. Therefore, I can vote for you if you can shave the dollars down. Leave something in there for those of us that got in at the end." There are more bipartisan compromises, more considerations taken, and people shaking hands. People will be talking about this over the course of the year, and certainly those last several months before the vote time. Over dinner or cocktails, the conversations can often turn to what you think about this bill we're voting on in Congress this month. "We need your vote. You're on the other side of the aisle. If we can get you to see things our way, then I can go to a lot of my colleagues on this side of the aisle and get them to okay your proposal for your state." Now we have a system where people are throwing out the partisan lines and working with each other so that they both can get something. There will be those that just can't, because of due diligence, pass a law that they don't believe in. It may make it difficult to get their proposal through. I think that most proposals will go through because not everybody reads every single one, and there will be a lot of people who just don't vote on it. What you need to do is just get a lot of yea votes, enough to override the no votes; that isn't that difficult when you have a number of Congress people simply not voting on that proposal. Now we've given everyone an opportunity to bring something *within reason* back to their people. They have an entire year (or at least nine months) to talk to their people and their governors, and decide what the best ideas are and how to get them in within a certain budget. I truly believe that this will be the beginning of a long time method of making friends on both sides of the aisle, so that we can get things done. We are throwing out the party lines and putting in a system where everyone, including the American people, can benefit.

This has nothing to do with energy. Since we're putting this bill into place, why don't we stick that in there? If not, let's do it at as a separate piece of legislation. Either way, I think it's a good idea. Since we're talking about taxes in this chapter, let's look at a couple of prudent moves in the tax code. Of course we can have in there things like flat taxes, removing loopholes for the corporate giants and making them pay a flat rate. But we will bring that rate down so it is competitive with the rest of the world, while assuring us that we will be able to calculate what the tax revenues will be. Therefore, we can increase revenues while making the capital gains and corporate rates competitive with the world. As of now, we are in last place. We have the highest tax rates. That is not good for business! As we talked about earlier, imports and exports will be huge as we bring prosperity to many countries around the globe. We don't want to lose our edge because of our tax rates. OUR EARMARKS PLAN ENABLES MANY IN-STATE PROJECTS AS WELL AS COMPELS OPPOSING PARTIES TO COMPROMISE.

We've entered into this discussion on taxes because it must be an integral part of our general plan. We have to be able to use the IRS as a collection, distribution, and refund entity. After all, we pay their wages. There should be no reason why we can't have that. Since we're into taxes, we're looking at taxes in a broader scope, hoping to kill several birds with one stone by adjusting corporate tax rates, etc.

CHAPTER 6

THE TEASE REVEALED

Here is something that I have been saving. I've had several opportunities in the course of writing this book to drop this in, but I postponed it so that we could save this chapter for this discussion and hopefully do something spectacular. That is the refunding of the investment capital, along with the tax rebates for our healthcare that our plan has made possible. Now, how do we set that up? Currently, the fiscal year for all taxpayers is the same as the annual calendar year: January 1st through December 31st. We have until April 15th to get our W-2s and 1099s altogether, get our taxes done, and get our tax papers in the mail. I see that as probably the worst fiscal year scenario that we could come up with. It just seems logical because our calendar year runs

from January through December. Let's look at our economic year, though. Winter is bad economically. Construction workers are out of work. The holidays have drained whatever savings we had. Now we're looking at coming into a period of the year where taxes are due. Many of us will get tax returns, some will not. By the time you get through April and things start picking up because of the summer months, you've already dug yourself into a hole. If you're getting a return and wait until April to apply, it could be another several months before you get the money. That's another reason why summer months are good; on top of getting back to work and getting a steady income, you may well be receiving a nice check from the government because of your overpayment on taxes during the year. For this reason, everybody loves summertime.

I have an idea. What if we were to change the fiscal year for taxpayers to the end of the year being May 15 and the beginning of the new year being May 16? You will have the four months that you generally have in the old system, which now takes you to September 15. September 15th will be your cutoff.

When you send in your tax return, you expect to get your money back in the next several months. Let's take a close look at something that's lying right under our noses and we haven't figured out yet. First, let's start with our plan. Our plan is not "maybe I get some money back, maybe I don't". It guarantees that every penny you put in, you get back plus whatever amount is due because of your healthcare rebates. We could be talking $500 or $1000 or even more per person. Some people have high medical expenses, and that 20% can really add up. You start putting it in there in May and it goes the whole year through. You apply for that return by September 15, as well as putting your money that you owe the government, or a refund if you get one, back in your pocket as well. When does this happen? Sometime in November. Are you starting to catch on? We have just created the sweetest of all Christmas funds. Even if you get no money back from your general taxes, you still get the money from your investment. If we decide to keep the fiscal year for tax- payers as a calendar year, that's okay; however, we want our fiscal year for our investment to come due on September 15. We want to get our money in time for Christmas.

What we're looking at aren't predictions as much as they are goals. From the national budget we set up our system so that

$200 billion goes into energy products. Our goal should be to have $100 billion in healthcare rebates across the board. That's 300 billion. Of course, in any given year we could get over our goals, or under, depending on how much money comes back as tax revenue. We need to be flexible on that so we can keep that goal of $130 billion in rebates. We would be putting in $230 billion and getting $330 billion in returns. That's a pretty good investment deal; I don't care who you are.

Here's the beauty: We have just made it possible to put $330 billion in the hands of the people in time for Christmas every year. Let's look at the value of this.

First of all, energy prices in winter go sky high. Many senior citizens end up turning down their heat and sit huddled around a kerosene heater, which then puts out carbon monoxide. It makes them sleepy, so they doze off but never reawaken - so many deaths in wintertime because of sky-high energy prices.

With our plan they could get a boost of $500 to $600. They could even see more because senior citizens have more health issues. They could keep their heat on. That's one advantage.

A Second advantage is doughnut holes. Doughnut holes come at the end of the year. October, November and December are when people fall into that doughnut hole. Christmas comes up, the holidays are there, you're laid off from your job, and now you have to pay out-of-pocket for your prescriptions. I think a $500 or $1000 check could do a lot of good toward solving that problem. If you are unemployed, you're going to see several bad months with low income. You get in trouble with your mortgage or they're talking about maybe turning off your electricity, that's not good. If you had $1000 in your pocket... that doesn't mean you could go running out to buy a new car, but it may mean the difference of surviving the winter.

Let's look at the big one: $330 billion dollars distributed throughout the nation in virtually every pocket of every person in the country means a Christmas of mega proportion. Last year's economy was bad, but we still did $450 billion in sales at the Christmas season. Imagine putting another few hundred billion dollars in on top of that! Talk about stimulus. This is about economic stimulus, quantitative easing, how to get money back into the economy, how to get money moving. If you give Americans $330 billion in time for Christmas, I guarantee you're going to see some job creation. You're going to see money moving all over the place. There may be some people that stick it into a savings, but I believe that most will put that money into the economy. It's every year. It's every person that benefits. The manufacturers of the goods that are sold during those holidays will have to be running at 100% capacity all year to store enough product to keep up with the demand at Christmas. We will create hundreds of thousands of jobs simply by changing the calendar date when people get their refunds from their taxes and their returns on their investments.

The $330 billion is only from the returns on the investment. What about if we do the whole thing and change the tax calendar as well? Hundreds of billions more will come into peoples' pockets through their refunds. That goes into the system at the same time. Instead of Christmas and winter being the most difficult, strenuous, stressful time of the year, it truly will be the season of joy! The kids, of course, will make out. The stress that is removed from their parents is the best present of all! All we have to do is change the dates. Since we have put this plan in place that returns all of this investment money plus dividends at the end of the year, we can double the amount of money that goes into the economy in just a couple of months. The people get to decide what they want to do with it. This beats the hell out of a nearly trillion-dollar plan, where the Obama administration threw money out the window, hoping it would land in fertile ground and grow a money tree. I'm sorry, Mr. Obama, but dollar bills aren't seeds. You throw them out the window, they're gone. This is one of my favorite parts of the plan, and it only exists because of the opportunities that our plan has presented us. Merry Christmas!

PART IV
ENERGY, ENERGY
AND MORE ENERGY

CHAPTER 1

BIO-METHANE

What did we just do? Did we just create a giant Christmas fund for all American investors? I think we just did. That in itself is enough to make our plan worthwhile. Just imagine $300 billion every year in the hands of the people at what is the most joyous time of the year, but in many cases the most difficult as well. People put a smile on their face and spread what we call the Christmas spirit to all who they come in contact with. Prior to that, we get together and give thanks for all the blessings that we have. It uplifts our spirits, gives us strength. Now we have truly given all Americans a reason to give thanks, a reason to have the joy, and a means by which we can celebrate.

This joyous spiritual uplifting, however, depends on whether we unite behind this plan. Without this plan, no investment dollars are collected and therefore no return on investment. Unless we have a separate bill that gives us the tax breaks that we will receive as a result of our plan, we lose that as well. Therefore, the Christmas holidays, as joyous as they are, return to the normal state of affairs with the normal downside that comes with the winter months. At this point, let's come together and say, "Let's do this. Let's join hands, shout out loud 'God bless America', and take the problems head on." So far in the plan, we've recognized our goal as sovereignty. We agree that the best path to sovereignty is through the effort to become energy-independent. If we're going to become energy-independent, let's take the opportunity to create that independence through means which give us clean, affordable, efficient energy sources. Therefore, the product that our corporation will produce will be energy. The energy comes in many shapes and sizes, and therefore our corporation will be multifaceted in its efforts.

It has finally come time now to look at the sources of energy and decide what they are, what they look like, how we accomplish the production part of our plan. At this point, we get to do something that I've been asking all along - that we put on our most imaginative, logical ideas and see if we can find a way to make this happen. This is going to be a very fun section. I say we start with the most obvious, the biggest problem. That is fuel.

We know that one source of energy comes from oxidation. Oxidation is a technical name for burning. Fire is produced in oxidation. We burn a number of things, and we list them all under the heading of fuel. Fuel is something that we burn to create energy in the form of heat. We use it many different ways.

Some we turn into steam by using that heat in combination with water, and steam turns a turbine that creates friction and releases electrons. Then we have energy. Another way we use it - and this is absolutely gigantic to our problem - is to take the fuel, compress it, add oxygen and a spark, and cause combustion. Combustion is the same as starting a fire, only it is much more rapid and more powerful in its release of energy. The engines that run our vehicles are internal combustion engines. We compress the fuel, explode it, and it drives the system that turns the wheels. In either case we find a great need for fuel. No matter how we look at it, especially in the transportation industry, it is the most practical and affordable means of transportation.

There are those that would like us to turn to electric driven vehicles. This has to be the stupidest idea I've ever heard, right up there with playing with nuclear fission to create electricity. It just is a bad idea! The cost of the electric powered vehicles will never, ever be affordable. The energy that is stored in the batteries of the vehicle must be produced in other facilities, mainly our power plants, which burn the fuel to produce that electricity. The whole idea of electric vehicles is to get away from having to use fuel. Yet we have to use fuel to produce the electricity to put into these monstrous, unbelievably heavy batteries that can only take us a few miles before they run out of charge, which we then have to put all of our 256 million passenger vehicles onto the electric grid system to recharge the batteries. It's not like we don't have enough problems with our grid system. In fact, they are so severe that we're going to completely renovate the system just to get it functional for our needs that we have now, let alone the need to make it capable of carrying that much more electricity. That is just insane! Most of the hybrid vehicles then require that you carry a gas tank full of gasoline so that when the electric battery runs out, you can switch to conventional fuel. Now you have to carry the weight of all of that fuel that you would normally carry, and on top of that carry the weight of that battery. The fuel burns in an internal combustion engine, while batteries turn an electric motor. Are you getting my drift? In order to make these things work efficiently together, we have to put in so many different components to that vehicle that now the vehicle costs us around $300,000.

They are still at times going to run on standard fuel, so what have we gained?

What we need to do is create a better fuel. Because of my background in chemistry, I can understand the simplicity of oxidation and combustion. Let's see if we can make this clear and simple, so that we understand what our new product should look like. First of all, standard gasoline starts with oil. The chemical composition of oil is one carbon and one hydrogen-CH-it's that simple. Although oil burns well, it cannot cause combustion. It won't explode when compressed, oxidized and sparked. That is very inefficient. So, we have to take an entire extra process, which we call refining, to take that carbon and hydrogen and turn it into gasoline. Basically, what we're going to do is bump up the hydrogen, oxygenate it so that when it's compressed and sparked, it will explode and drive the pistons of our engine. We add a little bit of hydrogen and add oxygen to that mix. But let's take a look at another fuel that without refining brings us an immensely more powerful combustion. That is methane gas, otherwise known as natural gas. It comes up out of the ground as a finished product with a chemical makeup of one carbon (same as oil) and four hydrogens, instead of one. When we combust, we burn the hydrogen.

Hydrogen is the most stable element in the universe. It is also the most abundant. Even water has two hydrogens. Someday we're going to figure out how to burn that water. In the meantime, we're looking at oil with one carbon and one hydrogen - a one-to-one ratio. We compare it to methane gas, which is one carbon and four hydrogens - a four-to-one ratio. It's plain to see that methane gas will be four times as efficient. When we oxidize these combinations, we release byproducts. The one that we're mostly concerned about, because it is light enough to go into the atmosphere and become a greenhouse gas, is carbon dioxide (one carbon, two oxygen). It is the result of the explosion caused when we combine our fuel with oxygen and the spark.

Some of the oxygen is connected to the carbon and goes off into space as a greenhouse gas.

If you look at the ratio of oil and even the ratio of standard gasoline - car- bons to hydrogens - we find that without any refinement at all, the methane is by far the most efficient, and therefore produces the least amount of carbon dioxide. With every molecule of carbon dioxide, there is only one carbon. Take standard oil, for example. To get four hydrogens burnt, you have to burn four carbons along with it. Again, we see that one-to-one ratio. Make it better by refining it; that's still not as good as the basic methane, and you don't have to refine the methane. Besides that, we have plenty of it right here in this country, and it is cheap. You don't need as much of it. There is an increase in your gas mileage. We look at this and say, "This has to be it! This has to be great!" No, we have to rethink this.

First of all, when we look at standard economic principles, we always have to look at supply-and-demand. If we convert all of our transportation vehicles to methane, the demand will be so greatly increased that it will drive the price up - maybe up to a point where it starts to become economically not feasible. One of the things we definitely want to do is create competition. First of all, we're not going to eliminate conventional gasoline. We're going to let conventional gasoline compete with our new fuel. In order to make this proposition even better, we add in a third means of combustion. This is what we call bio-fuels. These are basically alcohol created from sugar. There are a number of kinds of sugars. They are all carbohydrates. The makeup of sugar is one carbon, two hydrogens, one water; that's the very, very base carbohydrate. When we look at that, it means there is an atom of carbon attached to a water, H_2O. Therefore, we give it the name carbohydrate. All combinations of that are carbohydrates. It could be C2 (which is two carbons); then it would need two waters. It should be $C_2H_4O_2$, or $C_3H_6O_3$, and so on.

The way we've been making bio-fuels is to pull the sugar from corn. Corn is not the be-all to end- all. An even higher producer of sugar is plain old sugar cane - pure sugar. You can see by the combinations that the amount of hydrogen in a carbohydrate is always twice the amount of carbon and twice the amount of oxygen. Hydro- gen is the main component, and hydrogen is what we burn. This takes some extracting and refining processes that make it more expensive. Here's where it comes in handy.

First of all, it's renewable. We can grow it every year. Secondly, we can mix it with either gasoline or methane in any combination that we desire. In fact, we can mix all three of them together if we want. By adding the bio-fuel into the equation, we now have three burnable, combustible fuels. My idea is to combine the bio-fuel with the methane, giving us the cleanest burn for the best price. The price of methane can go up, but we can add more bio-fuels and bring it back down. We can combine in our gas tanks the bio-methane along with standard gasoline, getting better mileage and dividing the cost. This is why we will need these conversions so that our vehicles can take bio-fuels, methane, bio-methane, and standard gasoline, and do it in any combination that we want to produce the best bang for the buck.

We want to look at this from the position of our corporation. I say that one of the goals, one of the policies will be to attempt to make every single state fuel independent. I know this is impossible, but let's take a look at our options. We want every state to be able to produce enough bio-fuel to feed the needs of their state. They also need to come up with the right amount of methane gas.

They will need refineries, mixing stations that need to be strategically positioned so that the bio-fuels come to them from nearby producers to make the final product. We urge the farmers to add to their production whatever product grows the best and produces the most sugar. We don't want them to quit producing food and change to bio-fuel because it's worth more. We want to expand the growth. This may mean we have to supply machinery, equipment. We may have to put in irrigation systems. Whatever they have to do, we work with them through our corporation. They pay us back slowly out of their profits, and of course that money goes to the people of that state. The state then decides what the government will do with those revenues.

Down the road, there needs to be an actual bio-fuel production mechanism in place so the farmers can grow their crops and not ship them across the country, but just down the road, where a pipeline comes in from the producers of the natural gas to create the final product. Now that we have the fracking technology, I think that most states will be able to produce this natural gas at a high enough level to fill the needs of the people. Whatever infrastructure is needed - and this can include fracking mechanics, machinery, whatever is needed - we will happily supply. The natural gas company then, out of their profits, again pays that back over a long period of time. That money goes again to the people of that state.

On top of that, we have to think about national security. We need massive amounts of the bio-methane product stored in case of emergency. That's great! It works out even better this way. Each state will not only have the means of producing the fuel, but we will put the money up front in storage cylinders. What I would recommend would be that - for national security purposes - enough bio-methane will be stored to supply the people of that state for two years, thereby giving them chance to replenish the supplies even in adverse conditions. Also, when we say two years, we're talking about two years under a rationing program. If it's an emergency, we don't let people waste the fuel. On top of that, we add another 20%. We do an 80/20 combined total. The additional 20% that is stored will belong to the people of that state. The 80% for emergency is controlled by the federal government. The federal government can call an emergency and, by working with governors, access that fuel in case of catastrophe. What if the fields are flooded because of inclement weather? What if massive fires wipe out huge amounts of crops?

What if an extra cold season in spring kills off the crop? Whatever it is, they can attach some of that 80%, which of course needs to be replenished. That is fine, though. The governor also has control of the additional 20%. Once again, if adverse conditions cause a shortage, the governor can issue a mandate and open that 20% up for use in that state. This is one of the best inflation controls in the whole process. With that amount of fuel, if the prices for any reason go through the roof, they can put additional supplies into the market in their state and bring those prices down.

On top of that, as we go around the country, we'll see that some states are able to produce more methane than they need, but they lack in biofuels. They still have the refineries that we will build, they still have the containers for storage - we're going to do that for all states. They may be able to go over to another state and say, "You've got an excess of bio-fuel. We have an excess of methane. Why don't we talk turkey?" Again, we have an edge against inflation. In worst case scenario, one state can pump up the volume of their production and sell the product to another state that may be having difficulties.

Therefore, we have now created a competitive scenario of interstate commerce based on fuels. That gives us the power to hold down inflation while assuring the steady supply. We also are not going to run out of oil over the long term because we may be only using half as much gasoline as we were before. We're not going to run out of bio-fuel because it's renewable. We're not going to run out of methane because - in combination with the other fuels - it may only be a quarter or a third. That way we ensure that we always have enough supply to keep the wolves - which are the speculators - from getting too greedy. If they get too greedy on one and drive the price up, we simply will change to another. They operate on a future's market. When the future is stable, they want in. Of course, stable markets mean less risk, and less risk means less profit, but it also means less losses. A stable fuel market in this country is essential. All you have to do is look at the price of gasoline and see how what's going on in the Mideast affects that price on a daily basis. We are at the mercy of OPEC. We are not sovereignty. Most of what we do in the energy department, we do at their will. They have money to lobby politicians. They give out big contributions at election time. They control us. Not anymore! We are not only going to put American sovereignty at the top of the list, but it will be brought about through the sovereignty of the individual and the individual's relationship to the state. This is done by making each state their own sovereign entity as far as the production of fuel, as well as the consumption of other forms of energy, which we are just about to get deeper into in the next chapter. This is easily sustainable over decades and generations simply because we, as the members of this corporation, have in our wisdom put together a means for each state to have control over their own destiny as far as energy. Next, we're going to move on, and I'm going to show you some real exciting stuff. Stay tuned!

CHAPTER 2

SUNNY DAYS AHEAD FOR SOLAR POWER

We've managed now to scare the living daylights out of OPEC. This has been part of the plan that promises the low gasoline prices. Just the fact that we have signed into law a bill that enables us to start our new corporation is going to cause panic on Wall Street as far as oil speculators are concerned. We can expect oil prices to drop down significantly in a very short period of time, perhaps as fast as one or two days. Oil prices hitting $40 a barrel or less means that we're back to looking at a $2 per gallon (or slightly higher) price tag on conventional gasoline. We're going to add to that because it's our gas tax that is going to enable this plan to take place. Yet the amount of drop in the price could be considerably larger than the amount of gas tax we will impose. Those are just generic numbers, but the analyses I've done seem to indicate this is very feasible. Not only that, but we've now put into place a drive for people to convert their vehicles to efficiently utilize any of the fuels - the bio- methane, conventional gasoline, or any combination thereof.

The systems will have a sensor where gasoline is analyzed as it goes through the system, possibly using specific gravity or molecular density, to tell the engine what the fuel-to-air ratio needs to be. New spark enhancement technology that we already have should be a part of that, so that we get complete burn of the fuel and therefore enhance horsepower. What does this mean for the car manufacturers? Let's just take a look at this. There are 256 million passenger vehicles on the road today and approximately 8 million 18- wheelers. Many railways use diesel and therefore will need to be converted to take the biodiesel. For the car manufacturers, that means a huge boost to their bottom line. Millions of sales of conversion kits as well as new cars coming out with built-in ability to utilize any fuel. What a great day! I believe that as we're able to supply the fuel, there will be customers waiting in line with their already-converted vehicles to use the new fuel to their advantage. Of course, we get rid of the notion of electric cars, we stay with an internal combustion engine, and we manipulate the prices and availability through our plan. We are getting the hang of this, and I think we've got it nailed down pretty well. Now we have to look to the heavens. What else can we do? This section is all about creating new forms of energy, or at least utilizing the sources that we have in a new and more productive manner. When we look to the sky, we see the sun. That is one big ball of energy. Our sun is a medium white star, which means it has the power to generate enough energy to simply evaporate all the planets in our solar system if it was ever to go nova. Nova is when the star reaches its final days and implodes, and the fusion causes a massive escape of energy as well as an internal collapse that we know is what generates black holes. Anything short of that means that the sun will keep on burning for billions of years. The power from the sun is nuclear. You know that I have warned against playing with nuclear energy here on Earth, but the sun being 93 million miles away creates the perfect scenario. It can go ahead and be a giant nuclear reactor while we here on Earth get to utilize that power in so many ways that most of us can't even comprehend. The sun not only warms the planet, but it causes the growth of plants, molecular movement. We know the tip of the iceberg about what's involved, but even with that much knowledge we know that the ancient people were probably right to worship the sun, in that it is not a god but an incredible gift from God.

We know about energy, radiation, radiant heat, ultraviolet and infrared energy. We've been playing with the idea of making the sun our partner in our quest for clean energy and energy independence. Remember that our primary goal is energy independence, and sovereignty independence. Since the sun blesses every inch of the Earth with its energy, it only makes sense that we should utilize it. So far, the best we've come up with are solar panels that convert the rays of the sun into electricity. What we've run into are a number of road- blocks, most of them not having to do as much with technology as the cost of it. We know that the biggest problem with solar energy is the cost.

Barack Obama, through his stimulus package, decided to throw billions of dollars at the problem with one simple philosophy that has proven to be an utter failure. It is the philosophy of 'if you build it, they will come'. That philosophy worked for Henry Ford, but there was something very special that made that philosophy work. The companies before him that tried to market the automobile could not make a go of it for the simple fact that it cost too much. The product stirred peoples' imaginations and excited them, but there was simply no market because of the price. In order to make the 'build it and they will come' philosophy feasible, Henry Ford figured out how to mass produce the automobiles, bringing the price down to the rate that was afford- able to the average American. He then set forth on building huge amounts, and they did come. Without that part of the equation, it would never have worked. It is the same problem with solar energy.

We look at what we have in solar energy and in the way of technology. We know that it is going to get quite a bit better.

The industry is stifled. Investors don't want to put money into it because the risk is too high. You see what happened to Solyndra. Even with a half billion dollars in assets, they simply weren't able to sell their product. The few customers out there looking for solar power went to China to buy it, not because their technology was better but because their labor force was cheaper. Our problem is simply how to get the price down, how to make it affordable. The first thing we know is what worked for Henry Ford - mass production. When the engineers and the designers put their minds to it, they will come up with ways to mass produce the panels at a very reasonable cost. Why would they do that? What investor is going to get involved? Here's where we come in. Since we have started a corporation strictly for the purpose of investing in clean, affordable energy, we are set up to make the difference. We have the money in mass quantities, enough money to buy literally millions of panels. Of course, we want the technology to be state-of-the-art. I have heard of companies that are experimenting with panels that are made up of multiple cubes. The reason to use a cube is because it has six times the surface of a flat space. These cubes would have to be set up on a panel with some distance between each other, and reflectors on all sides and underneath that collect the light rays and bounce them around so that all six sides of the cube are bombarded with the sun's rays. We give up some space because we have to provide for spacing between the cubes, but we can double or even triple the amount of effective space by using this new technology. This also makes the units more compact.

Here's what I propose: We're going to invest the money not into the companies, like Barack Obama did, but into purchasing the product. This will stir the investors to pump billions of dollars into this new industry because they want a piece of the action. The action is going to be significant. We may pump $20 or $30 billion into this in the first ten years. This is how we'll do it. The first thing we have to realize is that terrain matters. Homes and businesses that are tucked into mountainous areas are at a disadvantage because the mountains block the sun. It's not enough that we only get to utilize the sun for a few hours a day, when it's nearly overhead; we want to be able to use it from the moment it breaks the horizon to the moment it disappears. Looking at terrain, there are several places that come to mind that would be excellent. The main place being what is known as the Valley of the Sun - Phoenix, Ari- zona. In Phoenix, Arizona, the minute the sun pops up on the horizon, it is right in your face, up to the very minute that it disappears.

There is so much open land all around it that there is nothing to block the sun. We get the full power of the sun for as long as the day lasts. Now we get into the guts of the plan. We're not going to spend money on building giant solar farms, gathering the energy, moving it through the grid for distribution.

Rather than that, let's look at individual residents.

I lived in Phoenix for 20 years. The last year I was there - which is about nine years ago - the electric bills in summer were brutal. They were $350-400 through the summer months, and nearly that much at the end of spring and early fall. I calculate my bill at that time to be about $3000 a year. What we want to do is equip these homes with solar systems that are capable of keeping up with the high electric flow rates that we see in the summertime. In the wintertime, the rates were down to under $100 a month. If you had gas heat, gas stove and gas water heater, it was quite a bit less. I did some math. I believe this plan works if we can equip a residence with a unit powerful enough to supply that much electricity at any given time. We will need to expend about $35,000 per home. Now you see why it simply has not been able to catch on. To put that much money into an electric-producing system, the odds are you're going to have to borrow the money. Much of what we'll target will be new homes, which means you put that $35-40,000 into your mortgage price and pay it over 15-30 years. With interest, your system ends up costing $70-80,000. You can't do it!

One of the important things we're going to do is make sure the home is connected to the standard grid. This is the new grid that we're going to be building for energy efficiency and cyber security. Houses that have the solar panels will need two meters, one for coming in and one for going out. When super-hot days hit, and they will - I have seen temperatures of 120 degrees - the system may not be able to keep up. Therefore, you need to draw some of your energy off the grid, which will go through your meter. Once every several months, the meter reader will assess what you owe, and you will have to pay that additional amount. Here's the upside: In the months where you do not use all of the energy that you're producing, which is virtually half the year or more, you send the energy back through the other meter and get a check in the mail for how much energy you have sold back to the power companies.

They'll probably give you 50 cents on the dollar so that they can redistribute that power and still make a profit. This takes an enormous strain off our power-producing companies in that area. In fact, we may even see energy prices dropping for the typical user because they're able to utilize the energy overage of all the homes with solar systems. That means there is no fuel being burnt. It means the nuclear fission-able material at the Palo Verde Nuclear Facility will be able to be used more sparingly, and hopefully the savings will be significant enough to bring energy prices down. How many homes can we equip with this technology in order to maximize the mass production and the value that comes from that mass production, to get us into that $35-40,000 per home range? I don't know exactly how many it will take, but I know how many we're going to build - 1 million. In ten years, we will equip 1 million homes with solar energy produced by their own units.

There will be massive growth in the industry, not just in production but in maintenance companies, installation companies, insurance that will cover any major damages to your system. I believe that we can put this package together at the rate of $300 per month for the homeowner. Let's look at how that works out mathematically. The solar systems that we have now are generally guaranteed to run efficiently for up to 15 years. This means at the end of 15 years you may have to do a massive renovation or even a complete changeover. In those 15 years, you've got to be able to make this affordable. At $300 a month, over the course of a year that is $3600. Remember, I claim that my costs were about $3000 a year. That was nine years ago. I'm sure the energy costs now are probably more like $3500 a year. That puts us right on target. The proud owner of this system on their residence won't be paying any more than they would if they were on the regular system. What about this? In the winter months, they sell back energy. We can't say exactly how much they'll get back, but they get back money on that energy. This means that suddenly that unit is more affordable than having the standard conventional form of energy brought to them through the grid.

As in every case, this money that we've invested is an investment by the people designed to give the people of any particular state approximately what they put in. this will go back to them in the way of assets and payments that they can get for those assets. Therefore, the $300 monthly payments from those 1 million people go to the people of the state, who technically own those units. They can then decide what to do with the money. We're looking at this plan at a 15-year time frame. By that time, the technologies will be so much better, the systems will be worn out, and we'll want to come in and either renovate or replace them. We will do that on our dime and start the process of repayment all over again. We want to install these in ten years, hoping that we have them all in before it's time to start replacement at 15 years. Over those ten years, with a million of these homes at $35,000, we've invested $35 billion. That's $3.5 billion per year, which may be more than Arizona's allotment, seeing as we have to replace the grid. We're going to do something with railways in that state as well - that's coming up. When you stretch it over the 15-year period, you find that it works out beautifully. We can do the other work that needs done as well as supply those million units. By that time, the companies will be making units in mass production with topnotch technology and probably at a lesser or equal price for a better product. With more of these projects that we put in place across the country, in the places that have the right terrain - middle America is perfect for these types of projects - we're going to realize such a great gain in energy production with such a lowering of the price. The people are going to want to get in on this all over. Many of these projects may even come up by the developers building new homes, where the person can opt in or out, realizing that the long-term benefits out- weigh the original cost. That's all because we have taken the responsibility to put in the money to get solar energy working for America.

California has already started a program which they put into law. I don't know exactly how it works, but there are going to be a lot of people forced to buy solar panels. This is just going to break their banks, especially in an economy like they have, which is going under faster than the Titanic. Yet if we start this project and we use it in southern California, we can accommodate hundreds of thousands or even a million people in that state as well. They don't have to suffer the monetary losses that they will have from having to borrow money at high rates of interest to comply with the state's wishes.

This is also a security issue. If we were under attack - either from cyber terrorists or from internal terrorists going around trying to blow up our energy producing facilities - having millions of homes on this system could save thousands of lives. The simple fact is that if we had to, we could turn off those air conditioners, only run them intermittently, save as much of that electricity as we can and put it through the grid to keep manufacturing running, to keep hospitals in control of the climate. There would be many places where an emergency plan would kick into place, and those that have the solar units would be an integral part of an energy plan. Not only are we heading for energy independence, we're knocking the prices down. We have a new thriving industry that creates hundreds of thousands of jobs with a trickle down of millions and massive amounts of tax revenue. The people of those states are getting their money paid back just as the plan says they will. We're not going to have the worries of the brownouts and blackouts. Of course, this one simple attack is not going to be the cure-all. There are numerous ways of get- ting energy, and we're going to continue to explore these means.

One of the best things about solar is its consistency. It does have cycles.

Sometimes the temperature of the Earth goes up a couple degrees; sometimes it goes down a couple degrees. We have mini–Ice Ages; we have hot spells.

Those are all because of the cycles of the Earth. The last time the sun had a major hissy fit, and combined with a lowering of energy from Earth's core, we had an Ice Age that lasted millions of years. If that were to happen, we could pretty much kiss it goodbye. There is nothing we can do about it. That's why we want to make sure that these units operate so efficiently that even in the low cycles of the sun, we still have enough energy to run a single household off of one unit.

It might be important to know that all of these calculations are built on my experience in Arizona and what I paid for my own home. My house was 2000 square feet. It had a large covered patio deck, it faced north (which is very good in Arizona). Homes that face east and west get beat up by the sun hitting the front of their houses, coming in through the back and front windows. North and south exposures leave the two ends of the house to be solid block, E.F.I.S. or stucco, whatever the builders use. That brings your utility prices down, so I think my utility estimates were actually conservative. Yet at $300 a month - especially with the ability to sell back in the wintertime - I would have made money on the deal. This is a win-win-win. Win for the solar industry, win for the homeowners, win for the people of that state. We have to seriously look at this issue and realize that the economics of sovereignty are based exactly on that economic feasibility. Throwing money at these things, giving the money to the corporations, having an "if we build it, they will come" philosophy is not going to work. We have to get our big guns in- volved. We need statistical analysis, we need proposals coming from capable and responsible entities, and we need to make the smart choices. I believe in my heart that this plan for solar is the smartest choice we can make as far as getting that ever so needed energy source working for us.

CHAPTER 3

C. A. A. T. E. S.

W hat an incredible gift we've just given ourselves - the power of the sun!

Along with that is an economical way to harvest that energy. The energy source is consistent, reliable and not going anywhere soon, at least let's hope not. The other great thing about it is it's free. The systems to utilize it are expensive, but the energy itself is free. When we look at its value compared to conventional methods, we see that we still have to build massive facilities to create power and we still have to have the grid to distribute power. What makes it different from our solar energy systems is that the conventional system requires massive amounts of fuel. That fuel is not only expensive, but it is the problem that we have with greenhouse gases. It is the use of that fuel which causes the pollution, as well as drives the cost up at abnormal rates any time there is a threat that the fuel supply may be interrupted. We've taken control of that by putting together a means to utilize systems that don't have fuel. This solar energy is the first we've talked about, and I think you'll agree with me that the plan is a viable plan.

Let's look at other sources now. The second thing we're going to look at is wind. I know what everyone says and what you're thinking right now, that wind is like solar energy and simply not efficient enough to be worth the cost. We've figured out a way to overcome the cost issue through our corporation and our investment power. Since the control of the finished products is in the hands of the people of each state, it can yield substantial revenues as well.

Wind is every bit as viable a source of energy as solar, and I'm going to show you exactly why and how it will be.

First of all, we have to look at the way we attempt to utilize wind. It seems a bit silly. We spend incredible amounts of money to put in what are known as wind farms, where we put hundreds of turbines in the open air, stretching over thousands of acres of land, in order to capture what we hope will be enough energy to make it worth our while. One thing that we do know is that wind does exist and will always exist. The amount of air that surrounds us has an incredible mass. The particles are small and light, and therefore travel easily. In any given area the amount of mass that the wind has is limited at best and is always unreliable. Another problem with these giant monsters, besides the cost, is that we have to try and find the level of height that carries the most wind. If you look at a flock of birds flying, they will always adjust the height to which they fly to utilize the strongest amount of wind at their backs, which pushes them along and makes their travel much easier. Our giant units can't adjust for different heights, trying to find that perfect stream of air that gives us the most efficient use of that energy source. In the instance that our energy stream coincides with the height of our windmills, which is usually more than not because we study the areas and determine what the best height would be, there comes a problem. At this point we are not working with Mother Nature; we are working against her. If a single bird flies through a wind farm, there is no problem. The bird will simply maneuver around the turbines and stay out of harm's way. But in the event that an entire flock- thousands of birds - sets their height for the best use of the airstream, which coincides with the height of the wind turbines, the birds always find themselves flying into the swinging arms of the wind turbines. Since the birds at that point are in a massive group, they lose the ability to maneuver around and through these turbines. Therefore, large quantities of birds get trapped and are forced to fly directly into the rotating arms of the turbine. This is what kills so many birds. We try to utilize air in order to work with Mother Nature, so that we don't pollute Her, so that we don't have the problems of dealing with fuel sources, most of which are brought in from other countries. As we've discussed early on, that is also what makes our country weak and makes us lose sovereignty.

We have to find a way to use wind so that it is cost-effective as a consistent amount of energy production and does not kill any of God's creatures.

Suddenly this task seems enormous. How do we do that? The first thing we have to do is look at energy. What is it? How do we measure it? Let's go back to some basic physics. Let's utilize the brain of one of our greatest scientists and mathematicians, Albert Einstein. He said "E = MC2." This stands for Energy = Mass times the Speed of light squared. We certainly can't and never will be able to take any mass and move it at the speed of light squared. This formula still has great potential for us to solve our problem. Let's look at a more simplified formula. Energy = Mass times Speed. Pure energy is released at the speed of light squared, but we can't do that. What we can do is maximize the amount of mass and maximize the speed at which it travels, confine that to a given area, and use Mother Nature to force this mass to impact the paddles of the wind turbine system, therefore converting mass and motion into electricity. The mass in motion carries with it energy, but it is not electricity. That's why we must create a collision between the mass and the turbine. That spins the turbine, and that's what transforms the wind into electricity, which then goes down through our brand-new grid for distribution.

Everything that we're about to do with our efforts to utilize nature and the free energy that She provides, means we must look at all factors involved.

Factor #1 is Terrain. We know that in different areas of the country, different areas of individual states, and certain areas around the counties that we live in have higher flow rates of air. It's because of the terrain. When air is moving along at a normal pace - let's call that 5-10 miles per hour because that is, in the absence of a storm system, what we usually see in wind movement - we find that we go through so much trouble to get our wind turbines in the right place at the right height to get more than the average flow. We look at the proposals to put wind turbines out along our coastal shores. Certainly, it's because the movement of the water creates turbulence in the air, and we get a higher flow rate. The optimum flow rate in these scenarios can be somewhere in the neighborhood of 300-400 feet in the air. They have to be anchored under the water into solid earth. They get in the way of airplanes. They are exposed to terrible hurricanes. The pedestals alone cost millions and millions of dollars. In certain conditions it becomes hard for ships and boats to maneuver in the turbulent water, therefore making passage through one of these wind farms treacherous. I guarantee you will see loss of life, not to mention the fact that they take away the natural beauty of the ocean. Let's forget about that. This is environmentalists forcing the government to clutch at straws to try to do something that will appease these overzealous people, while making it possible for them to tell the world that they are good stewards of Mother Earth. Come on, people! We are way too smart to let those kinds of ideas come to fruition. Let's find another way.

I'm about to ask you to consider my ideas for the use of wind. Once again, your input can be very useful. Perhaps you know where the specific terrain requirements exist that I'm going to explain are necessary, as you may live in or near such an area. All statistical analysis that we can provide is also needed, which means I'm talking to all you college students, engineers, mathematicians, designers. Take a close look at this and see what you can do with it. I will give you general dimensions. I have reasons for choosing these particular dimensions. I believe they will be efficient but possibly not optimum. This is where we need to come together. We are a team and will come together as a team. The best of the best will rise and take the future of America in our hands and return it to its glory.

I offer you now C.A.A.T.E.S. C.A.A.T.E.S. stands for Compressed Air and Turbines Energy System. What in that is different from the air energy system that we use now? It's the compression of the air. We use compressed air in so many ways. We use pneumatic tools in factories as well as mechanic shops, body shops - you name it. We've found that compressed air is easy to generate and very efficient. The way we do it in our businesses is to run air compressors. They are engines that compress air by jamming it into a container of a specific proportion. Obviously, the larger the container, the more air it can hold. The bottom line is that as we pump air into the container, we see that the mass of air is increasing while the size of a container does not... unless, of course, this air container would be a balloon. Even that is still compressed air. That's why the balloon grows in size. The compressed air applies pressure to the inside walls of the container as the air mass is increased. We find that when we get up to the pressure that pushes back on the engine that is compressing the air with enough force to stop that engine, the pressure has reached its optimum limit. You simply can't get any more air into that cylinder with that size of a motor. This is exactly the truth when we utilize Mother Nature. Another thing we see when we have the container filled with air is that if we open a small hole anywhere on that container, the air comes racing out at incredible speed. The faster we want the speed, the smaller we make the hole. Again, these forces will stabilize at an optimum speed for the pressure that is in the cylinder; as pressure drops, so does the speed at which the air is escaping. This is where we come back to our basic premise: We can utilize Mother Nature to give us increased mass at increased speeds. With our formula, mass x speed = energy, we therefore realize a much greater energy, more force on the turbines, and more electricity being produced.

Here's the problem that confronts us: How do we compress the air? We can't use compressors because any standard compressor must utilize either electricity or fuel for its operation. The amount of electricity or fuel that it consumes is greater than the amount of energy that can come from the air that it is compressing. We always will lose. Here we once again turn to Mother Nature. Along with our technology, we work as one. Remember the word that I mentioned earlier: Terrain. Mother Nature compresses air all the time. Let's just take a look at one scenario. Air as a whole move from west to east. Within that massive expanse of air, we have places where even though the air may be moving at 20 miles an hour, the air that is trapped in the funnel of a tornado can be moving 100, 150, even 200 miles per hour. If we go out west and realize that the general air pattern is moving as we discussed earlier at 5-10 miles an hour, a phenomenon occurs when it reaches the Rocky Mountains.

When the air reaches the mountain, suddenly it finds itself trapped between the mountain and the mass of air that is coming behind it, moving eastward. Something's got to give. By its own nature, the wind will find the path of least resistance. It can't go through the mountain, but it can go over the mountain. What we're interested in is between the mountains. When the air mass hits the mountains, you can go to one of any of thousands of canyons and gorges that make up the mountain range. You find that nature has compressed the air into that confined space. In order to accommodate the airflow, the air going through that enclosed space travels at a much higher rate of speed. This is the path of the least resistance. When we talk about terrain, this is what we're looking for. We're looking for places where the massive amount of air hits a wall and searches for a pathway between the walls. There we find a highly increased rate of airflow. Remember our formula: Mass times speed. As the air enters the canyon, the density of the mass - and therefore the mass itself - is greatly increased, being forced by the pressure of the air that has yet to reach the mountain. This provides opportunity. This is where we get clever.

First of all, we must confine the compressed air into a particular container. With C.A.A.T.E.S., it will be a cylinder. This cylinder will be miles and miles and miles long. It may stop for any reason and restart again. We can even take it right through obstacles that may be in the way (like a big, old mountain) with our tunnel-boring equipment. We'll just bore a hole right through the mountain so that our C.A.A.T.E.S. cylinder can continue its journey. Ultimately the cylinder comes out the other side of the mountains into free open space again. For purposes of construction, assembly, installation and maintenance, we will build C.A.A.T.E.S. with a diameter of 50 feet. At the entry to C.A.A.T.E.S., we're going to help nature along. She is already forcing the air into the canyon, but the canyon is much bigger than what we want to utilize. We put a funnel at the entry, of some dimension like 200 feet in diameter. This is a giant funnel that as nature forces the air into the canyon, the air hits the funnel, travels down the funnel, and is forced into our 50-foot cylinder. In the funnel, we can have ribbing that is in a corkscrew manner. That means that as the air is traveling down the funnel it begins to turn in a circular motion. To enhance this, we put a giant 50-foot fan just inside the entry to C.A.A.T.E.S., one that runs at low RPMs and needs low amperage, and therefore uses little electricity. This is to take the circular air movement coming down the funnel and spin it into the C.A.A.T.E.S. cylinder. The C.A.A.T.E.S. cylinder, throughout the entire operation in the entire system, will be lined with ribbing. These ribs will utilize most of the area and volume of the cylinder, therefore forcing the air to continue to move in a circular motion.

We look at this with very simple physics. If the air outside of the tornado is moving 20 miles an hour, the air in the funnel still has the capability of moving 200 miles an hour. Why? Because it is spinning. Picture this tornado lying on its side and being forced down the center of the cylinder that is C.A.A.T.E.S. We have now found a way to let Mother Nature compress the air into the canyon, down the throat of the funnel, and into the C.A.A.T.E.S. cylinder. The force of the air coming in behind from the mouth of the canyon continues to push the air through in a circular, spiraling manner. If we have a cylinder that is 50 feet in diameter, the air spinning through it will create a vortex just the way a tornado or a hurricane does. There will be an eye in the center that has virtually no wind movement at all. As it gets to the outer edge, because of the centrifugal force, the air moves faster and faster. That is because it has a further distance to travel. What we're looking for would be a ratio of something like 3 or 4 to 1. The distance that the air travels in a straight line, which would be down the center of the vortex, compared to the distance that the air travels as it spins down the cylinder can be adjusted by how close the ribbings are to each other. In other words, if in 50 feet of C.A.A.T.E.S. the air is spun in a circle and completes that circle four times before it reaches the end, we have increased the speed of the airflow by the circumference of the cylinder times four, plus the 50 feet that it has traveled. That gives us our rate of speed. Now what we have is compressed air spun, forced into a spinning motion. What started out as a 5 or 10 mile an hour air movement can reach 4, 5 or 6 times that speed at the same time that the funnel and the natural terrain have compressed the air. Now we have compressed air and turbine with an energy factor that is effectively measured with our formula, mass times speed equals energy.

The turbines in the cylinder have an excessive amount of resistance. It is this resistance, the turning of the generator that is at the core of the turbine and which will sit in the center of C.A.A.T.E.S., where the airflow is in that vortex. Therefore, this solid piece of equipment sitting in the center will do little to restrict airflow. The air will be spinning around it, and around it is where all the paddles are. The force of the air on the paddles turns the generator. The friction that is in the generator creates electricity. We need to have some good engineering done here to find out how much resistance we can put on the generator. This is important because the more resistance, the more electricity that is produced. When the resistance gets to the point where it overcomes the force of the air, then we've gone too far. We do have one thing in our favor; that is, momentum. It's hard to get the generators spinning, but once they do it only takes X amount of force to maintain that rate at which the turbine is spinning. It's like when you try to push a car down the street, it's hard to get it moving; but once you get it rolling, you can keep it moving.

What we're going to do instead of having these massive wind farms - which have all of those problems we just discussed - is have the wind contained in the cylinder, utilizing it over and over and over again. I said the C.A.A.T.E.S. can be miles and miles long, containing hundreds of turbines. We continue to utilize a spinning mass to generate electricity. This is where we want to be smart about it. How many can we put in a row? How close can we put them together? How much friction can we put into the generators with- out stalling them out? I have a couple other ideas. As we come upon a section of C.A.A.T.E.S. that has the turbine mounted in it, we create a cone-shaped induction port. This is like putting a cone-shaped collar on C.A.A.T.E.S. that is open. We know that as air moves through the cylinder, it creates suction. As it's coming upon a turbine, these induction ports, along with the suction, bump up the compression factor, giving it more mass and therefore increasing the speed once again. I believe we can utilize this to minimize the loss of speed because of the resistance of the turbine. This will be factored into how many turbines we can string along and still maintain optimum efficiency. We may even, in places where we see the speed slowing, take a little bit of that electricity that we're producing and install another fan, the same way we did at the mouth of the C.A.A.T.E.S. We will be able to pump up the speed with that method. If we have the collar with the induction ports and we put a fan right after it, that creates more of the suction we need to increase the mass and generate the speed. This is all to be considered. Something else we can consider is that all the induction ports as well as the mouth of C.A.A.T.E.S. will be covered with protective screens. It not only helps to keep debris out of the system but to protect birds from flying into one of the induction ports and being sucked in. We will have the screens to take care of that.

At this point we haven't done one single thing to hurt the environment. There are a couple issues. First of all, we're going to have to cut a pathway through the canyon in order to build C.A.A.T.E.S. Here's how I have it planned: First of all, the crew of logging companies come in to areas where rather than rocky canyon walls, we have walls that are covered with trees and growth. We can get them to pay us to let them take the trees out of the way. We allow them to go so far up on each side. If it turns out to be unprofitable for them to pay us - even if we get it removed for free - that saves us a lot of money. As the logging companies move through the canyon, we come behind laying railroad track. There will be two lanes with substantial distance between them, one for each direction. We can start C.A.A.T.E.S. on either end or in different places.

The best thing would be to start from one end as well as the other, with a plan to meet somewhere in the middle. As we go deeper, we have this railroad system that enables us to bring materials, even things as big as 50-foot diameter cylinders that have been prefabricated and huge 50-foot turbines.

Behind the railroad track that is being laid down, comes the crews building C.A.A.T.E.S. We follow synchronized, as closely as possible, the entire way through the mountains until the projects are completed. We have places where we build, places where we store materials that we will later convert into rest stops.

When I say rest stops, what is that about? Give me one minute. As we go through the mountains, we can turn our railroad into a huge city on wheels. It will have sleeping quarters, eating facilities, even recreation. As we get deeper in, instead of having to bring the workers a hundred miles or more into the center, we simply let them live on the trains. We get to work longer hours that way, which they will be handsomely compensated for, and we ensure that everybody is going to be there on time in the morning, don't we? Now we not only have the canyon made available, but we got some trees out of the deal. In cases where there are no trees but only shrubbery, we will do a controlled burn to burn out the things that would overgrow and cause problems with our system. Of course, we'll have crews that will maintain this. In the areas where we may get high water flow - as we're building C.A.A.T.E.S. - we build a canal.

That way we don't encounter any flash flooding. When we do, it hits a wall, travels into the canal and out the other side into a large basin. Therefore, we now are conserving water on top of everything else. In case there may be an avalanche, there will be a large retaining wall built along with the canal, on the outside edges of the C.A.A.T.E.S. course. This is a lot of work! A lot of work!

Let's not stop there. One of the problems that we've always encountered with these mountains is that in order to get through the mountain from one side to the other, it creates an extraordinarily complex set of problems. That is why there are only several interstates that go through those mountains. We're talking now about the Rocky Mountains, but we're going to look at the Appalachians and other ranges all over the country where we can utilize the terrain to install C.A.A.T.E.S. In each case we'll do it the same way. We pro- vide a course through the mountain so the travel from one side to the other becomes simple. We've already put in the railroad tracks, so we can hook up two railroad systems that will exist outside of the C.A.A.T.E.S. areas, on each side of the mountain. I'm going to explain that to you in the next chapter. We can then move people and freight easily through the mountains. On top of that, while we're at it, let's just go ahead and put in a four-lane highway. We have trucks, transportation vehicles, and railroad all moving through these canyons along with C.A.A.T.E.S. If we were to do this individually, we would face the cost of clearing a trail through those canyons three times over, once for a highway, once for a train, and once for C.A.A.T.E.S. Those expenses are so enormous that to date we have very few means of getting through those mountains. When we utilize our investment to accommodate all three means, we not only have a wonderful, clean source of energy, but we have opened it for transportation. We will be doing this all over the country.

We, the investors, will put the money up front. As always in our plan, we divide the resources up amongst the people in the states. As far as the look of C.A.A.T.E.S., the people that are traveling on the highways will utilize what we first created to be turned into rest stops. We want C.A.A.T.E.S. to not only be a testament to man's ingenuity and his commitment to Mother Nature but also to have it esthetically pleasing. We can have all kinds of cool things. We can paint it prior to installation, while it's still in the manufacturer's shop, to be camouflaged. We can paint beautiful murals of deer, bears and antelope, beautiful landscapes. I have the idea that at some of the rest stops we have created along our new section of interstate; we list the names of those members of the military who have died in the war on terrorism. We have the wall for those who died in Vietnam. We have the monument to those citizens we lost on 9-11. But those who are dying in service of their country in the Middle East - whether it is in Iraq, Afghanistan, or any country - need to have a monument of their own. This could be an exceptional opportunity to do that.

That is just one more option. Once again, I would like to hear from all of those out there who have ideas which may be used in any of our endeavors, whether it be physics, mathematics or simply a thank you to those who have died for our country. So let us take a moment and pray for those individuals and their families.

CHAPTER 4

ONE RAIL OR TWO

We have to look at means of saving energy. A smart grid is one of the ways. Also, new fuels are great, but there are still more options. I look now toward the railroads. It moved people, goods and military. It brought into our country the industrial revolution. The means of getting steel made in Pittsburgh or in Cleveland to California, Texas or the Northwest was precipitated by the railroad. It has the most valuable ratio of fuel to mileage per ton of goods of anything. A rivaling factor may be the huge barges that transfer materials from country to country across the ocean. I would venture to say that ton per ton, ton per dollar, they are pretty close. We have a system of railways that is rapidly dilapidating, while at the same time we have a highway system that is overloaded with passengers as well as product-carrying vehicles. The highways are dangerous and many of them are not kept up because of lack of funding. They are a critical part of infrastructure.

After the railroads, when automobiles became available, it was our highway system that grew the country for the next 50 years and beyond. They are still and integral part of what makes America the greatest country in the world.

When we look at the cost to move goods around this country utilizing our highway system, plus factoring in the cost of fuel, we find that it is a less than desirable scenario. In a perfect world, there would be balance between how we move people and product by trucks and passenger vehicles with the way we move people and products by utilizing an old concept and applying new technology. I am talking about revitalizing the railways.

Now I told you when we were speaking of C.A.A.T.E.S. in the last chapter that I had an idea that I was going to drop on you. It ties into the profile where we not only utilize the railway to build C.A.A.T.E.S. but we also put highways through those mountains; there would be a means to utilize what we did there in our everyday needs. It is this: Why don't we revitalize the train industry by taking some of our investment capital and installing a new network around the country of high-speed rail? When I speak of high speed I am not speaking of 200 miles per hour, though we certainly have the ability and the capacity. I am speaking of something a little more reasonable. Suppose we had freight lines that can be used as passenger lines while crisscrossing the country in pairs. One lane would go westward from the east and one lane would go eastward from the west. No sharing tracks and no worrying about perfect timing so that one train moves out of the way before an oncoming train hits it. It would have additional sections that can tie into the more local areas that we may need to get to. We would make the rails strong enough to handle high speeds, as well as make the engine strong enough to pull the cargo at high speeds. I would say that 80 miles per hour is a high speed.

How did I come up with 80 miles per hour? In the past I have lived in Pittsburgh and I have lived in Phoenix. I have, on occasion, had to travel the distance between in an automobile.

The distance is 2300 miles. At one point, I had a few days to get to Phoenix, pick up an automobile, and drag it to Pittsburgh. I left Pittsburgh heading for Phoenix and, with the help of caffeine, I was going to take a shot at driving straight through. Keep in mind that I was alone and there was no chance to take turns with another driver. This was a bold endeavor, but I figured I would see how far I could get. I managed to travel 2300 miles in 32 hours. This is one day and eight hours nonstop, other than to fill the gas tank, grab some donuts and more coffee, check the oil, wash the headlights and windshield, and get back on the road. When I got there, I was a basket case. I could not feel my legs or behind, and I could not focus on anything up close because I was so used to staring at things down the highway. I had a killer headache. This was one of the most insane and difficult things I have ever done. Let us look at this. Suppose I hop a train in Pittsburgh. I pay for very nice accommodations. I relax, have a few cocktails, watch some movies, meet some people, and go straight through to Phoenix. This is at 80 miles per hour, a straight shot to phoenix, even if I had to follow the interstates, which I had to do in my vehicle but would not have to do on a railway. This is because you could cut straight across the center of the country without having to go south to get on I-40 and then west to get to Phoenix. This would be even at the full 2300 miles. I would have still been there is less than 32 hours at the rate of 80 miles per hour. I used probably $400-500 worth of fuel, plus the other expenses that I found along the way (like munchies), quarts of oil, and of course more coffee. There is also the wear and tear on my vehicle - the wear on the tires, brakes, etc. It was also an experience I would never want again. If I had the opportunity and the system existed, why would I not want to utilize it? In my case, I had to pick up another vehicle and drag it back home again, so I needed to have my vehicle with me. On a train it is not that big of a deal and it is not that expensive to bring your vehicle along.

There are also other things that are positive about transporting people around the country. If we were to build the tracks, that would be our part of it. We would then expect for private companies to build the railroad cars, to purchase the engines that drive the train, and to create a revival in locomotive transportation. On top of the people that it would carry, what about freight?

Thousands of tons of freight can move at an optimal cost if the tracks were there and they were newly built, stronger than ever and able to handle the kind of weight that we are talking about at a pace of 80 miles per hour. The amount of energy in the form of fuel that we would save would be substantial. This brings down the cost of goods. Now we are not going to put a railroad through every single town, village and city that exists. We are simply going to make straight shots from one distribution point to another. We may go from Pittsburgh on a straight shot to Oklahoma City. From there we rely on our truckers.

Now the trucking companies may not like this because they are losing the business to the trains. Remember, this gives us a means of growth. Growth means expansion. Expansion means that the trucking industry will grow around these distribution centers and run the goods within what may be a few hundred-mile radius and back again. Truckers may like that because they would end up home at night to be with their families. It will save us money on road repairs, which will save the truckers money on the taxes they pay to have the repairs done. We know they cause most of the damage. There will be substantial growth in the nation and, with the additional competition of fuel prices, trucking companies may put less miles on their trucks. This is good, and they may realize higher profits. I do not think that adding the railway system is a bad thing. Let's look at our plan, how we have structured it, and how we utilize it to gain revenue.

We will put in the rail system. As the railway companies access our rail- way system to carry goods and people, they will pay a rate per car or per mile to whatever state that rail section exists in. Remember, we will have gifted our final product to the people of that state, who will decide what we will charge those rail companies to use our rail system. When you enter a particular state, you know exactly where your destination is and how far you are going. You will be expected to pay the people of that state accordingly. Once again, we have recuperated over a long period of time the cost to build the rail system.

We have cut the amount of fuel needed dramatically. This is another means by which we hedge inflation. We not only hedge inflation by creating the competition between different fuels that the truckers may use, but we have also created competition with the railway services. This means that we, the consumers, get a better deal.

As far as being a person traveling from Pittsburgh to Phoenix, a normal trip (which I have done), even when pushing hard, is three and a half days. That means you have three nights to spend in a hotel or motel. If you are carrying a family with children, that means maybe spending for two rooms. You also have to stop for meals. At the truck stops and diners, with four people you're looking at spending $50-70. When you add this up with the cost of the hotel, fuel and time spent for three and a half days, I think 32 hours in a luxury compartment of a railroad train sounds pretty good. Not only that, but as the train enters a state that allows gambling, the gambling cars open up and you are in a mini casino moving along at 80 miles per hour. They have room service, dining cars, and it is very similar to a cruise ship, with a lot more scenery than water. On a cruise ship for a week, you might spend $5000 per person. I would much rather take the long way around the country, where I can get off on certain tourist attractions and spend an evening with the kids hiking and taking pictures. I can then hop back on the train the next day and continue on. That sounds like a much better family vacation than trying to drag everyone around the country in an automobile. The cost would not be that far out of range from each other. It would be different than what you would picture on a regular passenger train. You would not have individual berths with a walkway down the center. The family would rent the entire car.

The car in its normal capacity is 8-9 feet wide, 20 or more feet long, and could be equipped with the latest technology that we see being used in travel motor homes. That is with a hydraulics system and with parts of the train that could expand several feet out on one end to make your living space bigger, while expanding on the other side to have a walkway where you can get from car to car without walking through the center of someone's room. Therefore, you have a hotel room with all of the amenities: computer hookups, mini bar, big screen TV, video games. And you can walk on the outside walkway down to the gambling and dinner cars. All of this would make it an extremely fun trip, a great way to see America, and cost effective. I guarantee you that with those types of accommodations, the industry would boom. At the same time, the states you are going through that allow the gambling get to collect a portion of the gambling revenue as a tax. This now really becomes a great investment opportunity for us, the owners of our wonderful new corporation. It is definitively energy efficient and exactly what we're looking for. We want to not only create new energy but save energy and make it affordable. This does exactly that.

You will see over the years that some of the private enterprises may even decide to tap into the main rail system to divert passengers through parts of the country into smaller towns that our macro rail system may not want to visit because of the investment cost. Just look at the opportunities. We started out with C.A.A.T.E.S. We needed a means to build C.A.A.T.E.S. and take us through the mountains. That provided the opportunity to go ahead and tie in additional rail lines across the country to generate jobs and investment opportunities that provide transportation for people and large quantities of products. It goes on from there.

We start thinking about vacation trips that are done by rail and lessen the traffic on the interstates. Of course, we are always in the investment business to make money and provide for our needs and still have something to show for it at the end of the day. This is money back in our pockets in time for Christmas, while the prices at the grocery store continue to come down. If nothing else, we are looking to hedge inflation. That's because through our investments, we are going to grow our economy so large and so fast that we don't want to be swamped with hyperinflation. Everything we have done so far provides revenue and pays us back our investment with benefits. It also enables prices to stay low because of competition. Sounds like a pretty good plan to me. We have not looked at the other side of the rail system.

Nobody wants to invest the money in monorail. They say that the ones we have built went so far over budget and ended up so expensive that the investors cannot get their money back. In most cases, that is the taxpayer.

That is what you get when the government tries to be a business or tries to be in the business of managing other businesses. The fact of the matter is that if we want to move in to the 21st century, we better damn well start planning for mass transportation into and back out of the big cities in this country so the population can expand into the suburbs while still being able to work in the cities.

The monorail systems are super high speed. The problem is that there are not enough of them, and you have to drive so far to access one from the suburbs into the city. Also, the cost to ride the rail, on top of everything else, actually makes it less desirable for some people than sitting for an hour-and- a-half in traffic every morning and every afternoon, plus drive 50 miles or more to finally make it there and back. At this point, life becomes a never-ending game of whack-a-mole. There is never enough time. No matter how hard you try, another mole keeps popping up. Would it not be better to take what has become the necessity to live in a fast lane society and make it more relaxing? We will absolutely have to provide rail systems into the cities. The highway systems, the bridges, and the tunnels just cannot handle the load anymore. When we start looking at the cost to replace, maintain and build new bridges and road systems, we find that we cannot do it fast enough to keep up with the population. Therefore, we are caught between a rock and a hard place. Once we dial in to the mechanics and methodology and efficiency of monorail systems, we will find that we can do this. The beauty of the monorail system is that even though it relies on electricity to operate, the number of passengers that it is capable of carrying, and the speed that they travel, makes it worthwhile for them to pay enough money to make the business profitable. Of course, we say, "Why hasn't that happened?"

Remember, profitability is a formula. We have to take all costs, direct and indirect, and we have to take the amount of revenue needed and balance it against cost. We have to be able to get the revenue needed and, in many cases, that means borrowing money. If it is a community project, we can sell bonds.

Either way, we have to give back more than we borrowed. The sloppiness of the way government regulates these businesses costs incredible amounts of money. That's what we discussed earlier in the book, as one of the things we're going to attack in our basic plan. The main thing is this: Once again, as we have discovered through C.A.A.T.E.S. and through our production of our new fuels and solar power, we find that the biggest hindrance is the startup capital.

The startup capital, once again, is furnished by us, the investors. We have $200 billion a year, and it takes a few billion dollars, depending on many different variables, to build a monorail. Once we have built it, the private industry will supply the cars and the engines. They will pay the electric bills and, if we are doing our jobs correctly, this will come down significantly because we're going to put cheap sources of energy at the heart of all of this.

Since we have made the initial investment to build the structures they will run on, their investment for the cars and engines will be significantly lessened, along with their energy costs. The system will be more complex, where people can enter and exit at a number of different places. They will be able to ride in comfort. I believe that many companies will make a deal with their people, one hour in and one out will be paid for by the company. Just because you are in transit doesn't mean you can't be getting some work done. You spend six hours at the office and you get two hours credit for getting work done while you're in transit. What a smoking deal that turns out to be! On top of that, the local authorities and the state get to share in revenues produced by the investment we have put into the monorail system. This is just like our other rail system, our solar system, and so on. We always get our money back at the end of the year with major opportunities to increase revenue potential by owning the assets we have developed. Just think of what this means to cities like Washington, D.C., Baltimore, Philadelphia, Atlanta. It even sometimes means getting people out of the outer suburbs of New York City to the places where they can get on the subway. This system would work great in Phoenix, Los Angeles, and in a number of other places where we find congestion is reaching critical mass. We can't put in enough roadways and maintain them.

We have to think about mass transit and we have to think about doing it in a comfortable and affordable manner.

We are the prime investors, so we can only expect to be paid back the amount that we have invested. It will take 10-15 or more years to pay us back, by which time we will have created even more newer and efficient systems.

This is our goal, our long-term goal forever and ever. We will continue to grow this country and supply the means of transportation and the energy necessary to make us prosperous and productive once again.

It was just yesterday on one of my favorite news channels, where I get a lot of my information, there was discussion about the state of California implementing a plan to build a monorail into and out of Los Angeles. Those that are pro-monorail see an opportunity to create jobs and ease the congestion. Those against the plan are saying this: "How can you spend several billion dollars on a project like that, which has shown in the past that the cost is too much to make the project economically feasible?" A project of that magnitude may cost several billion dollars, while at the same time California is teetering on bankruptcy, and it is inevitable that ship will flounder if something drastic isn't done. Several billion dollars could help pay down that debt. Not only that, but most likely in order to pay for the projects, taxes will be raised. No wonder everyone is leaving the state, at least in terms of major businesses, to find a friendly atmosphere. Now we come along with our corporation. We've already talked about a way to invest in the monorail systems to save on fuel, save on pollution and ease the congestion in and out of big cities. In such a plan, we the investors would cover the cost of the project.

Here's how it would work. The proposers of the monorail plan would naturally have put together all the statistical analysis to show costs, scheduling, etc. In our plan we require that as much as possible of the material and labor be from the state of California. The state that has the project gets the opportunity to utilize as much of their manufacturing, resources and labor as they possibly can. This should have been part of the proposal, which I really don't think in this case it is. There's a good chance that much of the benefits of building such a system will go to other states because that is where the companies that supply all the needs of the project are located. I really doubt if the proponents of this proposal took the time to evaluate that part of it. In our world that would have been incorporated. That proposal would have gone to the governor. He and his team would have gone through the proposal and decided whether it was feasible as a submittal to our corporation for funding. If they met the requirements that we've discussed, our corporation would say sure. In fact, Los Angeles is on our list of targeted cities, to utilize our two-rail and single-rail systems in a prudent manner. We would have allocated the funds. They would have been distributed into the small banks that we had decided to use. The companies that were outlined would be notified of their acceptance to the team. We would have set up our team to go in and oversee the operation to ensure full compliance at every turn. The project would go on for several years. The monorail is built. So far, it hasn't cost the state of California a single penny. Remember, the investors from California - the average residents - regain their investment money each year, along with the bonus that they receive from their healthcare deductions.

What we're going to do is build the monorail system. We're not going to buy the cars; we're not going to hire the people; we're simply going to build the rail. Once we're finished, we give it to the people of California, who, through voting on proposed methods of utilizing this asset, may decide to - let's say - pick one company. Let them invest in the cars, the people to operate, and the maintenance crew to run the system. They then charge the price to the passenger. Out of this price, there is part of that they're required to pay to the state as a repayment for the billions of dollars that it cost to build the system. They can do this over 10, 15 or 20 years. It doesn't have much effect on their bottom line. Perhaps add another dollar or two to the price of the ticket. If they run a successful operation, they can do well. There's nothing that says they can't pay the loan back fast. They don't get charged interest on it; we sim- ply want our money back.

Now you have all the jobs that are created in that state from the bottom up, from manufacturing through the finished product and to the people that are maintaining the facility. They are Californians. This gives a nice payment yearly to the state, which they can use to pay down their debt. By utilizing the small banks, we've created a means for Californians in that area to be able to get home loans, car loans, school loans, small business loans, etc. Once again, we've thrown another log on the fire. This is exactly how our system would work. Right now, I believe California is making a huge mistake. They have to get their fiscal house in order before they start coming up with these bright ideas of how to spend billions more dollars that they don't have. With our corporation in the mix, suddenly it's all doable. There's a perfect example right there of how we would operate.

CHAPTER 5

F. I. S. T. E. S.

This chapter moves us into another form of energy production, one that I have come up with and one on which I have spent an enormous amount of time and effect checking its viability. I have to tell you, I am excited. In fact, this is the last chapter in which I will offer my ideas on how to utilize the power of energy. This system is called F.I.S.T.E.S.- Forced Induction Submerged Turbine Energy System. It is a hydroelectric system, one that can be implanted in every major waterway in the world. What makes it tick?

Where are the guts of it? What is the most powerful force in the universe? This force creates galaxies from nebulae. It creates planets and moons and suns.

It's what locks them into orbit. It's what holds the people of this planet onto the surface of the Earth without flying off. We are going to use it for its effect on water. It is none other than Isaac Newton's friend, Gravity. The force is so powerful that if you were to dig a tunnel a mile deep into the Earth and drop a marble while you were at the mouth of that tunnel, it would fall at the exact same speed that it would fall if you dropped that marble from the top of the Empire State Building. It is an unstoppable force. It is what keeps our atmosphere in place. It is what makes water and other liquids travel downhill.

The main factor of this type of energy that is difficult at first glance is that the degree of slope has a major effect on the speed that the water flows. The steeper the grade, the faster it moves. Why does that concern us? Remember our calculations on the physics of energy that state energy equals mass times speed. We have so many large bodies of moving water that just don't have enough slope to them to get the water up to a speed necessary to efficiently spin the turbines and generate electricity. Once again it becomes a cost versus output equation that works against us. The first thing that I'm going to tell you is that slow moving water is a blessing. Rain and melting snow generate X amount of water. If the slope of the terrain is too steep, the water rushes downhill at a high rate of speed, but then suddenly there is no water left. We don't want to drain our rivers any faster than what they are now. So how do we create the speed and the force to make FISTES a smart bet?

At this point, in order to overcome the problem of mass times speed, we first look back two chapters to C.A.A.T.E.S. Remember in C.A.A.T.E.S. we have tracked the air into our cylinder. The cylinder has a defined volume. We increase that mass into the volume by compressing the air. That is done by the force of the air that is approaching the entry to a C.A.A.T.E.S. system into the opening of a canyon. This is a natural event; it follows the laws of nature. We then channel the air mass down the funnel, gathering more mass but condensing it into a smaller volume. In the cylinders we have put ribbing that spins the air in a tornado like manner, thus creating speed. We've increased mass and we've increased speed. We have a couple other tricks in there to help it along, but that's our basic formula. We optimize mass and have it balance with speed to give us the highest level of output.

In F.I.S.T.E.S. we will use these ribbed cylinders as well. This certainly will look different and be constructed differently. More than likely, there will be poured concrete sections, linked together in a manner that matches up the ribbing from one section to another to keep the cyclonic action of the water consistent. Since we don't have the air mass and the natural flow through the canyon, we have to come up with a new means of moving the mass, and doing so at a high rate of speed. We also have the problem that we don't have with C.A.A.T.E.S.- that is, drying up our supply of water. Once again, if water moves too quickly, the volume drops and eventually runs dry.

Now we require the help of nature, in many cases, at least in the water- ways of the east. I am specifically looking at the Mississippi River. It is not just the Mississippi river on its own. There is also the Allegheny River north of Pittsburgh joining with the Monongahela River east of Pittsburgh form the Ohio River at the Point in Pittsburgh, which flows for hundreds of miles into the Mississippi. All of these rivers carry a substantial amount of water. They all move at a nice consistent pace where, more often than not, there will be more water than what they can handle, rather than not enough. That brings us to another use for F.I.S.T.E.S. Let's keep our minds on the actual physical needs to make F.I.S.T.E.S. work. Picture this: You have a large tub of water. In the case of F.I.S.T.E.S., we're looking at probably 150 feet deep at its deepest point. When you release the stopper at the bottom of the tub of water, the weight of the water, because of gravity, pushes the water in the tub through the much smaller hole at a highly accelerated speed. This would be the equivalent of how we would feed F.I.S.T.E.S. Let's try to picture this. Along the Mississippi River - and I'll explain to you how we're going to actually go from Lake Erie to New Orleans with this system - we dig a basin. It's a huge basin. No big deal for us - we handle big earth projects all the time. The basin has dimensions, and these are certainly generic (my personal calculations) but to be used as food for thought. The basin on one end starts at O feet in depth.

It slowly slopes for the first 75 or 100 feet to where it suddenly makes a steeper decline, until it hits a level of approximately 125-150 feet in depth. This generally occurs over the space of what in length from north to south would be 3/4 of a mile - quite a nice-sized basin. In its width we will build it out to 3/8 of a mile. On the southernmost end, the slope of the basin at its deepest point will culminate in the weight of the water pushing down on the entire surface of the basin to distribute the weight down the slope of the sides to the exit of the basin, which is the mouth of F.I.S.T.E.S., at a depth of 150 feet. Right before we reach that level, we dig another 20- or 30-foot-deep trench across the bottom of the basin at the mouth of F.I.S.T.E.S., so that the mouth of F.I.S.T.E.S. sits slightly above that trench. The reason for all of this is that not only do we want to displace the force of the weight down to that point, but by having a very placid surface and very little undertow (because the basin is so large), the water that we're going to put into the north end, that may stir up the elements that would harm the system, will be nearly clean when it reaches the south end. The basin serves as a giant settling pond. Now F.I.S.T.E.S. can easily handle muddy water, gritty water, small particulates, but we want rocks and stones and that kind of thing to settle out. The final settling place will be in that trench that we've dug. Once every few months, or maybe once each season, possibly after a high-water event, we take a look at the trench and dredge it out if we need to, keeping the mouth of F.I.S.T.E.S. reasonably clean. At the same time, we put several layers of screening over the mouth of the system so that fish don't enter the system. Also, it will stop any rocks or debris that happen to make it past our defenses. These screens can be removed, replaced, cleaned as general maintenance. At that depth of water, you won't find the tiny fish, and they would have to be very tiny to get through our screen. They would have to be so tiny that they wouldn't hurt F.I.S.T.E.S. but we would have to worry about the aquatic population. That is another reason for the form of the basin. Small fish will be in the shallow water.

When it comes out and suddenly makes its drop, that's where the good fishing will be. That's where the food will succumb to the slope and be driven towards the fish that will be waiting right at that spot. Now we not only protect the fish but we create some decent fishing - and we will talk about that in a minute!

Once again, I'm working with the generic number of a 50-foot in diameter cylinder, with the turbines submerged in that cylinder to be the same size. The turbines are adjusted for the spinning water which will hit at an exact angle due to the configuration of our ribbing. We want to utilize force. This spinning action serves several purposes. If we just put a 50-foot hole in the bottom of the basin, the basin would drain faster than what the natural effects of nature could do to fill it up. The problem that we have to solve is that the water bypassing the system, traveling down the Mississippi in any pre-described distance, will meet the water coming out from F.I.S.T.E.S. at the same place.

Yet we want the water in F.I.S.T.E.S. to move 3, 4 or 5 times faster. That's where the circular motion comes in. Over the distance of the land on the surface the water in F.I.S.T.E.S. will travel the same distance in the same amount of time, but inside the cylinder the distance that it has to travel is greatly increased. As long as the water in F.I.S.T.E.S. doesn't get to its outflow faster than the water in its natural travel, we've conquered that problem. Now we can only get it to move so fast. With the depth of the water in the basin, it may be possible to move water through F.I.S.T.E.S. at such a high rate that we can generate enormous amounts of electricity but in the end destroy the system because we've sucked the basin dry. The basin will be attached to the Mississippi and as the basin drops in level, the Mississippi River will supply it with new water. The Mississippi River will have its level controlled by facilities that are connected to Lake Erie and/or Lake Michigan. In the end, we not only drop the basin level but, in order to compensate, the Mississippi gives up too much of its reserve and the level drops dangerously in the river itself.

This is a job for the physics department. This is a job for our engineers. How much ribbing should we install? At what intervals should the ribbing complete one circle? The more circles it completes, the faster it travels, as long as it maintains enough pressure from the basin to proliferate that speed. Either way, just as in C.A.A.T.E.S., we know that we can create a mass which can fill a 50-foot diameter cylinder and move it at a speed 3, 4 or 5 times faster than the water moving down the river bypassing F.I.S.T.E.S. They will come out at the same place at the same time; we have lost not one bit of water. We haven't dropped the level of the river one inch. The basins maintain a calm, placid surface because of their size.

I haven't looked at the topography of the river, but I do know that up in Pennsylvania, where it may be well over 1000 feet above sea level, in the end when it hits New Orleans, it comes out at zero. It comes right out at sea level. Here is why that's important: We can only install so many turbines in sequence in a single cylinder for the same reason that we talked about in C.A.A.T.E.S. The turbines represent a resistance. It is forcing them to turn against that resistance that creates the electricity. If we try to put too many turbines into a single cylinder, we find that as we go down river, we begin to lose efficiency. Our productivity per dollar is compromised. Of course, if we were to build a basin the size of the ocean, we could move the water so fast at such a high speed that we could suck that river dry in a matter of minutes.

That's why we have to be prudent about the size and depth of the basin, and the slopes of its sides. We of course want more than we need. There are a number of reasons for that. One is that as we need more energy, we may need to increase the flow into the cylinder by opening what is known as a weir, which is a giant gate, and letting the basin force more water. We add to the resistance of the turbine to balance out the same scenario as far as water flow to distance, so that it balances out with the water bypassing the system. That way we generate more electricity by using the same system. Also, we can split off of F.I.S.T.E.S., creating several F.I.S.T.E.S. cylinders and generating more electricity that way. Of course, we'll need additional pressure. After thinking about it, I went back to our basic plan: That is to create a means to reach our goal of sovereignty by making our country energy independent and doing it in such a way that we open doors of opportunity. We've gone through how many different opportunities that this has already created, everything from healthcare to immigration, education and so on.

Let's look at this from an opportunistic point of view. When we dig the basin and the trenches that will house F.I.S.T.E.S., we find ourselves with an odd problem. What in the world are we going to do with all of that dirt? I have something that I'd like to submit: One of the biggest problems we have with the Mississippi River is that it just loves to overflow its banks. It destroys property. It destroys lives. It wipes out crops. The only thing that we know how to do is to levy. Are you getting the picture? I wonder how much levy, of what size and dimensions, can we build down the sides of the Mississippi River with that much dirt. I would submit that if we utilize the entire river by putting in one basin after another, interconnecting the basins with the cylinders that house F.I.S.T.E.S., so that when the water from one basin travels through F.I.S.T.E.S. it empties into the next basin on the north side. On the south side of the basin, it's being sucked into another F.I.S.T.E.S. unit. As it travels X amount of miles, we put in another basin. The water drops into that basin. Keeping all things constant, the same water that we started on the very north end will feed every basin the whole way to the Gulf of Mexico.

That is a large amount of dirt that we're going to have to remove to build this on both sides. Remember, both sides will be utilized for maximum capacity as well as to present opportunities for the states on each side of the river to get their fair share of not just clean energy but the revenues that can be generated. I think we could levy this thing 40 feet high and 40 feet at the base, plant beautiful shrubbery and bushes along the side, build a giant fence on the top with enough room for animals to get in and out as they want.

Whenever that river decides that it wants to go over the top, it's going to have to have one hellacious amount of water to be able to breach those levies. In the meantime, the F.I.S.T.E.S. cylinders are submerging in the trench that is outside of the levy. The levy therefore protects any damage to the F.I.S.T.E.S. because of overflowing and flooding. We're just getting rolling here.

What else is it good for? Remember I said fishing? Oh, yes. Being opportunists that we are, we say this: As long as we're going to build this giant basin, why not make it a state park. It too will be gifted to the people of the state in which it exists. We will put sandy white beaches down part of it. On the north end, we need to increase water flow; therefore, we must tap into Lake Erie to feed the Allegheny so that we have adequate water flow to compensate the turbines. On the far north end, where the water from the previous F.I.S.T.E.S. unit comes in, we naturally have that sectioned off because there is going to be one heck of a force of water coming out of that 50- foot cylinder. We keep the people more on the east side, or on the west side of the Mississippi we keep them on the west side of the basin. We have things like this: Fishing boats, small boats, jet skis, all of which you can bring or rent. We have hot dog and hamburger stands. We have an entrance and exit that go overtop the levies, down into the sides of the basin, where picnic tables and pavilions will exist. There will probably be people renting out lawn chairs.

There will be people selling alcohol. It will be a miniature resort. All of this will be built in a way that when we predict the big water coming, we simply put it on our carts and remove it from the basin to a safe place. All parking will be outside the basin, on the other sides of the levies. We will not only levy the Mississippi but around the basin as well. Picture if we get 30,

40 or 50 feet high how much water that river with all of those basins can take, in addition to its normal amount. Now we have solved the gigantic problem of the Mississippi River overflowing and wiping out people and their property.

We've done it by solving another problem: what to do with all the dirt.

Because of the downward slope of the Mississippi, the F.I.S.T.E.S. cylinders will have to digress at a lesser slope than what the Mississippi has. What that will do is enable F.I.S.T.E.S. to eventually come from its 150-foot depth out to river level and above. That would make it possible for one basin to feed F.I.S.T.E.S., that would feed another basin that would feed F.I.S.T.E.S., and on down the river we go, winding and turning with the river. We would prob- ably be spending $100 billion or more over the next 15 or 20 years, putting enough energy out to feed most of the needs of the people within 100 miles or greater of that river. On top of that, the state would of course be selling permits for those that would set up shop at the state parks outside the levies. The entrepreneurs of the big resorts will be coming in asking for permits to build casinos, one or two small ones with a few hundred rooms here and a few hundred there. They will supply much of the patronage with access to small carts that would take them down to the beach and back. They may have bought up the permits to supply the alcohol and other amenities. Of course, the state receives a nice piece of change. On top of that, they would do the same as they would do with any of our other systems. The people would decide whether they want to operate the system themselves or lease the system to a subcontractor who will take care of it, make a profit, and pay back the cost of the system over time. Once again, we provide any major renovations or reconstruction or additions. That comes out of our corporation through the proposal system.

We've got stuff going on all over the place now. On top of that, what about all the traffic on the river? It will be fantastic.

You will find yourself showing up at a hotel at one of the many basin resorts along the river, traveling from basin to basin, resort to resort in water taxis. Perhaps we will even revive the paddleboat industry. Those that own their boat can come from the eastern side of Florida, down through the Keys, up through the Gulf, into the mouth of the Mississippi, and travel the whole way to Pittsburgh. Take a month off and just hit every casino on the river. What about the people that will decide that they like it in this particular area, say Memphis, and want to build their home there, work in that city, be able to take their kids up or down stream. They will need someone to park their boat. When you go to Florida, it's not just the cost to own a boat but the cost to have a parking place for that boat; that's what makes it a rich man's game. All along the Mississippi within the boundaries of where that state is, we can build boat docking and boat storage. Boating businesses for repair and dry dock will pop up and become a great industry there. They will be scattered up and down the Mississippi River on both sides. Boat docking will be one of the main concerns. Those that have the money will pay for their own private docking spot. These docking spots would be protected on both sides by walls that have bumper mechanisms built in that can go 40 feet above the river level. If we do have a huge flood, those boats will rise as the water level in the Mississippi rises; they will be protected on both sides from catastrophe. If you have the money and are going to play captain, you have to have it. Any time you want, you go out and hop in your boat, take off up and down the river and have all the fun you want. Can you imagine the amount of revenue that we're talking here over a 20-year period? Even if it costs us $150 billion to build it, you will probably quadruple that in revenue. I'm just guessing, but I think it will become the playground for not only the rich but for all of us average folks that want to go from the inland, get a room for a night, and take the kids out to play on the beach. We're going to build the F.I.S.T.E.S. anyway; why not add the extra money in to give everybody in each of those states a nice economic boost?

Here we are again, figuring out how to make money while reaching our goals at the same time. There will be other details like maintenance. How do you get a broken-down unit out of F.I.S.T.E.S.? I say we build a railroad track the full length of it, just the way we did under C.A.A.T.E.S. We can use our cranes and technology to lift out damaged units, take them to a place where they will be repaired, and reinstate a new unit in that spot in a matter of a single day. We will have built-in bypass systems so that we don't have to shut off an entire F.I.S.T.E.S. system in order to get to one turbine; we sim- ply reroute the water around that turbine and go back in line in time to hit the next turbine. We will need to look at what distance is the prudent and optimum distance between turbines. It all comes down to the genius, the innovation and the willpower that is America. It may seem out of reach at this time, but if we put together the working capital, the method for collection and distribution, get our top guns in there to set it up for us, it is a matter of simply doing one project hundreds of times over. There is nothing here that we can't do. We have the technology; let's get it done.

There is another problem that our country faces, that I believe F.I.S.T.E.S. can have a huge hand in solving. This one might take your breath away a little bit so before I start down that road, let me bring something to your attention that is factual. Nobody really knows exactly how long we can hold out or what the end results will be because we don't know what we'll eventually do year after year to try to solve the problem, but I'm proposing something that may seem radical yet is feasible. It will take a long time to implement, but we can do it within the time that we have. The problem that I speak of exists in the southwest part of the United States. The problem is none other than WATER! The same thing that we're trying to levy and conserve in our basins that we'll use for F.I.S.T.E.S. - in other parts of the country, we have that problem in reverse. There simply isn't enough water to maintain that part of our country. For generic purposes, I'll quote a number that I saw on C-span. They brought together a group of world-renowned physicists to speak in general of the greatest problems the world will face in the future. One of the experts brought up the issue of water. It's a global problem. We know that our situation here isn't nearly as bad as many other countries. He particularly spoke of southwest United States. The number he threw out was particular to Las Vegas, Nevada. That was that in 20 years Las Vegas will be a ghost town. That was an exaggeration, I'm sure. Basically, what he said was it's going to dry up and blow away out there in the middle of the hot Nevada desert. We need to look east, south, somewhat in the north from Las Vegas to see what the conditions are around it. They are dire. Arizona has slowed its growth considerably. It has very little of its own water resources. Hoover Dam has done miracles for that part of the country in helping to supply water. When the positive growth scenario that we're going to create kicks into full gear, and that high growth level comes back, we are facing the inevitability of water shortages. Not to mention - with all of the forest fires - we're going through water reserves like there is no tomorrow. What are we going to do?

There are millions of people in California and millions in Arizona, but Las Vegas is target #1. Not to mention, there is a lot of very good open land that we need to utilize. In order to utilize it, several things need to happen. First, they're going to need a strong source of energy. F.I.S.T.E.S. can deliver. On top of F.I.S.T.E.S., we have the Rocky Mountains to the west, where we can install numerous CAATES units to help with the energy part of that. They can help with energy on both sides of the mountains. We've been all over that. That will help. The second thing that we have to find a way to provide is water - a lot of water! If we supply the water and energy, we can turn that land into productive land that, I say, we earmark for the growth of the plants that we will use to create our bio-fuel, thereby being able to maintain the food supply while still being able to reach the vast amounts of bio-fuel that we're going to need to create our new bio-methane fuel to challenge conventional gasoline.

We get back again to the same thing: Where is the water going to come from? I have seen our technology at work. I've seen tunnel boring machines come up to a mountain and simply go through it. One machine or two would not be adequate. We would need a fleet of them. We're talking big bucks.

We're talking a lot of manufacturing jobs. Remember in our plan we want to utilize as much American productivity as we can. Here's where it gets a little crazy. I say we go up to Lake Superior and take some points in between, where the beginning of the Colorado River starts and where Lake Superior is. From different points, we start boring in both directions until we put several F.I.S.T.E.S. size cylinders the whole way from Lake Superior down to the beginning of the Colorado River. With a F.I.S.T.E.S. system, the very water that begins the system feeds the next system, and that feeds the next system. We need only to supply the initial amount of water flow to keep the systems all operating. There will be many places where we will be tunneling right

through the mountain and won't want to put F.I.S.T.E.S. units in place because we won't be able to get back at them to do repairs without having to disrupt the flow of the water, which means also the flow of the energy. In any place that the tunnel is near the surface, we simply dig in from the top, make a huge canal, put a basin in and let the water flow into the basin through the system and on down through the next mountain to the next opening, where there will be another basin starting another F.I.S.T.E.S. system. We do this on both sides of the Colorado River. The flow continues the whole way down and then spreads out in different directions to feed the needs of the people and of the growth.

We will have enough water utilized in this to irrigate that land so that we can grow our bio-fuels. As we get down to populated areas like Las Vegas, we will have units that split off from the river and head towards the city. They will bring electricity along with them, and the water then feeds the needs of the population. All along the way, we are building basins. We are digging major holes.

We may even want to bump up the size of the basins just for the specific purpose of holding more water. That way, we can use some other technology that will help us gather water coming from the mountains when the snow melts into other basins, which will also have F.I.S.T.E.S. units attached feeding into the main stream. We take all of the dirt that we use to dig all of this and utilize it the same way we did on the Mississippi River, by building the sides of the basin and the river where necessary the whole way down, so we can fill that to the top. We're not worried there about flooding.

Where in the east we need to leave half of our space available for floods, in the west we want to bump up the volume of water that we save by making the basins hold more capacity because the side walls of the basins are built much higher. This is the same way we would build a levy, only now we tap into Lake Superior to feed all of this. We try to catch as much as we can from the mountains and divert water so that it can be used in our system, but we will need some consistent flow from the northeast.

Lake Superior feeds the other lakes. Each lake represents a small drop in altitude. Lake Superior sends billions of gallons a day into Lake Michigan.

What we're looking at doing is borrowing some of that. Instead of letting all of it go into Lake Michigan, which eventually goes through all of the other lakes and ends up in the ocean, where it turns into salt water. In order to get it back, we would have to put in desalination units at God-only-knows what expense just to get back the water that we have in Lake Superior but let go. We need to continue the flow so we can have boating between the lakes. We want to carry products manufactured in that part of the country. Of course, we'll take a look at that and make darn sure that we have it. We will use a weir system to be able to increase the flow or decrease the flow. A weir is like a gate that blocks off part of the flow. It can also cut into a flow and split it, sending part this way and part the other way. The movement of the weir back and forth decides how much water goes to either stream. This is how we control the water flow. We have the same system where it comes out of Lake Superior into our canal system to be transported through the mountains down into the lower lands and into the southwest of the country. If we don't do this, we are looking at catastrophic events. One year of change in climate can completely dry up the southwest, simply because it didn't produce enough snow in the mountains to feed the Colorado River and bring the water to its collection point where it is distributed. I'm telling you if there is a drop in the water level at Lake Superior, it will be so minor they will hardly be able to notice it. If it looks like it's going to drop the water level more than we would like over a period of time, then we need to start building canals in the beginning to conserve the water in the north from Canada, making sure that Lake Superior gets an optimum flow of incoming water. We need to actually distribute water from melting snow in Canada down to the homes and businesses in the southwest, all along the way building huge reservoirs, setting up F.I.S.T.E.S. systems, irrigating land, growing our bio-fuels, providing for expansion in population in those areas, bringing huge amounts of revenue into those states that desperately need it, and making sure that Las Vega, Los Angeles and Phoenix are alive and well 20 years from now.

Think about it. It sounds like one hell of a challenge. There is nothing we haven't done before; it's simply a matter of doing it on a bigger scale. It will create quite a number of jobs and income. We may even want to collab- orate with Canada and work with them to put in some F.I.S.T.E.S. units as we channel their waters down into Lake Superior. We can work out something with them so that they too can benefit. After all, they live on that lake as well. Whatever we borrow from the lake affects them. I think it should affect them in a positive way. This is where we want to get our federal government involved and see what we can work out. It is doable and it needs to start now. According to my guy on C-span, we have about 20 years. We better start making it happen now. With that, I give you F.I.S.T.E.S.

CHAPTER 6

FINAL SUMMARY

In this chapter, we're going to take a look at how we've addressed the problems of this nation and what they mean for the future of our country, our children and our grandchildren. The first thing that we came to understand is that the freedom that is promised to us by the Constitution is a word on a piece of paper. It's a promise, it's a concept; it is an abstract. What makes it powerful is when we turn freedom into liberty. Another term for liberty would be actionable freedom, the ability to act in a free manner because we have the right to choose our own destiny. That is what sovereignty provides for us. Sovereignty protects freedom and enables liberty. Sovereignty is defined as independence. What we have realized is that not any of us, the individuals, nor the states we live in or our nation can be sovereign without a strong economic structure. It is the essence of our government system and our belief system. We are allowed to choose our own fate, our destiny. We are allowed to choose our religion. We can do this because we have provided independence from government control through economic means. We saw our country failing economically. When the country fails economically, sovereignty is lost. Our independence becomes dependence. When we are dependent, people get to tell us what to do. This is the core of socialism: when the government can tell you what to do because it provides for you. You lose independence. You lose you sovereignty, and with it goes liberty. We cannot let this happen. This country was made by the people. The government was designed to act for the people. When the people lose their ability to control government, we become slaves to those that can provide for us. This has been going on for thousands of years, and finally our Founding Fathers saw an opportunity to create something different.

The problem is now, how do we protect that sovereignty? Since that sovereignty is coming down to economic matters, we have realized that in order to protect sovereignty and redeem the sovereignty that we already have lost, we must fix the economy. We must do it in a manner that provides opportunities for everyone. We must do it in a manner that creates more jobs than we have lost. We have lost a lot of jobs. We have lost a lot of ground. We need to build an economy that can not only protect what we have but return us to what we were. This is an incredible endeavor. It takes a plan of massive proportion. It takes the involvement of everyone in the country. Citizens or residents, if you want to live here you must participate. This endeavor will dwarf the size and scope of anything that we have ever done in the past. It will be comparable to what we did in World War II, when we came together as a nation and stood up against dictators and tyranny. We know we can do it because we have done it. We are the most powerful, innovative, intelligent country that has ever existed. Once again, our will is being tested. The difference is that this time the pain and suffering and loss of life and treasure will not happen. This time it is strictly a matter of economics. Everyone keeps talking about the need to solve the problems, yet no one has a plan. Now we do.

Let's summarize the plan in a way that we can use it to solve all of the problems that we have as a society. The first thing we do is put a bill through Congress that enables us to use the IRS to collect funds. We will hire a team of the most brilliant, successful and patriotic people we have in our country to put together a corporation, a business entity, an investment entity. That investment will be in energy. We're not going to go out and buy up all of the oil in the world or continue to poke holes in Mother Earth. We're going to solve energy issues by using new technologies along with the laws of physics and the American know-how of innovation. By doing this, we will create a conservative figure of 15 million new jobs while at the same time saving another 30 million jobs. This is a projection for just the next ten years. It will continue on after that for generations. It will enable us to solve all of the problems and address all of the issues that we have as a nation. It will enable us to sustain entitlement programs which are meant to be a safety net, not a lifestyle. It will enable us to have strong healthcare. It will enable us to fix immigration. It will enable us to use education and training to prepare our children for the real world, a world where economic independence of the individual means liberty for those individuals and a higher quality of life. We will bring back manufacturing as a means to regain and then sustain economic strength. We will use our innovations in technology to build systems for energy that will save our environment. We will take away the overriding hand of government and put the power back in the hands of the people, where it was meant to be. The people will dictate to the states how to use the facilities and the funds generated from this plan in order to give the states a chance to regain the sovereignty that they have lost to the federal government.

Even though the Constitution promised that the states would have the power, the states' power would come from the people. The federal government would not dictate to the people but would be dictated to by the people through the state representatives that we send to Washington. The system is being broken. The economy is about to collapse. I have given you some likely scenarios of what will happen when the most powerful nation in the world collapses. These are not simple-minded predictions, but likely outcomes. It's not pretty. We're going to use our technology to create a means to use solar, wind, hydroelectric power. We will create a new fuel, causing competition between the new fuels and standard gasoline and other oil-based products. We figured out a way to make 300 million people all investors in this plan. We've defined the means by which the investors will recuperate their funds, along with dividends in the form of healthcare rebates. All of this is not only possible but is not very difficult. What makes it hard to fathom is the complexity. There is nothing in this plan that we haven't done before, and done repeatedly. Our Dream Team will be a group of the finest, most intelligent and patriotic businessmen and women that we have in the country today. They will go down in history as the ones that saved this country from annihilation. At the same time, we (the investors, the citizens and residents of this country) will continue to realize the liberty that we have come to treasure, the liberty that we have fought and died for, the liberty that our children are out fighting and dying for. We must sustain this liberty at all costs. This plan is a viable, simple plan of how to do it.

Before I go, I want to leave you with one more quotation. This quotation comes from one of the greatest blues artists this country has ever known. It is plain and simple but tells us quite a bit. The quotation comes from a song done by a man called B.B. King, a man that worked himself out of the ghetto and poverty into the limelight and success. He has a foundation to put instruments in the hands of our youths in order to keep them off the streets, off of drugs and away from violence. You should donate to this cause. In his song, he says something profound. I'm going to change the word 'I' to the word 'we' because it applies to all of us. This is his quote: "**AS LONG AS WE'RE PAYING THE BILLS, WE'RE PAYING THE COST TO BE THE BOSS!!!**" That, in a nutshell, is the essence of the Economics of Sovereignty.